CW01502101

THE MOTHER OF ALL CRIMES

The Mother of All Crimes

Human Rights, Criminalization and the Child Born Alive

EMMA CAVE
University of Leeds, UK

ASHGATE

Published by
Ashgate Publishing Limited
Gower House
Croft Road
Aldershot
Hants GU11 3HR
England

Ashgate Publishing Company
Suite 420
101 Cherry Street
Burlington, VT 05401-4405
USA

Ashgate website: http://www.ashgate.com

British Library Cataloguing in Publication Data
Cave, Emma
   The mother of all crimes : human rights, criminalization
   and the child born alive
   1. Fetus - Legal status, laws, etc. - England 2. Pregnant
   women - Legal status, laws, etc. - England 3. Women's rights
   - England 4. Fetus - Legal status, laws, etc. - Wales
   5. Pregnant women - Legal status, laws, etc. - Wales
   6. Women's rights - Wales 7. Fetus - Legal status, laws, etc.
   - United States 8. Pregnant women - Legal status, laws, etc.
   - United States 9. Women's rights - United States
   10. Substance abuse in pregnancy
   I. Title
   342.4'2085

Library of Congress Cataloging-in-Publication Data
Cave, Emma, 1974-
   The mother of all crimes : human rights, criminalization and the child born alive / Emma Cave.
     p. cm.
   Includes bibliographical references and index.
   ISBN 0-7546-2366-1
     1. Pregnant women--Legal status, laws, etc.--England--Criminal provisions. 2. Pregnant women--Legal status, laws, etc.--Wales--Criminal provisions. 3. Pregnant women--Legal status, laws, etc.--United States--Criminal provisions. 4. Fetus--Legal status, laws, etc.--England--Criminal provisions. 5. Fetus--Legal status, laws, etc.--Wales--Criminal provisions. 6. Fetus--Legal status, laws, etc.--United States--Criminal provisions. I. Title.

K5181.C38 2004
345.42'02--dc22
                                             2003064042

ISBN 0 7546 2366 1

Printed and bound in Great Britain by MPG Books Ltd, Bodmin, Cornwall

Contents

Acknowledgments

I would like to thank Barry Mitchell, University of Coventry, Professor Katherine O'Donovan, Queen Mary and Westfield College, London, Professor Celia Wells, Cardiff University and Professor Robyn Martin, University of Hertfordshire for comments on earlier drafts.

Introduction

With advances in fetal physiology, our perception of the fetus[1] has changed. We no longer view its passage from conception to birth as unaffected by human conduct, but as a time when medicine and human action are known to greatly impact on the health and welfare of the fetus and future child. It has become possible to link events that occur *in utero* with problems that can last the lifetime of the issue or cause its demise. There is a corresponding desire to prevent these occurrences in order to protect the interests of a number of parties. Not least amongst these is the pregnant woman who, in the vast majority of cases, wants nothing more than to bear a healthy child. Preventing harm *in utero* will also serve the interests of the fetus and the child born alive as well as the taxpayer who, in the UK, funds the treatment of damaged new-borns.

Damage to the fetus might result from genetic abnormality or innate deformity of the fetus itself. It might occur through the interventions of a third party such as the assailant who assaults a pregnant woman or the negligent driver who crashes into her car. It might also occur because acts or omissions of the pregnant woman somehow compromise the environment of the fetus, that is the womb in which it is carried. Pollution, illness, genetic abnormality, failure to exercise, over-work, smoking, alcohol intake, and drug use are but some examples. This book considers whether or not the criminal law should be used to punish pregnant women who act in a way that causes injury or death to the fetus born alive.

I personally feel that the pregnant woman has a moral duty to protect the future child from avoidable harm caused *in utero*. However, it is the role of the *law*, and in particular the criminal law, that is the subject of discussion. Though laws are enacted on the basis of morals, the two terms are not synonymous. What is moral often depends on the intricacies of a given situation. Law, on the other hand, must be of general application. Law invites a macro rather than a micro perspective. It is shaped by the majority view, which may or may not be the moral view. It evolves on the basis of precedent and must not contravene other laws. Consequently, my personal view that pregnant women owe a degree of moral responsibility to the fetus does not dictate that the law should criminalize her actions when she fails to reach the desired standard.

Current law in England and Wales[2] proclaims that the fetus is not a 'person' until birth when it achieves an independent existence from its mother.[3] This does not prevent legal protection of the fetus before that

1

event, but does ensure that protection is on a statutory basis and not on the basis of legal personhood. Once birth occurs, the fetus becomes a person and may act on certain injuries earlier received. The civil and criminal responses of the law are quite distinct. Though a civil law action against a third party who injures a fetus born alive is permitted under the Congenital Disabilities (Civil Liability) Act 1976, a similar action against a mother whose acts or omissions in pregnancy harm the fetus born alive, is barred. Yet, the same is not necessarily true of the criminal law. In certain circumstances the 'born alive rule'[4] treats as homicide the harming of a fetus that is later born alive and dies as a result of its injuries. To date the rule has been applied only to third parties, but the potential remains to apply the rule to pregnant women. The born alive rule has arisen out of recognition that though the fetus is not for legal purposes a person when the harmful act is carried out, it *is* a person when the act culminates in death. Hence, even though the act occurred when the child was a fetus, the perpetrator is convicted of a crime against a 'person' as defined by the law.

Certain states in the USA, most of which share their common law origins with England, have applied principles stemming from the born alive rule to criminalize recent mothers who harmed or killed the fetus born alive.[5] The extensions of the born alive rule in the USA not only generate interesting academic and political controversy, but also provide a means by which to determine the success of such a criminal law policy and thus its relevance as a potential solution in England and Wales. Lawyers and bioethicists have a duty to anticipate potential applications of law and policy and to explore and analyse them. The main objective of this work is to fulfil this role to the extent of my expertise. I do not consider in detail the potential impact of religion, social class, race, economics, or politics. This I must leave to eminent social scientists. However, as far as possible an attempt is made to arrive at a legally workable means of effecting a compromise in the specific dilemma of how to adequately protect the human rights of the pregnant woman, the state interest in protecting the fetus and the rights of the child born alive. This stems from the wider moral dilemma that it is neither acceptable to view the pregnant woman as a mere fetal container, nor is it acceptable to view the fetus as a being without intrinsic value.

The state interest in protecting the fetus is considered in Chapter 1 and the importance of autonomy of the pregnant woman is examined in Chapter 2. Chapter 3 demonstrates the means by which the born alive rule was extended in certain states in America and Chapter 4 looks at the potential for extension in the UK. Chapter 5 considers legal arguments against extended criminalization and it is argued in Chapter 6 that existing criminal, civil and family law measures together with adequate healthcare provisions offer a better solution than extended criminalization on both pragmatic and legal grounds. This chapter provides a backdrop for the ensuing debate. It looks in greater detail at the nature of maternal acts and omissions that can harm or kill the fetus born alive and then goes on to examine the 'born alive rule' which has enabled extension of criminalization in the USA and has potential for extension in England and Wales.

Harmful Acts and Omissions of the Pregnant Woman

Many acts or omissions of a pregnant woman may result in damage to the fetus. The diverse range of harmful factors is outlined in Table 1.

Some of the hazards referred to, such as passive smoking, the effects of pollution and even infectious diseases and genetic conditions of which the pregnant woman is unaware,[6] are not solely the responsibility of the pregnant woman.[7] Other, preventable harms are caused by specific acts or omissions of the pregnant woman. The inability of the fetus to protect itself, its total dependence on the pregnant woman and the supposed 'natural bond' that society expects her to forge with her fetus makes preventable harm caused by the pregnant woman particularly abhorrent in the eyes of the public. Failure to abstain from tobacco, alcohol or illicit drugs, to take the appropriate dietary supplements, to rest and to submit to certain pre-natal tests all potentially contain an element of culpability.

Some harmful acts are currently illegal. In North America a 'bio-underclass' of neonates has emerged due to their mothers taking cocaine whilst pregnant.[8] The American Medical Association Board of Trustees reported that as many as 11 per cent of American pregnant women used an illegal drug during pregnancy, and of these 75 per cent used cocaine.[9] There is evidence that hard drug use is becoming more common in England, especially amongst the young,[10] and there is a corresponding recognition that England must develop a clear policy to deal with the growing number of drug-addicted new-born babies that result. The criminal law already imposes sanctions when an individual engages in illicit substance use. The question remains whether or not to impose additional sanctions based on the person's pregnant status. If policy dictates that the additional harm caused to the fetus by the illegal drug habit warrants further sanctions, then the next question is whether to impose sanctions for harmful activities which are not currently outlawed. Depending on the extent of use, smoking tobacco or drinking excess alcohol can be as harmful or more harmful to the fetus and resulting child than the use of illicit substances in pregnancy.

Intake of (Currently) Legal Substances by Pregnant Women

Of the legal but preventable activities in which a pregnant woman can engage, the two most obviously harmful to the fetus include smoking tobacco and drinking alcohol. The former is not illegal under any circumstances, though it is recognized as harmful to the smoker, to passive smokers, and can result in the low birth-weight of the neonate. This in turn increases the incidence of jaundice, hypoglycaemia, neonatal

Table 1   Strickland and Whicker, 'Prenatal Hazards: Estimates of Exposure and Adverse Effects'[11]

Types of Hazards/Risks	Estimates of Exposure/Adverse Effects
Crack/cocaine	Ten thousand to 100,000 infants per year are affected by exposure to crack/cocaine. Harmful effects: premature birth, low birth-weight, tremors, genital-urinary tract disorders, irritability, and fetal tachycardia.
Other illicit drugs (i.e. Marijuana, amphetamines, opiates, PCP)	Approximately 350,000 to 375,000 infants may be exposed to some illicit substance. Harmful effects: lethargy, premature birth, low birth-weight, skull malformations, neurological disorders, developmental problems, tremors, wakefulness, and heightened risk of sudden infant death syndrome.
Tobacco	Approximately 750,000 infants are exposed to cigarette smoke and by-products each year. Harmful effects: spontaneous abortion, decreased birth-weight, increased likelihood of sudden infant death syndrome, tremors, and abnormal responses to sound.
Carbon Monoxide	No estimates exist of fetal exposure to carbon monoxide concentrations in major urban areas or of those living near industrial plants. Harmful effects: same as exposure to one pack of cigarettes a day.
Lead	Over 40,000 prenatal exposures occur annually. In the United States, the average woman is not exposed in high-risk employment industries but rather the exposure comes from lead-based paints and leaded gasolines. Harmful effects: post-birth delay in cognitive development, neurobehavioural problems, and impaired hearing.
Alcohol	As many as 6,000 to 8,000 infants per year are born with fetal alcohol syndrome. Harmful effects: irritability, lowering of IQs, mental retardation, hyperactivity, facial abnormalities such as malformed lips or misaligned teeth, impulsiveness, lack of concentration, and social withdrawal.
Genetic conditions	An estimated 30,000 infants per year are born with a major genetic condition. Harmful effects: vary according to the condition.
Infectious diseases	It is expected that 4,000 to 5,000 infants per year will contract HIV from their mother during pregnancy. Harmful effects: neurological problems, frequent illnesses, stunted physical growth, and death.

infant death, poor physical growth and retarded intellectual development.[12] The White Paper 'Smoking Kills'[13] recognized that smoking in pregnancy is harmful to the fetus as it passes on harmful carcinogens and can lead to pre-term delivery and lower birth-weight.[14] Smoking is also associated with miscarriage, sudden infant death syndrome[15] and respiratory problems in young children.[16] In 1997 in the UK, 24 per cent of women smoked in pregnancy and of these, only 33 per cent gave up whilst pregnant.[17]

A recent American study[18] claimed that pregnant women who smoke during pregnancy collectively do more harm to their children born alive than the high profile cocaine abusing pregnant women. The study showed that up to a quarter of American pregnant women smoke and that nicotine inflicts serious damage on the fetus, even if the levels are not high enough to cause low birth-weight. Yet some states have introduced harsh criminal sanctions for cocaine use in pregnancy, but have been unable to criminalize the activities of smoking tobacco due to human rights objections.

Conversely, drinking alcohol is potentially illegal if coupled with certain other activities, such as driving a car. Some states seek to make excessive alcohol intake illegal in a similar manner, when coupled with pregnancy. It is one of the best documented preventable causes of birth defects potentially resulting in 'fetal alcohol syndrome' (FAS) and 'fetal alcohol effects' (FAE).[19] One study reported the worldwide rate of FAS to be 1.9 cases per 1,000 live births.[20] The Fetal Alcohol Study Group of the Research Society on Alcoholism recognized three main symptoms of FAS; pre-natal or post-natal growth retardation; central nervous system impairment; and types of facial dysmorphology.[21] Hyperactivity is often evident as the child progresses, and the adult is likely to maintain subnormal intellectual functioning, poor concentration, memory deficit and impaired judgement.[22] The effect of such a preventable syndrome comes not only at the cost of expenditure by the state in terms of medical treatment,[23] but also at the cost of the possible link between FAS and criminality.[24] FAE is less severe and usually results in behavioural problems.

In the UK, the Royal College of Physicians of London issued guidance in 1987[25] advising practitioners to be aware of the ill-effects of heavy alcohol consumption during pregnancy. Further, the Advisory Committee of the Royal College of Obstetricians and Gynaecologists issued guidance[26] to aid the diagnosis and establish the causes of both FAS and FAE. The guidance recognized both heavy alcohol consumption and social consumption (of over 15 units per week) as potentially harmful to the fetus.

FAS/E is potentially caused not only by the woman who drinks excessive amounts of alcohol during pregnancy, but also by the imbiber who abstains from the onset of pregnancy. The effects of alcoholism can remain in the woman's blood stream during the early stages of pregnancy and pass through the placenta to damage the fetus.[27] This presents an additional problem for proponents of criminalization, for a society that wishes to prevent damage to the fetus through FAS, needs not only to control the woman's behaviour during pregnancy, but also prior to it. With the present state of medical knowledge it is also difficult to gauge how much alcohol is needed to cause ill-effects to the fetus and child born alive. One serious drinking bout is potentially as harmful as regular, but smaller sessions, and ill-effect is dependent upon the gestational stage of the fetus. Yet, despite the causational problems involved in prosecuting women for imbibing alcohol during pregnancy, there have been a number of cases in the USA,[28] where pregnant women have been charged with fetal abuse for drinking during pregnancy and causing FAS in the resulting child.

Intake of Illegal Substances by Pregnant Women

A pregnant woman taking illicit drugs passes the effects of her conduct through the umbilical cord to the fetus. Cocaine, for example, reduces the flow of blood and oxygen to the fetus, retarding its growth and increasing incidents of fetal fatalities.[29] Drug-addicted pregnant women are more likely to give birth prematurely and to suffer *abruptio placentae* during which the placenta tears from the uterine lining, reducing the oxygen flow to the fetus and increasing the incidence of still-birth and brain damage.[30] Babies born to cocaine- or heroin-addicted mothers face the ordeal of withdrawal from the drug involving symptoms of vomiting, diarrhoea, seizures and shrill crying. Following this, babies will often present with neurological and behavioural abnormalities and cognitive deficits.[31]

The extent of harm often relates to the stage in pregnancy when the drug is used. Substance abuse in the first months of pregnancy often has the direst effect, because the development of the brain is particularly susceptible to damage at this stage. However, at this point the offending user may not realize that she is pregnant. For this reason she may lack the necessary culpability for the particular crime. It is drug use in the later stages of pregnancy that is more frequently criminalized in the USA due in part to the ability to detect the drug in the neonate's blood stream.[32] Following the birth of the child, the continuing drug use of either parent can increase the risks of harm to the child, especially where the child has behavioural and health problems associated with its exposure to drugs *in utero*. One study suggested that incidents of child abuse are increased,[33] partly due to the infant's inability to bond to the mother, for which it is blamed. Certainly, financial constraints are placed on drug-using parents due to the high costs of the substance.

It is not only 'Class A' drugs that harm the fetus. Ammenheuser and colleagues at the University of Texas[34] conducted a recent study comparing 17 pregnant women who smoked marijuana but not any other illegal drug or tobacco, and 17 women who used no such drug. They found that the frequency of mutations in the DNA of neonates was nearly three times as high in the marijuana users.

To punish currently legal acts, such as alcohol consumption, on the basis that a person is pregnant may be criticized on the ground that as the fetus is not a person in law, such a policy would discriminate against pregnant women and offend their human rights. Illegal activities, on the other hand, already have the force of society's condemnation behind them, and it might therefore be argued that the additional harm caused to the fetus by the illegal activity deserves extra punishment. Yet the mere fact that the offending substance is already illegal does not necessarily make it any more harmful to the fetus and child born alive than use of some legal substances. If sanctions are extended on the basis that a currently illegal activity also harms a fetus/child born alive, then there is a powerful case for extending sanctions where an equally harmful activity is currently legal. The 'slippery slope' argument counsels against the extension of the criminal law where pregnant women are already in breach of existing law. Instead, the same sanctions should be indiscriminately applied to the pregnant and non-pregnant alike and alternative means of aiding the fetus employed.

Four Possible Crimes under the 'Born Alive Rule'

Evolution of the principles contained in the born alive rule could ensure the successful criminalization of recent mothers for their harmful acts and omissions in pregnancy. Four categories of extension are examined in detail in Chapter 3. The first category represents the original rule as currently applied in England and Wales which, depending on *mens rea* and causation, criminalizes third parties who injure a fetus *in utero* which is later born alive and dies as a result of the injury.

In the United States the rule has been extended to incorporate a second category; the recent mother who has given birth to a baby which then dies as a direct result of her acts or omissions during pregnancy. The third category involves a further extension in the USA: in this scenario the recent mother has given birth to a baby which does not die, but is *injured* as a direct result of her acts or omissions during pregnancy. Third party acts are punishable in a similar way. The greatest extension involves the causation of injury or death to a child who is not actually 'born alive' at all, but has died *in utero*. In this case, the particular state's statutory definition of 'person' includes within the term, the viable fetus.[35] When the viable fetus dies or is injured as a result of third party or maternal action, some states criminalize the act under a deviation of the born alive rule, or when the judge or jury refuses to extend it thus, under special statutes created for the purpose.

It is contended that the extension of the born alive rule beyond the first category breaches the pregnant women's human rights. These rights should be protected to the extent that women are not subjected to additional criminalization for acts or omissions whilst pregnant which kill or injure a child born alive. Yet this is not to say that the pregnant woman should have unfettered rights to act to the fetus's detriment during pregnancy. In Chapter 2 a distinction is made between the stronger state duty not to interfere with an individual's competent choices, and the weaker duty to act positively to his benefit. Protection can be given to the fetus by curbing her positive choices, through abortion laws for example.

Notes

1   In medical terms, the embryo is that which exists between conception and 8 weeks gestation, and the fetus is that which exists between 8 weeks and birth. However, for present purposes, the term 'fetus' will encompass both fetus and embryo.
2   Hereafter, where the law in England is referred to, it should also be taken to include the law in Wales.
3   *Re F (in utero)* [1988] 2 All E.R. 193.
4   In England and Wales, the born alive rule states that a child born alive and dying of injuries attained whilst *in utero* is potentially a victim of a homicide provided that the relevant *mens rea* and causation can be proved. The *Attorney-General's Reference* (No. 3 of 1994) [1997] 3 All E.R. 936. To date the rule has been applied only to third parties.
5   By 1996 200 women in 35 states had been charged with abusing a fetus born alive. S. Lehigh, 'Common Sense, or a New Way to Ban Abortion?', *Boston Globe,* 15 September 1996, D1 (citing a study by the Center for Reproductive Law and Policy).
6   Even where the mother *is* aware of a potentially harmful condition that she may pass on to the child, whatever her perceived moral obligation, the standpoint adopted here is that the law should not operate so as to limit her procreative rights. In the USA it has been feared that statutes criminalizing the wilful or neglectful transmission of HIV might be applied to mothers who pass it to the child *in utero*. See M.L. Closen, S.H. Isaacman, 'Criminally Pregnant: Are AIDS Transmission Laws Encouraging Abortion?' (1990) 76 *American Bar Association Journal* 73; D.A. Weiczorkowski, 'From Mother to Child ... A Criminal Pregnancy: Should Criminalization of the Prenatal Transfer of AIDS/HIV Be the Next Step Against this Deadly Epidemic?' (1993) 97 *Dickinson Law Review* 383; S.H. Isaacman, 'Are we Outlawing Motherhood for HIV-Infected Women?' (1991) 22 *Loyola University of Chicago Law Journal* 479.
7   Prescribed drugs might for example, cause problems. See V. MacDonald, Health Correspondent, 'Prescribed Drugs do More Harm to Babies Than Heroin', *The Sunday Telegraph,* 21 September 1997, 18 (b), which suggested that babies born to mothers addicted to common tranquillizers are more likely to be admitted to intensive-care units than babies born to heroin or methadone addicts.
8   See J.V. Greer, 'The Drug Babies', *Exceptional Children* 56 (1990), 382 at 382 quoting Dr. H. Nickens of the American Society of Addiction Medicine who uses the term 'to define an entirely new, organic brain syndrome, based on the physical and chemical damage done to fetal brains by drug-abusing mothers'.
9   American Medical Association Board of Trustees, 'Legal Intervention During Pregnancy', *Journal of the American Medical Association*, 264 (1990), 2663.
10 See A. Travis 'Youngsters Targeted in New Heroin Epidemic', *The Guardian,* 15 August 1998, 1 col. 2.
11 R.A. Strickland and M.L. Whicker, 'Fetal Endangerment Versus Fetal Welfare: Discretion of Prosecutors in Determining Criminal Liability' in Patricia Boling (Ed.) *Expecting Trouble: Surrogacy, Fetal Abuse and New Reproductive Technologies* (Westview Press: San Francisco and Oxford, 1995) at 56.
12 See S.S. Balisy, 'Maternal Substance Abuse: The Need to Provide Legal Protection for the Fetus' (1987) 60 *Southern California Law Review* 1209 at 1218.

13 Department of Health, *Smoking Kills, A White Paper on Tobacco* (Department of Health: London, 30 November 1998) Cm. 4177.

14 *Ibid.*, para. 5.1 citing S.S. Hecht, et. al. 'Metabolites of the Tobacco-Specific Lung Carcinogen 4-(methylnitrosoamino)-1-(3-pyridyl)-1-butanone (nnk) in the Urine of Newborn Infants', *American Chemistry Society* 216 (1998), 32. For other harmful effects of smoking on the fetus see Department of Health, *Report on the Scientific Committee on Tobacco and Health* (Department of Health: London, 20 March 1998) para 6, which concludes at 6.4.5, 'Maternal smoking in pregnancy may increase the risk of congenital defects. Prevention may require smoking cessation before conception.'

15 E.A. Mitchell, J. Milerad, 'Smoking and Sudden Infant Death Syndrome', in World Health Organisation, *Tobacco Free Initiative, International Consultation on Environmental Tobacco Smoke (ETS) and Child Health* (World Health Organisation: Geneva, 1999) at 105, indicating that infants of mothers who smoked in pregnancy are at a five-fold increased risk of sudden infant death syndrome when compared with those with non-smoking mothers. Importantly, where the mother did not smoke but the father (present during pregnancy) did, the risk of sudden infant death syndrome was increased by 1.4 fold when compared with children of non-smoking parents.

16 K. Bolling and L. Owen, *Smoking and Pregnancy: A Survey of Knowledge, Attitudes and Behaviour* (Health Education Authority: London, 1997), v.

17 Department of Health, *Smoking Kills op. cit.*, para 5.2 citing K. Foster et. al., *Infant Feeding 1995: Office for National Statistics* (The Stationery Office: London, 1997).

18 T. Slotkin of Duke University, North Carolina writing in the *Journal of Pharmacology and Experimental Therapeutics,* reported in *The Guardian,* 3 June 1998, 5 col. 3.

19 It was first used in 1973 by British physicians, K.L. Jones, D.W. Smith, C.N. Ulleland and A.P. Streissguth, 'Patterns of Malformation in Offspring of Chronic Alcoholic Mothers', *Lancet* (i) (1973), 1267.

20 E.L. Abel and R.J. Sokel in 'Incidence of Fetal Alcohol Syndrome and Economic Impact of FAS-Related Anomalies', *Drug Alcohol Depend.* 19 (1987), 51, considered 19 worldwide studies on FAS frequency.

21 H. Rosett and L. Weiner, *Alcohol and the Fetus* (1984) as quoted by S.S. Balisy *op. cit.,* 1212.

22 See The Committee on Substance Abuse and Committee on Children with Disabilities, 'Fetal Alcohol Syndrome and Fetal Alcohol Effects', *Paediatrics* 91(5) (1993), 1004. Also A. Pytkowicz Streissguth et. al., 'Fetal Alcohol Syndrome in Adolescents and Adults, *Journal of the American Medical Association* 265(15) (1991), 1961.

23 E.L. Abel and R.J. Sokel, *op. cit.,* 112, estimate that treatment in the United States costs over $321 million a year.

24 See for example, M.D. Bellew, 'Fetal Alcohol Syndrome, Fetal Alcohol Effect and Genetic Influence on Alcoholism', *Capital Concerns (Kentucky Capital Litigation Resource Center – a Branch of the Kentucky Department of Public Advocacy)* 6 (1991), 1 at 6. In *Harris v. Vasquez*, 913 F.2d 606 (9th Cir. 1990), FAS was raised as a mitigator.

25 Royal College of Physicians of London, *A Great and Growing Evil – The Medical Consequences of Alcohol Abuse* (Royal College of Physicians of London: London, 1987).

26 Royal College of Obstetricians and Gynaecologists 'Alcohol Consumption in Pregnancy' (RCOG: London, 1999) website: http://www.rcog.org. uk/guidelines/alcohol.htm. Valid until November 1999.

27 Bellew, *op cit.*, 2.

28 For example, *State v. Pfannensteil* No. 1-908CR (Wyo. Cty Ct. Albany Cty Jan. 5 1990).

29 See J.W. Steverson 'Stopping Fetal Abuse with No-pregnancy and Drug Treatment Probation Conditions' (1994) 34(2) *Santa Clara Law Review* 295, at 302.

30 Steverson, *ibid.*, 303.

31 See for example S.S. Balisy, *op. cit.,* 1217.

32 The rationale and inappropriateness of this system are examined in Chapter 5 p. 90.

33 I.J. Chasnoff, 'Drug Use In Pregnancy: Parameters of Risk', *Pediatric Clinicians of North America* 35 (1988), 1403.
34 N. Boyce, 'Bad Dope', *New Scientist,* 25 July 1998, 16.
35 See Chapter 3 p. 47.

Chapter 1

The Status of the Fetus

In England and Wales the law gradually increases the protection of the fetus as it comes nearer to legal personhood, which is achieved at birth. Though this does not necessarily bring the rights of fetus and woman into conflict, it has the effect of gradually increasing the potential for conflict.

In the USA, the law operates in a similar manner, increasing the protection of the fetus as it progresses in gestation. The US Constitution, which is defined and protected by the Supreme Court, governs the entire federal system. The Constitution protects the human rights of the citizens of America and has had a major role in defining the abortion rights of pregnant women. Each individual state is left to develop its own laws to the extent that it does not conflict with the Constitution. States have different definitions of the onset of legal personhood and operate different mechanisms to ensure that the fetus is protected adequately before that time. The 'born alive rule' that operates in English law has also been adopted by many states in America. There it has been adapted and extended in various ways. In its narrowest form (and its current state in England and Wales) it declares that a third party who injures a fetus which is later born alive and dies as a result of the injury, may be guilty of homicide. Three possible extensions were examined in the Introduction. The first extends the rule to criminalize women who, whilst pregnant, harm the fetus which is born alive and dies as a result of those injuries. The second category extends the rule to include third parties or women who, whilst pregnant, cause *injury* to a child born alive. The third includes third parties or pregnant women who cause injury or death to a *fetus,* which for the purposes of the state law is defined as a person. Alternatively, the born alive rule has been overridden with existing or newly enacted legislation.

The government has an interest in protecting the fetus, but that protection proceeds on the basis of its potential to become a person in law, and its human derivation. As there is potential for the interests of fetus and pregnant woman to conflict, a balancing exercise must take place to determine the respective legal rights of each. A theory of autonomy is expounded in Chapter 2 in an attempt to fulfil this criterion. It is then argued that criminalizing pregnant women does little to overcome problems caused by maternal activities that harm the fetus and child born alive in practical terms, and is theoretically unsound in terms of ethical and legal theory.

The Importance of Autonomy

The balancing of the rights of the pregnant woman and fetus is an exercise not only of moral philosophy but also of law. It has been stated in the Introduction that, though law and ethics are entwined, the law is bound by rules of precedence and general applicability. This and the next chapter therefore consider moral arguments purely in the context of their potential application in law. This chapter considers the appropriate legal response to the need to protect the fetus. The next attempts to balance this with the human rights of the pregnant woman. Of the various rights that potentially conflict with the interests of the fetus, autonomy is given precedence. It is argued that the key to an appropriate balance of interests and rights lies here.

Gerald Dworkin put forward a theory of autonomy with a procedural rather than a substantive definition.[1] Once the definition is examined and accepted, it is suggested that *negative* rights to freedom from intervention warrant greater protection than *positive* rights to demand it. In the unique circumstances where the woman's human rights potentially conflict with the interests of the fetus and potential child, it is argued that a pregnant woman's negative rights should be protected to the same extent as a non-pregnant individual's. Any conduct that would not be considered illegal in the absence of pregnancy, should be tolerated in law.[2] Thus, it is contended that the pregnant woman has a right to insist that others do not damage the fetus she carries, or end its life without her consent. She has a legal right to continue activities that are considered legal in the absence of pregnancy, such as smoking tobacco, working or drinking alcohol, even though harm may result to the fetus.

It cannot be stated as a general rule that all individuals should be treated equally with regard to their negative rights to shun state intervention. There are cases where the law rightly reacts by prohibiting acts that may harm the human rights of other persons. An epileptic may be banned from driving until his condition is stabilized. A driver may be criminalized for driving under the influence of alcohol. Why then can we not prohibit a woman from drinking, smoking, working, or over-exercising whilst pregnant? The answer is a complex one. It is based on the necessity to reach a compromise between the rights of the woman and the interests of the fetus and potential child. The drunk driver and epileptic driver risk damage to the human rights, and in particular the right to life, of other individuals. The consequent limitations on their activities are well defined and the damage to their autonomy small. Balancing the two, it is possible to prevent substantial harm whilst impinging in only a minor way on the driver's autonomy.

In the case of the pregnant woman, her activities may cause harm or loss of life to a potential being, which does not yet carry full human rights. Due to the fact that the fetus is contained within the womb of the woman and therefore utterly reliant on her for life, protecting it from potential harm would involve considerable limitation of the pregnant woman's autonomy. The balance here is quite different; it is unsustainable.

Conversely, the value of autonomy is not always important enough to warrant third parties following the whim of the pregnant woman to the detriment of the fetus. Therefore, positive action involving third parties, such as abortion, genetic engineering or fetal surgery, should not be granted to the pregnant woman without consideration of the state interest in protecting the fetus and potential child. This position is not uncontentious, but is suggested as a legally applicable means of protecting both fetus and pregnant woman. It does not accord with every sector of public opinion but, like the legal definition of personhood at birth, it compromises between the various moral standpoints.

The Status of the Fetus

The status of the fetus is considered in this chapter in order to support two propositions. The first is that the woman's right to reject state intervention with regard to her otherwise legal acts and omissions in pregnancy overrides the state interest in fetal health or life. The second is that the state has a duty to protect the fetus, potential child and child born alive through curbing the pregnant woman's demands for intervention. A charged debate surrounds the area and it is not possible within the scope of this work to voice each of the numerous religious, cultural and political standpoints. Instead, some of the arguments are eliminated and others are commended in an attempt at compromise, and to reach a legally workable conclusion.

There is a wide divergence in views as to the relevant moral status of the fetus. For Peter Singer[3] killing is wrong when it frustrates the desire of a self-conscious being to live. On this basis, killing a fetus is different to killing an adult. Even the death of a neonate, caused by acts or omissions of the mother whilst pregnant, might be viewed as acceptable on the basis that the child is not yet self-conscious. At the opposite end of the spectrum the Roman Catholic Church takes a fundamentalist position, contending that the fetus has a soul from conception and that its sanctity of life should be respected from that point. There are various positions that view stages in-between conception and autonomous thinking as the all-important time when the fetus should be protected in law as a person.[4] In English law personhood is not achieved until birth, and the same is true in many American states.[5] Lack of personhood status does not prevent protection of the fetus on other grounds, but to ascribe legal personhood to the fetus would be to ascribe all the corollary legal rights that personhood entails. This, it is submitted, is legally unworkable. If the law labels a fetus a 'person,' it should have the full rights of a person resulting in the potential conflict of legal rights between fetus and pregnant woman. Consider, for example, the pregnant woman whose life ultimately depends on medical treatment that will kill the fetus. If both are persons of equal legal standing, then it becomes essential to determine whose rights should take precedence. Even where both would die without the treatment, the law would have difficulty permitting the intentional killing of the fetus person.[6] In fact the equal rights of both fetus and pregnant woman lead to quite bizarre scenarios. In Missouri, where a fetus is defined as a person from conception for the purposes of certain laws, a pregnant woman serving three years for forgery and theft claimed, though she was ultimately unsuccessful, that the state was unconstitutionally imprisoning her fetus who had committed no crime whatsoever.[7]

Brody[8] argued that fetuses are persons and that though there is no duty to *save* another fetal-person, there is a positive duty not to *harm* him. On this view, all the acts in-between harming and killing would become illegal. This would mean that the woman's right to smoke, drink, exercise, not exercise, work, or live in a polluted area could be jeopardized if the fetus is also labelled a person. The fact that pregnant woman and fetus are inextricably linked means that the potential for conflict in rights and interests is immense. The legal label 'person' becomes empty and irrelevant if what really matters is not when personhood physically begins, but when it becomes morally important.[9] The argument that the law should ascribe the fetus personhood rights from conception is therefore flawed. Other moral arguments warrant the legal protection of the fetus, not as a person but as an entity capable of achieving personhood.

The Argument of Potential for Life

The fetus has potential to become a person. On this basis it might be offered protection from a particular point when its potential becomes so significant that it should be regarded for all intents and purposes as a person; it might be afforded gradually increasing protection as its potential increases; or retrospective protection when its potential has been realized because it has been born alive. Each of these claims is examined in turn. The first is rejected whilst the second and third are accepted as offering useful guidance as to the appropriate level of protection to afford the fetus.

The first argument envisages protection from a particular point in gestation, such as conception or viability, when potential becomes pertinent for some reason. At this point the fetus should be protected on an equal basis with born persons. As a *child* is given protection and valued highly, the proponents argue, so too the fetal potential for becoming this child should be valued from that point in time.[10]

Some commentators argue that the point in gestation where potential should result in legal personhood status is viability.[11&12] This is because the fetus can potentially survive independently of and externally to the woman from this point. Various states in America have legislated to this effect.[13]

However, there are problems of legal certainty in this argument, because as technology advances, the point when a fetus becomes viable changes. The fetus is a potential person, but the argument fails to provide any firm method by which to afford the fetus protection and for this reason it is subject to criticism. Onset of personhood rights at birth has the advantage of certainty, though this is not to say that protection (on a basis other than legal personhood) cannot gradually increase throughout gestation as the fetus nears childhood.

An alternative view is that the fetus should be protected from conception by virtue of its potential to become a person. Marquis[14] argued that to deprive the fetus of its future is similar in moral terms to depriving an adult of his future. Abortion is therefore justifiable only when it would also be morally acceptable to kill a competent adult. Brown[15] contended that the 'future like ours' argument is flawed because it is derived from equivocation on what constitutes 'a future of value'. The term, he argued, can be taken to mean 'potential future of value' or 'self-represented future of value'. As to the latter, the fetus does not have any concept of self. Brown stated:

> [O]ne should not fall into the trap of thinking that the fetus as it was at the time of an abortion had a self-represented future to lose. One may mourn the absence of the child the fetus would have become, but in doing so one is coming to terms with a painful mental representation in one's own mental life, not acting on behalf of a person who had a future of his or her own.[16]

As to the former, Brown maintained that it is not presumptively seriously wrong to deprive someone of a potential future of value. People can and often do die in ways that do not violate their rights, such as the person who dies because the resources are not available to give him a kidney transplant. The potential future of value is dependent on favourable external circumstances and the fetus has no right to this. It relies on the woman to provide the environment that will enable it to realize its potential. The woman has no duty to provide this because it would involve the sacrifice of her own rights to autonomy and bodily integrity.[17]

Marquis responded,[18] acknowledging that the potential future of value theory does not entail a fetal right to its mother's uterus. Thus, the fetus has a right to life, but not the right to its mother's uterus. Therefore the fetus is just like a child. A child's parents have strong obligations to protect the well-being of their offspring. Abortion is therefore the killing of one's own child, which is abhorrent.

The future of value theory is valuable in its attempt to define the content of the right in the context of abortion. However, the theory is flawed in that it is incompatible with abstinence and contraception. A sperm and egg have a potential future of value as do human cells, which could be used to clone the donor. Savulescu[19] acknowledged that the future of value theory gives us a good reason not to kill the fetus, but argued convincingly that 'whether it is wrong depends on whether there are other good reasons, stronger reasons, to destroy it'. Arguably the protection of the pregnant woman's human rights presents a strong reason for limiting the protection afforded to the fetus. Though its potential for a future of value should prevent us from viewing it as a mere appendage of the pregnant woman, so too the rights and interests of the pregnant woman should prevent us from viewing her as a mere fetal container.

The second argument states that the fetus should gradually be afforded greater protection as its potential to become a person comes closer to realization. As the potential grows (as gestation proceeds) so the respect owed to the fetus is increased, and as the fetus always has some potential to become a person, it should always be protected to some degree. As it is not a person but merely a potential person, arguably protection should not be as great (or at least it should exist on a distinct basis) as that owed to a legal person. As Engelhardt[20] stated: 'If 'X' has potential 'Y', it follows that 'X' is not 'Y' and does not have the properties of 'Y' ... If 'X' has potential to be President, he does not have all the Presidential rights.' This argument is convincing. It provides a valid rationale for gradually increasing the protection of the fetus and represents the current legal stance in England and Wales. Of course, the theory provides no way of ascertaining the relevant degree of protection at each particular stage in gestation. A number of different religious perspectives might be used to illustrate this point, though there is not the scope in this book to consider them in detail. From the Jewish perspective, for example, Jakovits[21] contended that though full human status does not occur until birth, the potential for being human should be respected even before conception. Hence the seed must not be wasted because the sole purpose of procreation is the production of children. The theory of autonomy put forward in Chapter 2 presents a legally workable model to ascertain the required degree of protection owed to the fetus by virtue of its potential personhood.

The third position in the potentiality argument, suggests that only the future child has enough potential to warrant protection. These commentators can be sub-divided into those who look prospectively and those who look retrospectively at the rights of the fetus. The former group believes that the fetus has no significant human potential as long as there exists the woman's right to abort. Hence Radcliffe Richards proclaimed that once the mother decides not to terminate the pregnancy, the mother's autonomy can be overridden because the fetus is now a definite future child.[22] Yet it is impossible to say that a fetus is a definite future child, first because the decision of whether to terminate pregnancy is ongoing and secondly because there is always the unfortunate possibility of miscarriage or stillbirth.

The latter group proposes that the future child (fetus) deserves protection from a retrospective stance. In other words, rather than looking from the perspective of the fetus, the situation must be viewed from the perspective of the child. Hence it is the baby that has retrospective rights once it is born and has become a person.[23] Because these rights are retrospective, third parties are unable to tell if the fetus will later become a future person, and hence some protection is offered to all fetuses in the form of a deterrent. It is from this principle that Coke's 'born alive rule' stems. The *Attorney-General's Reference (No. 3 of 1994)*[24] is an example of its application.

Though the retrospective standpoint represents a valid state interest, the means of protecting that interest must take into account the rights of the pregnant woman and the wider legal and social consequences. It is suggested that the current application of the born alive rule in England and Wales recognizes the fetal potential for life whilst also protecting the pregnant woman by criminalizing the conduct of third parties whose actions cause death to the fetus born alive. A wider construction of the rule that imposes restrictions on the actions of pregnant woman would unduly impose on her human rights.

'Humanness'

The fetus is afforded a degree of retrospective protection out of a concern for the well-being of the future child. However, it is also protected prospectively (by the Abortion Act 1967, for example) because the fetus is human-derived and therefore has special significance. Kennedy[25] recognized the flaws in the 'fetal-person' debate, but argued that the fetus is special, not because it is a person but because of its 'humanness'. He stated that the fetus is sufficiently human-like to deserve special status and protection. It has the potential to become a person, he claimed, but more than this is needed before the state should afford it protection. That extra factor is provided by virtue of the fact that there is something that commands moral respect in human products.[26] Thus, research on the human embryo is acceptable only until it is 14 days old.[27] The embryo is to be destroyed after research, which arguably thwarts its potential to become a person. Yet research is carefully controlled out of a respect for the human derivation of the embryo.

The fact that the fetus is human-derived gives added force to the potentiality argument. The former argument taken alone is subject to criticism because, though the fetus is human-derived, so too is the sperm, the ovum and a myriad of other human products. Similarly, where the prospective potentiality argument is taken alone, it is seen that potential can be thwarted at any point. Take the two arguments together, however, and it becomes clear that the 'humanness' of the person, coupled with the fact that it is capable of becoming a person, make it important to gradually increase protection as the 'humanness' becomes more apparent and the potential more real.

This still leaves the appropriate level of protection uncertain. To what degree must the fetus be protected in view of its potential and humanness? On the basis of the above, the fetus should be protected, but its protection does not take precedence in all cases. There is a strong case for the proposition that if the fetus is not a human but is merely potentially so (with the added 'humanness' factor), the fetus is adequately protected by controlling the woman's right to demand state intervention (reducing her autonomy as the fetus grows in gestation as occurs currently under the law in England and Wales), so leaving her right to be free of intervention as unfettered as that of other non-pregnant individuals.

Ronald Dworkin[28] provided some support for this view. Looking in particular at abortion, Dworkin recognized two stances in the argument against it. First is the argument that the fetus is a person and has the same rights and interests that other persons have. He called this the 'derivative objection' to abortion. Second is the 'detached objection' that human life is sacred and that it begins when biological life begins, at conception. According to the latter view, abortion is wrong because it insults the intrinsic value found in any stage of human life. Dworkin argued that one of the main reasons for the huge controversy over abortion is the false representation of the first objection. In fact, the second objection is the more realistic and constructive. According to Dworkin, arguments based on the fetus having the same rights and interests as persons should be rejected:

> The belief that human life in any form has intrinsic, sacred value can therefore provide a reason for people to object violently to abortion, to regard it as wicked in all circumstances, without in any way believing that a tiny collection of cells just implanted in the womb, with as yet no organs or brain or nervous system, is already something with interests and rights.[29]

This view is similar to Kennedy's assertion that the 'humanness' of the fetus makes it worthy of protection. Though some might assert on this basis that abortion or other injury of the fetus is wholly wrong, Dworkin contended that there is no inconsistency in believing abortion to be wrong on the basis that life is sacred and yet recognizing that the decision to end fetal life in early pregnancy should be left to the pregnant woman; 'the person whose conscience is more directly connected to the choice and who has the greatest stake in it'.[30]

Therefore three arguments for the protection of the fetus have been accepted, based on the retrospective value of the future child, the prospective potential of the fetus, and the fact that the fetus is human-derived and special to us. The state has an interest in protecting the fetus, but that protection need not equal that accorded to actual legal persons. The next chapter considers the legal rights of the pregnant woman.

Notes

1   G. Dworkin, *The Theory and Practice of Autonomy* (Cambridge University Press: Cambridge and New York, 1988). The pregnant woman's autonomy rights are defined in Chapter 2. Dworkin laid little importance on substantive freedom (an autonomy with a

particular content) separating it from the all-important procedural independence (an actual independence). Provided the individual considered his higher-order preference in coming to a decision, the decision is autonomous even if the higher preferences obey authority. This makes autonomy compatible with human values of love, loyalty and commitment and avoids the unrealistic fixation of autonomy with a particular content.

2   Though, in order to give her real choices, issues regarding the best way to promote fetal health should be brought to her attention through educational measures. See Chapter 6.

3   P. Singer, *Practical Ethics* (Cambridge University Press: New York, 1993). See also M. Tooley, *Abortion and Infanticide* (Oxford University Press: Oxford 1983).

4   R. Gillon, 'Is there a "New Ethics of Abortion"', *Journal of Medical Ethics* 27 (2001),
5   charts the various points in gestation which have historically been assigned significance as the point at which the fetus develops personhood status. These include conception, the 'quickening' (usually around 20 weeks gestation), brain life (around 20-24 weeks), viability (currently around 22-24 weeks), birth and autonomous thinking.

5   UK: *Re F (in utero)* [1988] 2 All E.R. 193. USA: *In Re Peabody*, 5 N.Y.2d 541 at 546, 158 N.E.2d 841 at 844, 186 N.Y.S.2d 265 at 269 (1959). The New York Court of Appeals stated 'a child *en ventre sa mere* is not regarded as a person until it sees the light of day'. Note, however, that some states have enacted statutes to override this common law rule, as seen in Chapter 3.

6   The courts faced a similar dilemma in *Re A (Conjoined Twins: Medical Treatment)* [2000] 4 All ER 961 where the court authorized the separation of conjoined twins that would inevitably lead to the death of one twin on the basis that it was in the best interest of the other twin and was justified under the criminal law doctrine of necessity.

7   Editorial, 'Fetus Illegally Jailed, Inmate's Lawyer Argues', *Washington Times*, 4 August 1989, 4.

8   B. Brody, *Abortion and the Sanctity of Human Life: A Philosophical View* (MIT Press: Mass. USA, 1976), chapter 2.

9   See J. Harris, *The Value of Life: An Introduction to Medical Ethics* (Routledge and Kegan Paul: London, Mass., Melbourne, Henley, 1985), 14. Also J. Eekelaar 'Does a Mother have Legal Duties to her Unborn Child?' in P. Byrne (Ed.) *Health, Rights and Resources: King's College Studies 1987-8* (Oxford University Press: London, 1988), 55. Eekelaar argued at 58 that trying to solve moral issues by recourse to definitions, such as the definition of 'person' is flawed: 'Definitions are descriptions of factual phenomena; their applicability in the present context is, as a matter of language, uncertain. They cannot in themselves resolve the moral issues of how people should behave.'

10 For example see J.A. Parness and S.K. Pritchard, 'To Be or Not to Be: Protecting the Unborn's Potentiality of Life' (1982) 51(2) *Cincinnati Law Review* 257.

11 Viability is a term given to the stage when the fetus is developed enough to survive outside the pregnant woman. Viability shifts as science advances and babies have been known to survive birth at 22 weeks gestation. The Infant Life Preservation Act 1929, Section 1(2) defines viability as follows: 'For the purposes of this Act, evidence that a woman had at any material time been pregnant for a period of twenty-eight weeks or more shall be *prima facie* proof that she was at that time pregnant of a child capable of being born alive.'

12 For example, P. King, 'The Judicial Status of the Fetus: a Proposal for Legal Protection of the Unborn' (1979) 77(2) *Michigan Law Review* 1647. For an opposing view, see C.J. Dougherty, 'The Right to Begin Life with Sound Body and Mind: Fetal Patients and Conflicts with Their Mothers', (1985) 63(7) *University of Detroit Law Review* 89 at 115.

13 See Chapter 3 p. 47.

14 D. Marquis, 'Why Abortion is Immoral', *The Journal of Philosophy* 86 (1989), 183. ' ... we can start from the following unproblematic assumption: it is wrong to kill *us* ... when I am killed I am deprived of all the value of my future. Inflicting this loss on me is ultimately what makes killing wrong. The future of a standard fetus includes a set of experiences, projects, activities and such which are identical with the futures of adult

human beings and the futures of young children. Since the reason that is sufficient to explain why it is wrong to kill human beings after the time of birth is a reason that also applies to fetuses, it follows that abortion is *prima facie* seriously wrong.' At 189, 202.

15 M.T. Brown, 'The Morality of Abortion and the Deprivation of Futures', *Journal of Medical Ethics* 26 (2000), 103; 'A Future Like Ours Revisited', *Journal of Medical Ethics* 28 (2002), 192.

16 *Ibid* (2000), 107.

17 'Since the fetus will become a person who has the capacity to enjoy its life and derive meaning from it only if it has access to the reproductive system of a woman, abortion would be presumptively wrong only if women had no presumptive right to control access to their reproductive systems. The fetus certainly needs its uterine environment if it is to realize its potential, but persons do not in general have a right to satisfy their needs at the expense of the autonomy, bodily integrity and wellbeing of another person. If I need a bone marrow transplant in order to realize my potential future of value, I do not thereby gain a right to your bone marrow, even if you are my mother.' *Ibid.*, 104.

18 D. Marquis, 'A Defence of the Potential Future of Value Theory', *Journal of Medical Ethics* 28 (2002), 198.

19 J. Savulescu, 'Abortion, Embryo Destruction and the Future of Value Argument', *Journal of Medical Ethics* 28 (2002), 133.

20 T. Engelhardt in 'Viability and the Use of the Fetus' in Bondeson, Engelhardt, Spicker and Winship, *Abortion and the Status of the Fetus: Philosophy and Medicine Volume 13, A Collection of Essays* (Reidel: New York, 1983), 184. So too, J. Harris *op. cit.*, 10 argued that one day we will all die, but do not want to be prematurely treated as dead. R. Gillon, 'Human Embryos and the Argument from Potential', *Journal of Medical Ethics* 17 (1991), 59, at 61 states: 'The crucial moral question remains: at which phases of human development should individuals within those phases be accorded the intrinsic right to life that we all agree must be accorded to individuals who are in the person phase of human development? And alas the argument from potential, in whatever version, does not ... give us an answer to that question ...'

21 I. Jakovits, 'Respect for Life: Embryonic Considerations', in D.R. Bromham, M.E. Dalton, J.C. Jackson and P.J. Millican, *Ethics in Reproductive Medicine* (Springer-Verlag Ltd: London, 1992), 47.

22 Radcliffe Richards, 'Maternal-Fetal Conflict', in S. Bewley and R. Humphrey Ward (Ed.), *Ethics in Obstetrics and Gynaecology* (RCOG Press: London, 1994), 34.

23 See Congenital Disabilities (Civil Liability) Act 1976 s. 1(1). Also see R. Gillon, 'Pregnancy, Obstetrics and the Moral Status of the Fetus', *Journal of Medical Ethics* 14 (1988), 3. As T. Engelhardt, *op. cit.*, 186 stated: 'Potential persons have no actual rights, however the actual persons they become will have strong rights and claims. Therefore, actions harming future persons are immoral due to a causal chain that is part of the gestational history of the body of that person.'

24 *Attorney-General's Reference (No. 3 of 1994)* [1996] 2 All E.R. 10, [1997] 3 All E.R. 936. See Chapter 4 p. 56.

25 See I. Kennedy, *Treat Me Right: Essays in Medical Law and Ethics* (Clarendon Press: Oxford, 1988), 125.

26 See J.E. Myers 'Abuse and Neglect of the Unborn: Can the State Intervene?' (1984) 20 *Duquesne Law Review* 1; B. Steinbock, *Life Before Birth: The Moral and Legal Status of Embryos and Fetuses* (Oxford University Press: New York and Oxford, 1992), 40; S.L. Barron, 'The Galton Lecture for 1992: The Changing Status of the Fetus', S.L. Barron and D.F. Roberts (Eds.) *Issues in Fetal Medicine,* Proceedings of the 29th Annual Symposium of the Galton Institute 1992 (Macmillan Press Ltd: London and New York, 1995), at 1-24 for commentary on the gradually increasing symbolic significance of the fetus.

27 Department of Social Security, *Report of the Committee of Inquiry into Human Fertilisation and Embryology* (London: HMSO, 1984), 58-66.

28   R. Dworkin, *Life's Dominion: An Argument about Abortion and Euthanasia*
      (HarperCollins: London, 1993).

29   Dworkin, *ibid.*, 12.

30   Dworkin, *ibid.*, 15. Dworkin states, 'That combination of views is not only consistent but
      is in keeping with a great tradition of freedom of conscience in modern pluralistic
      democracies. It is a very popular view that government has no business dictating what
      its citizens should think about ethical and spiritual values, especially religious ones. ... If
      the great battles over abortion and euthanasia are really about the intrinsic, cosmic value
      of a human life, as I claim they are, then those battles have at least a quasi-religious
      nature, and it is hardly surprising that many people believe both that abortion and
      euthanasia are profoundly wrong and that it is no part of the proper business of
      government to try to stamp them out with the jackboots of the criminal law.' At 15.

Chapter 2

The State Interest in Protecting the Pregnant Woman and the Significance of Autonomy

Just as the state has a legitimate interest in protecting the fetus, potential child and child born alive, so too it has a duty to protect the rights and interests of the pregnant woman and mother. It is undesirable to protect the state interest in the fetus through extended criminalization of pregnant women and recent mothers, on the following grounds. The woman's human rights would potentially be breached through such a policy.[1] Her rights must be balanced with the state interest in protecting the fetus, future child, and child born alive, but some grading of rights is inevitable. As the fetus is only a potential child, it cannot claim human rights until it is born alive. Even at that point it cannot claim a full complement of rights retrospectively: it cannot claim that all injuries received *in utero* are actionable upon live birth without unduly limiting the human rights of all pregnant women and indeed women of child-bearing capability. Were extended criminalization to produce only a limited effect on the rights and interests of the pregnant woman and a valuable effect on the fetus and future child then such a policy might be considered. However, according to Chapters 3 and 5, extended criminalization has undesirable consequences for the fetus and future child, and potential far-reaching adverse effects on the woman's rights, and in particular her right to autonomy. A better effect can arguably be achieved through education and treatment,[2] which both aid the fetus and protect (and enhance) maternal autonomy rights.

Autonomy is only one of the human rights threatened by a policy of extended criminalization. It forms the crux of this chapter because the principle can be utilized to achieve a legally effective compromise between the state's interests in protecting the fetus and the pregnant woman. To respect an individual's autonomy may imply a state duty to act positively to his benefit, or it may involve a duty not to interfere with his competent choices. Gillon[3] contends that in the context of the healthcare arena the latter aspect of autonomy is the stronger. Thus there is a negative obligation on the state to withhold interference, which is stronger than the positive duty to intervene on her behalf and to the detriment of the fetus. By enforcing the negative obligation, the rights which the woman enjoyed prior to pregnancy are not withheld. She can continue to drink, smoke and work, but cannot in all circumstances demand an abortion, or fetal surgery. Positive obligations are not considered in detail in this work. However, though the state's negative obligation is of primary importance, this is not to say that the positive obligation is non-existent. Careful balancing is needed to ensure fairness and justice when comparing the weaker, positive duty of the state to aid the woman to the fetus' detriment with the mere potential capacity of the fetus to achieve personhood. In Chapter 6 it is contended that the state has a positive obligation to commit adequate resources to healthcare treatment and educational initiatives aimed at women likely to harm the fetus born alive. Though it is acknowledged that this in itself might be viewed as a form of paternalism, it is viewed as an acceptable method of aiding both fetus and woman through empowerment of the latter.

Autonomy

Having illustrated the particular importance of autonomy in this debate, it is necessary to define the term. The concept involves 'self-government', however the concern in this instance centres on individual, as opposed to state autonomy. Autonomy is closely related to the concepts of liberty and freedom, and in order to come up with a legally workable definition of the term it is first necessary to consider the historical context. Debate centred on two forms of liberty: negative and positive. In order for the principle to be enforced in legal practice, the concept of autonomy must be separated from these terms. Instead, a contemporary theory of autonomy is adopted as proposed by Gerald Dworkin.[4]

The 'Negative Theory'

Negative libertists believe that liberty or freedom constitutes first a lack of constraint, and second, a willingness to consider the options available. Milne described the theory in the following terms: 'You are free or at liberty to the extent that you are not subject to constraint in the shape of compulsion, coercion or interference by any other human being.'[5] Positive liberty, on the other hand, demands much more of an individual before he is to be considered free, or at liberty.

Of the many negative liberty theorists it is only possible here to briefly consider a few. Cranston,[6] a negative theorist in the purest and possibly most basic form, stated as a general premise that any society in which there is wide agreement is considered free, regardless of the political ideals within that society. To state a complicated theory in simplistic terms, he did not believe that freedom is best preserved through a total lack of constraint. Instead, he saw a free society as one which governs its people according to two considerations; that constraint is not used unless it is to enforce rules that have pragmatic or substantive justification; and that such constraint is only used when it is advantageous to society to do so. This involves wide agreement within society before it can be considered free. Therefore curbing the freedom of one set of people according to the majority view would be acceptable.

J.S. Mill is a negative liberty theorist, but embellished the pure form that was subsequently supported by Cranston. He added to the negative theory by arguing that certain features, such as freedom of speech, must be present before an individual can consider himself free. He argued that constraint is wrong, even when exercised for the individual's own good.[7] On this basis, to force a pregnant woman to give up smoking on the ground that it harms her would not be acceptable. However, Mill did recognize that constraint to prevent harm to *others* is acceptable, provided that it is a fair constraint organized by the state.[8] Mill did not comment directly on the status of the fetus, which presents a particular dilemma here, because though it is not legally 'another' during pregnancy, it becomes so if it is born alive. Nevertheless it is questionable that Mill would have sanctioned constraint to prevent harm to a mere potential other.[9]

The 'Positive Theory'

The positive theory demands more of the individual before he is considered free or at liberty. It requires an inner consciousness of responsibility for individual actions. A man is not free if he is constantly at the mercy of his desires and inclinations. Instead, he must consider his well-being and his responsibility to others. Green,[10] for example, argued that freedom is dependent upon rationality, whereas for the negative theorists the most important factor in freedom is the lack of restraint. Equally, Bosanquet[11] contended that one is free to the extent that one achieves what he termed 'real selfhood' which is achieved to the extent that one is a rational moral agent. For him, liberty is something to be achieved. Hence only a rational decision by a pregnant woman would be considered a free decision.

Positive theorists contend that there may be a single way of life in which each of us can become the best we have in us and that there is always a rational way to resolve a conflict. Berlin[12] on the other hand, stated the view that not all human values are compatible; that men must 'choose between ends equally ultimate'. For Berlin, the rational solution is not necessarily a free solution. Therefore a man who is coerced is not a free man, for a man cannot be forced to be free. Berlin criticized the positive theory for leading too easily to the conclusion that coerced people are free provided that they are coerced for their own good. A woman forced to exercise, or give up smoking for the benefit of the fetus and her own health would not, on this view, be free, even if she should consider the effects of the coercion valuable. The self, Berlin suggested, is not a metaphysical concept: it does not comprise of two elements, the natural side and the rational side. Splitting the personality in two in this manner arguably leads the positive theorists to think that if only the rational side of the personality could overcome the natural side, then people would voluntarily do what they are being forced to do. In this way they see such a coerced individual as truly free. Berlin supported the negative theory because it recognizes the individual's ability to choose and the importance of that ability.

Milne, however, defended the positive theory against Berlin's attack, claiming that Berlin takes the theory to illogical extremes and that his conclusion is reached by abusing it.[13] Milne claimed that the positive theory incorporates the negative theory and then builds upon it. Pure negative theorists see freedom as comprising only an external side. Positive theory adds to this, also comprehending an internal side to freedom.[14] However Milne argued that the theory as postulated by Green and Bosanquet could be improved upon by recognition of the distinction between two types of self-determination; personal and moral.[15] To be free, individuals must be self-determining in respect of both their personal and moral freedom. This is achieved by placing the importance of social responsibility and justice over personal well-being. A woman who cannot place the social responsibility to her future child above her desire to continue smoking is not, on this view, fully free. Moral freedom is important because if we concentrated on personal freedom, morality would be undermined. A rational agent at the level of social morality, rather than the level of personal well-being, is the most fully free. Self-determination, then, is not just a matter for the individual in his personal capacity (as Green and Bosanquet suggested). It is also a matter of being a moral agent and being self-determining in that role. In order to be able to carry out such a role, social morality is a necessary constituent.[16]

So for the pure negative theorists, agreement is the only criterion for a free society, no matter what system is used. Green and Bosanquet modified this, as positive theorists, demanding that laws and rights protect the individual's external freedom. A society of free individuals (for them) must be self-determining. Milne went further still, and argued that an individual is free only if he is both morally and personally self-determining, which is possible only if each individual is on an equal footing.

When applied to the scenario of the pregnant woman, ambiguities develop. The acceptable constraints on the woman's freedom would depend on the perceived status of the fetus. One might take the view that the pregnant women must be on an equal footing with other, non-pregnant woman, so protecting her freedom. Alternatively, it might be thought that the pregnant woman and fetus should be on an equal footing, so necessitating forced intervention of the woman in order to protect it. It is largely this ethical ambiguity and its legal inapplicability that makes both positive and negative theories unacceptable for the purposes of this book.

Gerald Dworkin: Procedural, Not Substantive Autonomy

A definition of autonomy is needed that is applicable in a legal context rather than a purely theoretical one. Clearly neither the positive nor negative liberty definitions entirely fit this criterion. However, they provide a useful basis on which to build a theory. Gerald Dworkin is a contemporary positive theorist who refers expressly to 'autonomy' rather than to 'freedom' or 'liberty' as general concepts. He cannot be called a negative theorist because he does not contend that substantive independence is necessary for a person to be autonomous, he merely demands that individuals be procedurally free. On the other hand, he does not fully accord with the positive theorists, because though he believes (contrary to the negative theory) that a person must be able to reflect on his own desires and preferences, he does not believe that they need to satisfy particular moral criteria as positive theorists advocate. Dworkin argued that neither the positive nor the negative theory exactly fit the concept of autonomy and therefore a third theory is necessary.

Dworkin defined individual autonomy thus:

> Autonomy is a second-order capacity to reflect critically upon one's first-order preferences and desires, and the ability either to identify with these or to change them in light of higher-order preferences and values. By exercising such a capacity we define our nature, give meaning and coherence to our lives, and take responsibility for the kind of person we are.[17]

This is a subjective definition of autonomy. We have first-order desires, second-order desires and perhaps third and fourth and more. Dworkin gave the example of a person who desires to smoke (his first-order desire) and also desires not to have that desire (his second-order desire). In accentuating the difference between first and second-order desires, he delivers us from the mistake of thinking that autonomy merely comprises of a person's wishes. Dworkin argued that it is that person's ability to reflect upon his desires that makes him potentially autonomous: 'It is not the identification or lack of identification that is crucial to being autonomous, but the capacity to raise the question of whether I will identify with or reject the reasons for which I now act.'[18]

Though reflection and the ability to change one's first-order desires is necessary for autonomy, Dworkin did not demand that the individual exercise this autonomy in any particular way, and it is here that he differs greatly from Milne, Green and Bosanquet. His theory also clearly differs from the negative theorists for whom the key is substantive independence. They argued that lack of interference from the state constitutes greater freedom; that laws should not be obeyed without reflection. Dworkin on the other hand laid little importance on substantive freedom (an autonomy with a particular content) separating it from the all-important procedural independence (an actual independence). Provided the individual considered his higher-order preference in coming to a decision, the decision is autonomous even if the higher preferences obey authority.[19] This makes autonomy compatible with human values of love, loyalty and commitment and avoids the unrealistic fixation of autonomy with a particular content.[20]

This is not to say that substantive independence lacks any importance in Dworkin's view. Liberty (as defined by Dworkin as recognition of first-order preferences) is important and the individual should have a good reason for abandoning procedural independence.[21] Dworkin defined liberty as 'roughly, the ability of a person to do what she wants, to have (significant) options that are not closed or made less eligible by the actions of other agents'.[22] Autonomy, on the other hand, he sees as the power of self-determination. The two are different, he claimed, because only coercion and force can interfere with liberty, but to interfere with autonomy, deception will also suffice.

Yet independence is arguably a freedom from coercion rather than a freedom from influence, for we are influenced in every action that we undertake. Hence a person can be acting autonomously even if his choice is not independently deduced. The only independence that Dworkin demanded is independence in the form of choice; not independence in the form of freedom from all influences. A pregnant woman is not necessarily autonomous merely by making a choice, for she must first follow her personal preferences. However, subject to this, should she choose to follow the advice or even the whim of her doctor or her partner, or any other group, individual or God on issues relating to her pregnancy, then for Dworkin, she is still acting autonomously.

Dworkin's view is subjective and can be likened to the positive theorists in that he sees autonomy as an internal as well as external concept. It is a condition of the mind rather than just a condition imposed upon the mind. However, unlike Bosanquet, he does not see rationality as the key to autonomy; it is not, he argued, necessary to be a rational moral agent. Milne, on the other hand, emphasized the need for moral as well as personal freedom and that a free person must be self-determining in both respects in order to be free.

Hence Dworkin differed from the positive theorists, for according to the latter theory, the pregnant woman could perhaps have been coerced for her own good and remained at liberty; she could have been forced into an action that she herself would have undertaken had she been rational, and remained at liberty. On Dworkin's model, such action would breach her autonomy. What *can* be done, however, is to educate the pregnant woman in order to convince her of the harm she may do to her fetus through smoking, drinking or drug taking. This is no way harms her autonomy and may in fact enhance it. Dworkin's view is logically consistent with other concepts, empirically possible, ideologically neutral and has judgemental relevance.[23] For Dworkin, the concept of autonomy is not theoretical but practical.

What is the Value of Autonomy?

This still begs the question: what value is autonomy to an individual? McCormick[24] argued that autonomy is extrinsically valuable and therefore if a better result could be achieved without it, it should not be the primary goal. R. Young[25] on the other hand, argued that autonomy has more than mere instrumental value. He used as an example the scenario of the famous novel *Brave New World* by Aldous Huxley, in which the characters were content but were not autonomous. The rationale of the book is that the vital autonomy was missing from their lives and that being content was not enough, for it is important to be the *author* of that contentment. Hence R. Young argued that autonomy has intrinsic value:

> According to this position, autonomy is part of the moral basis of personhood. To the extent that a person is at the mercy of his (or her) urges or impulses, or lacks scope for actively placing and then achieving goals and purposes, it is the person's circumstances, not the person himself (or herself), that governs. Accordingly the person's life lacks self-direction.[26]

Even a prisoner of war can be autonomous. Being able to think for oneself is enough because ' ... to the extent that we are able to shape our lives in ways that we consider worthwhile, our self-esteem will be enhanced'.[27]

Therefore, there is much to be said for Young's belief that autonomy can be instrumentally valuable, but that its primary value is intrinsic.[28] Hence it is important that an individual has the opportunity to be autonomous even if his autonomy leads in an irrational direction or creates additional hardship. It is important that the legally competent pregnant woman is given the opportunity to control her pregnancy to the extent that she can legitimately prevent others from interfering, even if the reasonable man would view her decisions as irrational.[29]

Why Might the Pregnant Woman's Autonomy be Overridden?

This is not to say that autonomy is the only value of importance, merely that it is a good basis upon which to found the pregnant woman's rights with regard to the fetus. It enables the law to effect a compromise between the state interest in protecting the fetus and the rights of the pregnant woman. It is thus argued that the duty of the state to respect an individual's autonomy by withdrawing interference with his competent choices is greater than the duty to act positively to his benefit. This is so in the context of many medical dilemmas. Hence, the right of a competent patient to decline treatment, even if he should die as a result, is protected by law. On the other hand, the right to demand that a physician deliberately puts an end to one's life is not protected by law, and is in fact prohibited.

In the United States, the criminal law has been called upon to protect the fetus from harmful actions by third parties and the pregnant woman herself. In England there are few such criminal law cases, and those that do exist are, to date, based on a limited application of the retrospective potential theory outlined in Chapter 1.[30] The law has so far been limited in its application to the fetus born alive and dying as a result of a pre-natal injury caused by a third party. Nevertheless, the temptation to increase protection of the fetus by means of criminal sanctions exists not least because of the limited application of the civil law following *Re F (in utero)*.[31] There it was held that the fetus has no civil legal personality. The local authority wished to make an unborn child a ward of court, but the Court of Appeal held that it had no jurisdiction to do so. However, *obiter dicta* May LJ showed some sympathy for the local authority's case.[32] In *Re F* the pregnant woman already had one son in care (with adoption proceedings initiated) and had disappeared. The Court, however, was bound by *Paton v. Trustees of BPAS*[33] where the pregnant woman's husband was refused his action to prevent the abortion of the fetus due to a lack of *locus standi*, and *C v. S*[34] where, again, the father was said to have no *locus standi* because the fetal rights crystallize at birth and not before.

In *Re F* however, Balcombe LJ[35] feared the consequences of allowing the claim (having recognized that it could not proceed on the authorities). He said:

> Approaching the question as one of principle, in my judgement there is no jurisdiction to make an unborn child a ward of court. Since an unborn child has, *ex hypothesis*, no existence independent of its mother, the only purpose of extending the jurisdiction to include a foetus is to enable the mother's actions to be controlled.[36]

Balcombe LJ then went on to quote Lowe on the dangers of such a concession:

> It would mean for example, that the mother would be unable to leave the jurisdiction without the court's consent. The court being charged to protect the fetus' welfare would surely have to order the mother to stop smoking, imbibing alcohol and indeed any activity which might be hazardous to the child. Taking it to the extreme were the court to be faced with saving the baby's life or the mother's it would surely have to protect the baby's.[37]

In other words, over-zealous protection of the fetus, despite its values, would create a serious deficit to the pregnant woman's rights. Morgan recognized that both the 'slippery slope' argument and the consideration of 'therapeutic conflict' between the parties lay behind Balcombe LJ's argument.[38]

The potential for criminalization to erode the pregnant woman's autonomy is not lost on the American judiciary. One judge stated:

It is, after all, the whole life of the pregnant woman which impacts on the development of the fetus. As opposed to the third-party defendant, it is the mother's every waking and sleeping moment which ... forms the world for the developing fetus. That this is so is not a pregnant woman's fault: it is a fact of life.[39]

In the Canadian case, *Winnipeg Child and Family Services (Northwest Area) v G*,[40] an addicted glue sniffer had given birth to three children, two of which were harmed as a result of her addiction. When she became pregnant for a fourth time, the Queen's Bench ordered her detention until the birth of the child, in order to protect it by preventing her sniffing glue. The court did so by making the unborn child a ward of court. The Court of Appeal overturned the order and the appeal was rejected in the Supreme Court. Applying *Re F* (*in utero*), it was held that an unborn child cannot be made a ward of court.

In the UK, the civil law is currently protective of autonomy in pregnancy, but judicial sympathy for protection of the fetus over maternal autonomy is evident not only in the *obiter* judgements in *Re F*, but also in cases of court-authorized Caesarean section operations,[41] and a case involving care proceedings of a child injured by maternal behaviour whilst pregnant.[42] Both of these areas are examined in Chapter 4. Both the judicial sympathy for the fetal rights, and the legal limitations of the civil law to uphold them, are worrying in the light of potential extensions of the criminal law. As technology advances and regulators in England more fully appreciate the ill effects that maternal behaviour can have on a fetus, the danger of traversing a similar slippery slope increases. Third parties are increasingly condemned for harming the fetus, and the ease with which the law can be extended to apply to pregnant women harming the fetus is exemplified in the USA. On the theory of autonomy put forward in this chapter, together with an analysis of the state interest in protecting the fetus, and the rights of the pregnant woman, it is put forward that extended criminalization is inappropriate. This position is supported by utilitarian arguments that demonstrate the harmful effects of criminalization.

Feminist Perspectives on Autonomy

Feminist perspectives on the value of autonomy provide context to the debate. Historically pregnancy has been viewed as a medical problem and 'all women became potential patients subject to the surveillance and ministrations of male members of the medical profession'.[43] Attempts to rebel against social constraints were medicalized. For example, the term 'hysteria' emerged in the nineteenth century and comes from the Greek word for uterus. Hysteria was thought to be prevalent amongst unmarried, divorced or working women of the middle and upper classes, and the suggested cure was marriage and childbirth. Further evidence of constrictive medical dominance exists in relation to the 'rest cure' by which nervous or hysterical women were subjected to long periods in bed with constant nursing supervision. The fact that concurrently, working class women worked extremely long hours lends power to the argument that such illnesses were socially constructed.

According to Lupton[44] the technology to develop the contraceptive pill existed 13 years before pharmaceutical companies began to research and develop it and 22 years before it was licensed. At first associated with prostitution, contraception gradually became more respectable with the development of the feminist movement. However, whilst absolving the man from responsibility, the contraceptive pill arguably forces the woman into long-term, potentially health-threatening medicalization. This is a trend that according to Lupton[45] has been perpetuated with regard to childbirth over the past two centuries.[46] She charted the prominence of the female midwife, which gave way to an eighteenth century struggle for dominance between the midwife and the male practitioner, who had exclusive knowledge of life-saving techniques such as forceps and Caesarian section delivery. Lupton further questioned the current prominence of hospital, as opposed to home, births on the basis that it emphasizes the curative aspect of labour and reduces the individuality of the woman.

Wells[47] recognized two characteristics of the medical model of pregnancy. The first is that it emphasizes the potentially adversarial relationship between pregnant woman and fetus. The second is that it artificially separates pregnancy into discontinuous stages into which medicine can intervene, including assisted conception, screening, fetal medicine, and others. According to Jinnett-Sack,[48] what is lacking in the autonomy debate is the public discussion of the various ideas of private and public good. Wells counselled that the debate is moved beyond the simple ethical or medical model so as to incorporate the fact that the pregnant woman does not view the fetus as a separate entity but as a 'total bodily indwelling'.[49] Law and medicine, she argued, must listen to women's account of pregnancy and childbirth. Though this will not make the answers any easier, she stated, it might give increased integrity to the debate.

New reproductive technologies invite a range of feminist views. Radical feminists might argue that they offer potential benefits to women by freeing them from the constraints of childbirth altogether. On the other hand it might be postulated that they simply place increased control over reproduction in the hands of men. What emerges is a tension within feminist writings between recognizing the value in the uniqueness of being a woman with reproductive capacity and the desire to reject such uniqueness in the interests of equality. However, consistency exists in the call to ensure that in preference to a system that medicalizes reproduction and childbirth in a patriarchal way, women should be able to choose the extent to which medical intervention might benefit them. To this extent, feminist writings offer support to the position maintained in this book.

The use of autonomy as a guiding principle might legitimately be criticized from a feminist perspective for over-emphasis of the separateness of pregnant woman and fetus. Yet, in the context of this book, autonomy is not put forward in isolation. It presents a useful means by which the law can achieve a compromise in the moral dilemma that, on the one hand, prohibits our viewing the woman as a mere fetal container and, on the other hand, makes abhorrent the view that the fetus is an organism without intrinsic value. By protecting the rights of the woman to shun state intervention and curbing her right to demand it, the law can both honour the legal rights of the pregnant woman whilst also protecting the state interest in the fetus as proposed in Chapter 1. An attempt is made here to supplement theory, based on autonomy and human rights, with a utilitarian consideration of the potential effects of extended criminalization. In the context of this debate, there are, for example, a number of factors that operate against the value of autonomy. These are considered in the next section.

Factors Opposed to Autonomy

The Burden of Responsibility

Cases of conflicts of interest between the pregnant woman and the fetus are thankfully rare. In most cases the pregnant woman is keen to do all she can to aid the fetus. However, a woman might fervently wish to do the best for her fetus but prove unable to do so. She may, for example, be addicted to cigarettes, or face social pressures to drink alcohol. In such circumstances a paternalistic policy of preventing her from acting to the detriment of the fetus might prove viable. Alternatively it might be argued that the potential harms to the health of the pregnant woman caused through miscarriage, her own remorse or even social condemnation warrant a policy that overrides her autonomy *for her own good*. However, in all but the most severe cases of addiction (which warrant voluntary and occasionally non-voluntary treatment)[50] such a policy is in reality a thin veil masking the true goal of protecting the fetus. It is argued that though autonomy can be burdensome, it is nevertheless valuable. Thus Dworkin suggested that the appropriate maxim for limiting choice is as follows: 'A decent respect for autonomy of individuals will lead us to be very wary of limiting choices even when it is in the rational self-interest of the individuals concerned.'[51]

With choice comes the burden of responsibility. This may take the form of legal responsibility or the social need to conform.[52] Failing to mitigate possible harm does not remove the original aspect of the harm, but the choices involved may present additional burdens. Dworkin gave the example of a pregnant woman who decides to consent to amniocentesis to screen for Downs Syndrome. Under the Abortion Act 1967 termination of the fetus might be an option if the fetus is so afflicted. Once she has consented to the amniocentesis and heard the results, she and her partner are responsible for bringing the child into the world (or aborting the fetus).[53] On the same basis it might be argued that a woman who chooses to smoke, or drink excessive alcohol in pregnancy makes a choice. If she also fails to exercise her positive choice (in the limited circumstances that it exists) to abort and chooses to bring the child into the world, she must accept the burdens of social condemnation and guilt, should the child be born alive and die or suffer as a result. Thus, the mere existence of the choice to smoke or drink in pregnancy might constitute a burden. Were the choice removed (by making the actions illegal), the burden would also be removed.

Conversely, Bayles[54] proposes the theory that the more extensive our choices, the more content we are. This is first, because the greater the number of alternatives, the lower the risk of being dissatisfied, and second, because our actions express our character and desires, and the more options we have, the better we can express ourselves. However, such claims are subject to criticism. Young,[55] commenting on Bayles' first point, argued that mere proliferation of choices does not as such promote autonomy (as has been previously noted), and on the second point he answered that often the greater the number of choices, the more agonizing the choice is to make.

The question is whether the intrinsic value of autonomy is important enough in the light of potential ill effects resulting from the individual's responsibility for the act. It is argued that whilst a particular act is illegal regardless of pregnancy (such as using Class A drugs) then state intervention is acceptable, but where an act is otherwise legal, such as drinking alcohol or smoking, the responsibility is rightly placed in the hands of the pregnant woman, however onerous it may be.

Coercion and the Prevention of Harm

Rules are necessary to allow certain actions and prohibit others. This in turn involves restraint (refusing to allow an individual to act in a particular way) and coercion (forcing a person to act in a particular way). Coercion is less likely to be tolerated for it constitutes a greater intrusion on an individual's autonomy.

Of the many commentators on the subject, Bay called coercion 'the supreme political evil'.[56] Similarly Hart found it abhorrent: 'I shall advance the thesis that if there are any moral rights at all, it follows that there is at least one natural right, the equal right of all men to be free.'[57] Mill concentrated specifically on the question 'when is constraint justified?' He did not advocate constraint for the person's own good because he was of the view that we are each the best guardian of our own well-being, but nevertheless, he advocated constraint to prevent harm to others.[58]

There is some uncertainty, on Mill's principle, whether or not harm caused to a future person or persons is sufficient to allow constraint. In law, the pregnant woman is a person, but the fetus is not. Nevertheless, the fetus may become one, in which case the pregnant woman's actions could be said to harm another. Also, where damage caused to the fetus by the pregnant woman causes injury, it could be said to harm those in society who take on the emotional and financial burdens of treating and caring for the child. Thus Kaplan[59] stated that laws predominantly enforced to prevent harm to the actor, such as failing to wear a crash helmet, usually also exist to prevent harm to others. Examples include the pedestrian who is injured when the motorcyclist loses control when stones from the road hit his face, society's expense in treating him when he is injured, or injuries to others who copy his actions. Harm to others may thus be primary, where harm occurs directly to others, or secondary, where the harm is indirectly caused to others. Harm to others may also be actual or, as in the case of the pregnant drug addict (or female addict of child-bearing age), contingent.

The pregnant woman who uses legal or illegal substances may be said to harm the fetus. If harm to 'others' is taken as harm to other legal *persona* (rather than harm to the fetus) then the harm she causes is often indirect and contingent. There is not a sound basis for submitting her to criminal prosecution at this stage. Even after the baby is born and is *actually* harmed by her action, the law criminalizing the harm must be fair and indiscriminate. In prosecuting a pregnant woman for actions harmful to the child born alive, unfairness is generated both because she is singled out from general liability and because scientific knowledge cannot yet define how, or by what or whose particular conduct the harm was caused;[60] discrimination is arguably achieved because acts that are otherwise legal, such as drinking alcohol or smoking tobacco, or failing to exercise or follow the doctors advice, would become illegal on the basis that the woman is pregnant. Her moral culpability would then be further dependent on whether or not she knew that she was pregnant, whether she was negligent as to the fact and whether or not a justification or excuse could be provided in defence.

In the same way that this chapter has proposed that autonomy is not a universal good, but has intrinsic value, Mill argued that even if the good of the individual is best served by interference with his liberty, that interference should not be tolerated. It is only for the sake of 'others' that liberty should be compromised. In other words, to curb the liberty of an individual is wrong because it is his right to be free. But to curb the liberty of a society in order to achieve the general good of that society is acceptable. Take the example of substance abuse; it clearly harms those who participate in the activity, though there are arguably benefits to society and therefore certain types are allowed, such as drinking alcohol and smoking tobacco. Even these may be universally limited, for example driving a car whilst over the legal alcohol limit is a crime. However, as soon as individuals are unfairly refused the right to participate in the activity, the constraint becomes unacceptable. To refuse all of society the right to take cocaine is acceptable, but to allow society to smoke tobacco and refuse that right to women who are pregnant is not. There are a number of differences between the drunk driver and the drunken pregnant woman. Driving is something that all licensed drivers may participate in and other people may be harmed by the action. Only women may become pregnant and the harm is contingent and often indirect. Other difficulties include problems relating to causation, lack of culpability (perhaps due to a lack of knowledge of pregnant status), and limited means of enforcement. This is not to say that actions harming the fetus are morally right, or that there is never moral culpability on the part of the drug user, but that means other than the criminal law are usually better equipped to tackle them.

The view that coercion must not be used against the woman in a way that leads to any gross inequality between her and the rest of society, is contended (from an American perspective) by Johnsen:

> By creating an adversarial relationship between the woman and her fetus, the state provides itself with a powerful means for controlling women's behaviour during pregnancy, thereby threatening women's fundamental rights. A woman's right to bodily autonomy in matters concerning reproduction is protected by the constitutional guarantees of liberty and privacy. Furthermore, the Fourteenth Amendment guarantee of equal protection of the laws should be interpreted to prohibit the state from using women's reproductive capability to their detriment.[61]

Clearly, autonomy must be overridden by constraint, restraint or coercion in certain instances. Yet this should not be undertaken lightly, and respect for individual autonomy should be promoted. A pregnant woman may harm her fetus by refusing to undergo a Caesarean section or by continuing to act or omit practices that are considered legal in the absence of pregnancy. However, this and the last chapter have attempted to justify a ranking of interest in which the fetal interests in life and health are often placed below the woman's right to autonomy. As Feinberg stated,[62] some ranking of interests is inevitable because of the unavoidable conflicts of different persons and non-persons:

> The interests of different persons are constantly and unavoidably in conflict, so that any legal system determined to 'minimize harm' must incorporate judgements of the comparative importance of interests of different kinds so that it can pronounce 'unjustified' the invasion of one person's interest of high priority done to protect another person's interest of low priority. Legal wrongs will then be invasions of interests which violate established priority rankings. Invasions that are justified by the priority rules are not legal wrongs though they might well inflict harm in the non-normative sense of simple setback of interest.[63]

Once the child is born alive, it cannot be retrospectively claimed that the pregnant woman owed a duty to act towards the fetus in a particular way without unduly curbing her autonomy in pregnancy. On the other hand, it can be said retrospectively that third parties owe a duty to the child born alive not to harm him,[64] because their autonomy is not unjustly or discriminately curbed by this restriction. Hence, a person who sets a bomb to explode in ten years time cannot claim a defence on the ground that the child killed in the explosion was not conceived at the time of the act. In England and Wales this is how the criminal law currently stands. In the USA the law stemmed from a similar basis which some states have eroded in order to subject women who harm their fetus later born alive to criminal law sanctions.

Conclusion

The actions of a third party who intervenes in the course of a woman's pregnancy so as to injure or kill the fetus or fetus born alive, are redressable under both civil and criminal law. The reasons for this are twofold. First the fetus is a potential human, it has symbolic value to society and it has a human origin. Once born alive, it is a person in being with human rights. For those reasons it deserves a measure of protection. The second reason is often overlooked. A pregnant woman's autonomy deserves legal protection and any third party harming the fetus without the consent of the pregnant woman breaches her autonomy.

Respect of the pregnant woman's autonomy not only involves punishment of individuals who intervene in the course of the pregnancy, but also prevention of state intervention. A society that authorizes a Caesarean section operation on a pregnant woman who withholds her consent for the operation is exercising coercion. A society that prohibits smoking or drinking alcohol is exercising constraint. Both these analogies prevent autonomous action of the pregnant woman. The state has an interest in preserving the autonomy of pregnant women and it also has an interest in preventing harm to fetuses and future children. The consequences of harming a rational and autonomous person are often greater than the consequences of harming a non-autonomous non-person.

But her right to autonomy is not absolute. It is limited in that she cannot demand action of other individuals or the state if that action causes unacceptable harm to the fetus. Therefore, her rights to demand abortion are correctly limited. However, what she can demand is the right to prevent action of the state or other individuals that interferes with her and the fetus. Even this is limited, for actions that are universally considered illegal do not stop being illegal as a result of pregnancy. Therefore a pregnant woman who insists on using cocaine can rightly be criminalized for her action, not on the basis that it harms the fetus, but on the basis that it is illegal whether or not she is pregnant. Conversely, a woman who smokes tobacco, or imbibes excessive amounts of alcohol cannot be criminalized for her actions without her autonomy being unacceptably breached. Having said this, educational and treatment initiatives aimed to inform pregnant women are warranted, as they effectively increase the woman's choices.

Autonomy is particularly useful in this context because it offers a workable legal compromise between the state interest in protecting the fetus and the assertion of human rights by the pregnant woman. However it is not the only important consideration in the debate. As the feminist discourse on autonomy reveals, rather than seeking to artificially separate the fetus and the pregnant woman, legal policy should address potential conflicts on the basis of the symbiotic relationship between pregnant woman and fetus. Utilitarian arguments are put forward to show that, within the context of the rights and interests of fetus and pregnant woman, extended criminalization is harmful. The next chapter demonstrates how extended criminalization was achieved in the USA, Chapter 4 shows how easily the same could be achieved in England and Wales and in Chapter 5, pragmatic criticisms are added to the theoretical of this chapter. Finally, Chapter 6 shows that important though lack of state interference in pregnancy is, the state needs to actively empower the pregnant woman by giving her realistic options to give up the harmful addiction, whether it concerns cocaine or the cigarette.

Notes

1   The potential breach of human rights is considered in Chapter 5.
2   As examined in Chapter 6.
3   R. Gillon, 'The Four Principles Revisited – a Reappraisal', in R. Gillon (Ed.) *Principles of Health Care Ethics* (John Wiley and Sons: Chichester, 1994), 319.
4   G. Dworkin, *The Theory and Practice of Autonomy* (Cambridge University Press: Cambridge and New York, 1988) at 108: 'The central idea that underlies the concept of autonomy is indicated by the etymology of the term; *autos* (self) *nomos* (rule or law).'
5   A.J.M. Milne, *Freedom and Rights* (George Allen and Unwin Ltd: London, Humanities Press Inc: New York, 1968), 17.
6   M. Cranston, *Freedom, a New Analysis* (Longman Green and Co.: London, 1953).
7   'The only freedom which deserves the name is that of pursuing our own good in our own way so long as we do not attempt to deprive others of theirs or impede their efforts to obtain it. Each is the proper guardian of his own health, whether bodily or mental and spiritual. Mankind are the greater gainers by suffering each other to live as seems good to themselves than by compelling each to live as seems good to the rest.' J.S. Mill, *On Liberty* (Basil Blackwell: Oxford, 1946).
8   Mill, *ibid*. 'The only purpose for which power can be rightly exercised over any member of a civilised community against his will is to prevent harm to others. His own good, either physical or moral, is not a sufficient warrant, he cannot rightfully be compelled to do or forbear ... because in the opinion of others to do so would be wise or even right.'
9   This question is analysed at p. 33.
10   T.H. Green, *Lectures on the Principles of Political Obligations* (Longman Green and Co: London, 1941), 3.

11 B. Bosanquet, *The Philosophical Theory of the State* (Macmillan Press: London, 1951), 118.

12 Sir I. Berlin, *Two Concepts of Liberty* (Clarendon Press: Oxford, 1958). Berlin is a negative liberty theorist.

13 Milne, *op. cit.*, 36.

14 'On its internal side it is the condition of mind and character of the rational moral agent. Such an agent is emancipated from subjection to the natural impulses and inclinations which make up his merely empirical self and is free to become the best that he has it in him to be. But the significance of the external side of freedom is also recognized. What is important is not the absence of external constraint as such but its absence in the form of interference by anyone, with anyone else's rational moral conduct and hence with his self-realisation. This external freedom can be secured by a system of rights maintained by law, and a society in which it is secured as a free society.' Milne, *ibid.,*146. In effect, this is to say that 'the negative aspect of personal freedom is a by-product of its positive character as self-determination'. Milne, *ibid.*, 148.

15 For Milne an individual's 'personal freedom' is his own survival. More than this is needed in order to be free, according to Milne. Participation with others is indispensable to us. 'But there can be fruitful co-operation only where there is mutual trust. ... It follows that there is a sense in which morality is relevant to rational activity at the level of personal well-being.' (Milne, *ibid.*, 151.) At the level of social morality, the individual will do his best to promote his personal well-being, but the social morality will take precedence. Self-determination at its highest level involves social morality over personal well-being.

16 Milne, *ibid.*, 155.

17 G. Dworkin, *op. cit.,* 108.

18 G. Dworkin, *ibid.*, 15.

19 '... there is a tension between autonomy as a purely formal notion (where what one decides for oneself can have any particular content), and autonomy as a substantive notion (where only certain decisions count as retaining autonomy whereas others count as forfeiting it).' G. Dworkin, *ibid.,* 12. And later; 'Suppose we have a person who has not been subjected to the kinds of influence – whatever they turn out to be – that interfere with procedural independence. Suppose the person wants to conduct his or her life in accordance with the following: Do whatever my mother or my buddies, or my leader or my priest tells me to do. Such a person counts, in my view, as autonomous.' G. Dworkin, *ibid.*, 21.

20 '... it is only through a more adequate understanding of notions such as tradition, authority, commitment and loyalty, and the forms of human community in which these have their roots, that we shall be able to develop a conception of autonomy free from paradox and worthy of admiration.' G. Dworkin, *ibid.*, 47.

21 G. Dworkin, *ibid.,* 26.

22 G. Dworkin, *ibid.*, 14.

23 These criteria are outlined by G. Dworkin *ibid.*, 7-12.

24 R. McCormick, *How Brave a New World? Dilemmas in Bioethics* (SCM Press Ltd: London, 1981), 359. 'A moral right is always with regard to a good. The good in question is self-determination in the acceptance or rejection of medical treatment. This self-determination ... is a conditional or instrumental good – that is, it is a good precisely insofar as it is the instrument whereby the best interests of the patient are served by it. If, for example, the best over-all good of patients would be better achieved without self-determination, it would be senseless to speak of self-determination as a right.'

25 R. Young, *Personal Autonomy: Beyond Negative and Positive Liberty* (St. Martin's Press: New York, 1986).

26 R. Young, *ibid.,* 25.

27 R. Young, *ibid.*

28 R. Young extrapolates two models from the intrinsic value standpoint. The first is put forward by G.E. Moore, *Principia Ethica* (Cambridge University Press: Cambridge), who argued that autonomy is intrinsically valuable for its own sake. Hence it has value

even when there is no valuer to value it. Young prefers the second opinion, which has previously been contended by C.I. Lewis in *The Theory of Knowledge and Valuation* (La Salle: Illinois, 1946). This is the view that autonomy is intrinsically valuable only if it is worth having for its own sake.

29 With the proviso that where the pregnant woman is deemed legally incapable of making a particular decision, that decision need not be respected.

30 Chapter 1 p. 16.

31 *Re F (in utero)* [1988] 2 All E.R. 193, reaffirmed in *Rance v. Mid-Downs Health Authority* [1991] 1 All E.R. 801.

32 May LJ offered the following view, *obiter*: 'On these facts... I have no doubt myself that if the court had the power I would give leave to issue the necessary originating summons and make the unborn child a ward of court.' *Re F (in utero), ibid.*, 194.

33 *Paton v. Trustees of BPAS* [1979] QB 276.

34 *C v. S* [1988] QB 135.

35 Contrary to May LJ.

36 *Re F (in utero), op cit.,* 200.

37 Lowe, 'Wardship and Abortion Prevention – Further Observations' (1980) 96 *Law Quarterly Review* 29 at 30. As referred to by Balcombe LJ in *Re F (in utero), ibid.*, 200.

38 Morgan, 'Judges on Delivery: Change, Continuity and Regulation in Obstetric Practice' in T. Chard and M.P.M. Richards (Eds.) *Obstetrics in the 1990s: Current Controversies* (Mac Keith Press: Oxford and New York, 1992), at 28.

39 *Stallman v Youngquist* 531 N.E.2d 355 (Ill. 1988), 360.

40 *Winnipeg Child and Family Services (Northwest Area) v G* [1997] 3 BHRC 611.

41 See *Re S (adult: refusal of medical treatment)* [1992] 3 W.L.R. 806, *R v. Merton Borough Council and Ors, ex parte Sutherland* [10th July 1997] I.L.R. Document Number C800046 and *Re MB (Adult; Medical Treatment)* [1997] 2 FCR 541. These cases are analysed in Chapter 4.

42 See *D v. Berkshire County Council* [1987] 1 All E.R. 20 (Div. Court); 27 (C.A.); and 33 (H.L.). This case is analysed in Chapter 4 p. 71.

43 D. Lupton, *Medicine as Culture* (Sage Publications: London, 1994), 136.

44 D. Lupton, *ibid.,* 138.

45 D. Lupton, *ibid*, 146.

46 The medicalization of pregnancy and childbirth is charted by Ann Oakley in *Women Confined: Towards a Sociology of Childbirth* (Martin Robinson: Oxford, 1980*); The Captured Womb* (Blackwells: Oxford, 1984); *From Here to Maternity* (Penguin: Harmondsworth, 1986).

47 C. Wells, 'On the Outside Looking In: Perspectives on Enforced Caesareans', in S. Sheldon and M. Thomson (Eds.) *Feminist Perspectives on Health Care Law* (Cavendish: London, 1998), at 242.

48 S. Jinnett-Sack, 'Autonomy in the Company of Others', in A. Grubb (Ed.) *Choices and Decisions in Health Care* (John Wiley & Sons: Chichester, 1993). 'To the extent that the only public vocabulary we have developed is one where I insist on the testing of the dominance of my rights over yours, we should not expect non-litigious resolution or any sense of community good or of personal obligation.' At 132.

49 C. Wells, *op. cit.,* 255.

50 See Chapter 6.

51 G. Dworkin, *op. cit.,* 77.

52 G. Dworkin, *ibid.,* 68. See also A.M. Capron, 'Informed Consent in Catastrophic Disease Research and Treatment' (1974) 123 *The University of Pennsylvania Law Review* 356: '... autonomy is centrally associated with the notion of individual responsibility. The freedom to make decisions for oneself carries with it the obligation to answer for the consequences of those decisions.'

53 G. Dworkin, *ibid.,* 67. 'The defective child, if they choose to have it, can no longer be viewed as bad luck or a curse or an act of God.'

54   M. Bayles, *Principles of Legislation* (Reidel Publishers: Detroit, 1978).

55   R. Young, *op. cit.*, 27.

56   C. Bay, *The Structure of Freedom* (Stanford University Press: Stanford, California, 1958), 92.

57   H.L.A. Hart, 'Are There Any Natural Rights?', *Philosophical Review* 64 (1955), 174.

58   ' ... the sole end for which mankind are warranted individually or collectively interfering with the liberty of action of any of their number is self-protection; that the only purpose for which power can be rightfully exercised over any member of a civilised community against his will is to prevent harm to others.' J.S. Mill, *On Liberty* (Basil Blackwell: Oxford, 1946), 5.

59   J. Kaplan, 'The Role of the Law in Drug Control' (1971) 65 *Duke Law Journal* 1065.

60   See Chapter 5 p. 90.

61   D.E. Johnsen, 'The Creation of Fetal Rights: Conflicts with Women's Constitutional Rights to Liberty, Privacy, and Equal Protection', (1986) 95 *Yale Law Journal* 578, at 579.

62   J. Feinberg, *Harm to Others: The Moral Limits of the Criminal Law* (Oxford University Press: New York and Oxford, 1987), 35.

63   *Ibid.*

64   Feinberg, *ibid.,* 96 explained the fetus's contingent right not to be harmed *in utero* stating: 'A negligent motorist who runs over a pregnant woman may cause damage to the fetus that causes it later to be born deformed or chronically ill. Sometime after birth that infant will have an actual welfare interest in self-locomotion or health that may be harmed (doomed to defeat) right from the beginning. The child comes into existence in a harmed state caused by the earlier negligence of a motorist whose act initiated the causal sequence, at a point before actual personhood, that later resulted in the harm. The motorist's negligent driving made the actual person who came into existence months later worse off than she would otherwise have been. If the motorist had not been negligent, the child would have been born undamaged.'

Chapter 3

Criminalization of Pregnant Women and Mothers in the USA

Because the fetus is not a person for purposes of the English common law, it is only when it is born alive[1] that it achieves full legal status. There is no crime of feticide in England and Wales (though the law may treat the ending of fetal life as unlawful in certain circumstances). However, once it is born alive, it achieves legal personhood status and can be the victim of homicide. A legal dilemma ensues when the fetus is unlawfully injured, but is born alive and subsequently dies. As it was not a person at the time of injury, the question is whether or not the illegal killing can be viewed as homicide. In 1997 the House of Lords reluctantly accepted the validity of the 'born alive rule' in the *Attorney General's Reference (No. 3 of 1994)*.[2] In that case, which is examined in Chapter 4, it was held that a third party[3] who causes injury to the fetus which is later born alive and dies as a result of that injury may, depending on *mens rea* and causation, be guilty of homicide.

The precedent is worrying on two grounds. First, the ancient born alive rule is of limited use and applicability today: there are other more effective means of affording legal protection to the child born alive. Secondly, there is potential for application and extension of the rule to apply to recent mothers in a manner that is inconsistent with their human rights.

The 'born alive rule' was first postulated by Coke[4] in 1680, so called because the appropriateness of a homicide charge is entirely dependent on the fetus achieving independent existence from its mother (and so becoming a person in law) and subsequently dying as a result of pre-natal injury. Coke argued that the charge should not be dependent on foresight or even recklessness as to the life of the born child. Subsequently the rule became a feature of the common law.

When Coke devised the 'born alive rule', the felony murder rule operated so that intention to commit an unlawful act resulting in death was sufficient *mens rea* for murder. Temkin[5] argued that since the felony murder rule was abolished by section 1 of the Homicide Act 1957, the rule has become anomalous, unjust and unnecessary. It is anomalous for the fetus is not a person in English law, so there can be no liability for its murder when the defendant intended to do no more than kill a fetus *in utero*. The only way to achieve liability for murder is by extending the malice aforethought rule to incorporate an intention to kill or seriously injure a fetus, which is later born alive and subsequently dies.

Temkin further claimed that the rule is unjust.[6] Temkin noted that the stigma and sentence attached to the practised and successful abortionist would be unjustly light in comparison to that applied to the failed abortionist. Finally, contending that the rule is unnecessary, Temkin recommended the potential application of section 58 of the Offences Against the Person Act 1861.[7] Though this section has not been applied in this context before, she asserted that there is no reason for it not to be so applied in the future. Otherwise, transferred malice can be used, providing the *actus reus* is the same in the mistaken and intended act. A manslaughter charge might be brought without invoking the born alive rule either where a defendant was grossly negligent as to the death or serious injury of the child once it was born alive, or by following *Kong Cheuk Kwan v. The Queen*,[8] if there was an obvious and serious risk of causing physical injury to the child when it was born which the defendant failed to consider.[9] Also the crime of abortion is appropriate; this carries a maximum term of life imprisonment.

Despite such criticism, the rule received support in the Hong Kong Court of Appeal case, *R v. Kwok Chak Ming (No. 1)*[10] and was subsequently accepted by the House of Lords in the *Attorney General's Reference (No. 3 of 1994)*.[11] Various cases were cited in support of the rule. In *R v. West*[12] a charge of murder was brought against a third party following his attempt to kill a fetus of six months gestation which was born alive and subsequently died. In *R v. Senior*[13] a midwife was found guilty of manslaughter for his negligent assistance in the birthing process which resulted in the live birth and subsequent death of the child.

Temkin[14] argued that *Senior*, *West* and *R v. Kwok Chak Ming*[15] do not necessarily support Coke's rule. '[They are] authority for no more than that liability for murder or manslaughter may ensue provided all the requirements for these offences are fulfilled but irrespective of whether the relevant injury is inflicted pre-natally.'[16] On this basis the House of Lords might have rejected the rule and found alternative means of criminalizing the third party's behaviour. Instead the rule was reluctantly accepted.

The second cause for concern regarding the acceptance of the rule in the *Attorney General's Reference (No.3 of 1994)* is that the rule's application, as Coke formulated it, was not expressly limited to third parties. Though there has yet to be an English case against the mother of a child which is born alive and dies as a result of injuries received *in utero*, this undoubtedly remains a possibility as is evidenced by practice in certain US states.

An application of the rule to recent mothers would have a potentially devastating effect on her rights and interests and would upset the careful balance currently maintained in England and Wales between the interests of the fetus and the pregnant woman. Namely, the state has only a limited obligation to provide the pregnant woman with choices in pregnancy, so protecting the fetus from harm. Meanwhile, the negative obligation on the state to refrain from exercising constraint on the woman during pregnancy is preserved, so achieving a workable balance between the interests of fetus and pregnant woman.

This chapter explores the possibility that the born alive rule, or principles derived from it, could be extended to protect the fetus, later born alive, from harms caused by its mother, as was achieved in certain American states. The similar common law origins shared by England and Wales and many states in America make this a useful comparison and measure for the success of such a policy.

Four Extensions of the 'Born Alive Rule' (and an Alternative)

Since healthcare professionals first made the link between acts and omission of the pregnant woman and the state of health of the resulting neonate, most pregnant woman have been keen to learn how to achieve optimal fetal health. Those cases where the baby is born alive but damaged by its mother's intentional acts are treated with abhorrence by sections of American society. Not only does society bear potentially huge financial costs, but the status of the fetus is a highly contentious issue in terms of religion and politics. There is fierce debate between the pro-choice movement, which advocates freedom of choice for pregnant women, and the pro-life movement which campaigns for the protection of the fetus as a person. States with a strong pro-life bias are keen to protect the fetus from the ill-effects of maternal acts and omissions. Elections are won or lost on such issues. Though most states have drug and alcohol treatment and education programmes, such schemes are costly and slow-acting. Criminalization is swift and serves retributive goals, having far greater political impact, but its effectiveness and constitutionality are constantly called into question.

Those American states which employ criminalization measures to curb and punish acts by the pregnant woman that harm the fetus, have taken the concept of the born alive rule in a number of directions. Some have extended the common law, others have enacted legislation.[17] Therefore the combinations for criminalization are numerous; both in terms of the relevant victim (be it fetus, potential child, child born alive or pregnant woman[18]) and the relevant perpetrator (be it third party, doctor, or pregnant woman).[19]

In the Introduction, extensions of the born alive rule were examined under four categories. The first retains the rule as it currently exists in England and Wales, applying to third parties who injure a fetus, which is later born alive and dies. The second extends the rule to incorporate women who, whilst pregnant, harm the fetus later born alive and dying of the injuries. In these two categories the potential crime is homicide. The third category extends the rule to include a third party or woman whilst pregnant who causes *injury* to a child born alive and the fourth includes injury or death, caused by a third party or woman whilst pregnant to a *fetus* which, for the purposes of the state law, is defined as a person. Alternatively, the born alive rule is overridden altogether, with existing or newly enacted legislation which makes it a crime to kill or injure the fetus.

Category 1: A Third Party Injures a Fetus Which is Born Alive and Dies as a Direct Result of the Injury

To date, the born alive rule has been applied in England and Wales within the narrow confines of this category. In the *Attorney-General's Reference (No. 3 of 1994)* the rule applied when a man stabbed his girlfriend whom he knew to be pregnant. The baby was born prematurely with a knife wound to the abdomen. It died 120 days later from a condition related to its prematurity.

A similar US example is *Williams v. State*,[20] though this case involved the application of the doctrine of transferred malice. Jones believed that Williams had become involved with his girlfriend and so chased him with a bow and arrow. After yelling at a pedestrian to 'watch out' he released the arrow, which struck the pedestrian who was nine months pregnant. The pedestrian died, and her baby was born alive but died 17 hours later as a direct result of the injury. Williams was convicted on two counts of manslaughter (one against the pregnant woman and the other against the baby) and one of carrying a weapon with intent to injure.

Category 2: A Woman Whilst Pregnant Harms the Fetus Which is Later Born Alive and Dies as a Direct Result of the Injury

In *State v. Ashley*[21] in Florida, a 19-year old pregnant woman shot herself in the stomach at 25 weeks gestation. The child was born alive and lived for 15 days before dying as a result of the woman's action. She was charged with third-degree felony (illegal abortion) and manslaughter. Though the first count failed because the child had been born alive, Ashley was convicted on the second count.

The extensions of the born alive rule under the second category have largely occurred in the context of substance use. There are a number of cases where women using Class A drugs in pregnancy have been prosecuted following the death of their children born alive. For example, in *Alaska v. Grubbs*[22] a two-week old boy died from a heart attack that resulted from his mother's use of cocaine before his birth. She was sentenced to six months in jail and five years probation for criminally negligent homicide.

Category 3: A Third Party or Woman Whilst Pregnant Causes Injury to a Child Born Alive

There are three methods of achieving the prosecution of women whose actions in pregnancy cause injury to the neonate. The first involves enacting legislation specifically criminalizing such actions. For example, a 1989 bill presented by Peter Wilson, the 'Child Abuse During Pregnancy Prevention Act of 1989'[23] suggested a three-year prison sentence for harm caused to a fetus through both illicit (such as cocaine) and licit (such as alcohol) drug use. The purpose of the bill was to prevent substance abuse and effect rehabilitation. This option is examined in more detail in Chapter 6. Many such bills suffer defeat due to criminal justice and constitutional criticisms, which are examined in Chapter 5.

The constitutional constraints on enacting new legislation force prosecutors to consider the application of existing laws to criminalize pregnant women who harm the fetus born alive. Accordingly, the second method has nothing to do with the born alive rule and involves proving that the injury occurred after the birth of the child. Some states have prosecuted women for supplying drugs to a minor in the short space of time between birth and severance of the umbilical cord. This was true in three Florida cases, *Florida v. Johnson*, *Florida v. Black* and *Florida v. Hudson*.[24] Similar charges have been made in Georgia, Massachusetts and Michigan.[25] The theory is that the child is physically separate from the woman and therefore a person in law, and the cocaine is passing through the umbilical cord so satisfying the *actus reus* of the offence. In many cases the charges have been unsuccessful, as in *Michigan v. Hardy*[26] where charges of supplying through the umbilical cord were dismissed because the court 'cannot reasonably infer that the legislature intended this application'.

Prosecutors often charge a variety of offences in the hope that the jury will indict for at least one. In *North Carolina v. Inzar*,[27] a woman allegedly smoked cocaine the day before giving birth to a brain damaged child and was charged, though not successfully prosecuted, with assault with a deadly weapon and distributing cocaine to a minor.

The third method is an extension of the born alive rule by which existing rules enacted to protect child victims are extended to protect children from retrospective injury *in utero*. For example, in *Connecticut v. Baez*[28] a pregnant woman who swallowed a quarter of an ounce of cocaine was later charged with 'risk of injury to a child'. Probably the most common charge against pregnant women who injure a fetus born alive is 'fetal abuse', which is an extension of existing child abuse laws.[29] The charge of criminal neglect is similarly used as a means of prosecuting women who have given birth to drug-dependent children. For example, the American Civil Liberties Union (ACLU) reports that over 20 women in Charleston and Greenville have been charged with criminal neglect or distribution in South Carolina.[30] Annas criticized the application of criminal neglect laws to pregnant women. He argued that it places a duty on the pregnant woman that is far more onerous than that placed on the parents of a born child and involves an inherently sexist application of the law.[31]

In the English civil case of *D v. Berkshire County Council*,[32] the House of Lords held that when considering whether to make a care order under Section 1(2)(a) of the Children and Young Persons Act 1969 in respect of a baby born with drug withdrawal symptoms, the juvenile court could properly consider events and circumstances prior to the baby's birth. This worried some English commentators[33] who believed that this represented a step down the slippery slope toward criminalization for fetal abuse. Though the case concerned civil law, a corresponding US precedent illustrated how the principle contained in D could be applied to extend criminalization. In *California v. Stewart*[34] Stewart became the first woman in America to be charged with a criminal offence for her conduct whilst pregnant. Stewart allegedly contributed to the death of her son on the basis that she failed to take proper medical care for her viable fetus which was born alive and died five weeks later. The grounds for this charge were that she had ignored the doctor's advice and refused to give up amphetamines during pregnancy. Stewart was hospitalized in her eighth month of pregnancy complaining of pain and bleeding, returning again a week later with similar symptoms. She was sent home and instructed to rest, avoid sexual intercourse and return if bleeding should recur. Allegedly, she was informed that she had *placenta previa*, but she denied any knowledge of this. Nearly a fortnight later, she engaged in sexual intercourse, and imbibed marijuana and amphetamines. Stewart was convicted of failing to provide for a minor. The case caused considerable controversy not only because of its novelty, but because in addition to criminalizing her positive acts, it also criminalized an *omission* (namely, refusing to take the advise of the doctor). On appeal, the conviction was overturned on the basis that it would involve perverting a statute to impose such liability on a pregnant woman.

Attempts to use the common law to liberally construe statutes enacted to protect children and adults is popular because it avoids the constitutional scrutiny which is a necessary constituent of enacting new legislation. However, there are three disadvantages to this method of prosecution. The first is that following *Liparota v. U.S.*[35] criminal legislation must be strictly and narrowly interpreted with any ambiguity resolved in favour of lenity. In many of the above cases prosecutors failed to secure convictions because the relevant statute was designed to protect children from injuries caused after birth as opposed to pre-natal injuries.[36] Consequently in *Ohio v. Andrews*[37] a charge brought under a child-endangerment statute was dismissed on the basis that it only protected children born at the time of the endangerment.

The second disadvantage is that existing laws do not properly fit the harmful activities of pregnant women. For example, existing laws criminalizing the supply of a drug to a minor cannot be used to criminalize the supply of alcohol or the failure to heed the doctor's advice. The third disadvantage is that the court is often restricted to prosecuting only when the child is born alive by which time the damage is already done. Again, legislation could theoretically enable prosecution during pregnancy and thereby limit harm.

The apparent solution is to enact legislation specifically to protect the child born alive from the actions of the pregnant woman. Legislation might take a number of forms. It might impose sanctions against the third party or mother who can be shown to have harmed or caused the death of a child born alive. Alternatively, it might define the fetus as a person at a particular point in gestation (such as conception or viability), so that other statutes designed to protect the child and adult will also protect the unborn child. Finally a feticide statute may criminalize actions of third parties and pregnant women that cause the death of the fetus.

The latter two options are discussed in the next sections. Of the first option it appears that states are reluctant to legislate in this manner for fear of contravening the Constitution. The Constitution demands that punishment is fair and that it effectively meets the goals of the particular state. Further, any statute must respect the woman's liberty, privacy, autonomy and equal rights. Constitutional criticisms are examined further in Chapter 5.

Category 4: A Third Party or Woman Whilst Pregnant Causes the Death or Injury of a Fetus Which, for the Purposes of the State Law, is Defined as a Person

Though it seems somewhat incomprehensible to include under the 'born alive rule' a category in which the crime is committed against a fetus which is not actually born alive, this nevertheless forms an extension of the original rule. The original emphasis on the child being born alive exists because it is at this point that the fetus becomes a person. If a state defines personhood as beginning earlier than birth, then murder or manslaughter can also occur at that earlier stage. Thus in *Hughes v. State*[38] the Oklahoma Supreme Court prosecuted a third party for the murder of a viable fetus following his attack on a pregnant woman. It was held that the legal emphasis on rights occurring when the child is born alive was antiquated and no longer useful.[39] In *People v. Chavez*[40] the Californian Court of Appeal prosecuted a mother for murdering her child during labour. The court held that for the purposes of the particular statute the term 'person' incorporated the fetus.

It has been seen that the courts showed a marked reluctance to construe statutes enacted to protect children from injury after birth, to protect *children* injured pre-natally. The US courts have proven stricter still when asked by prosecutors to apply statutes protecting children to the *fetus*. In *Hollis v. Commonwealth*,[41] the defendant forced his hand into the womb of a pregnant woman, assaulting her and aborting the fetus. Due to the violence and premeditation involved, the prosecutors charged Hollis with murder of the fetus. The Court of Appeal reversed the decision at first instance,[42] holding that the relevant statute should be construed as incorporating the fetus within the definition of person. The Kentucky Supreme Court reversed this decision, holding that the fetus was not a person under the statute, and that the statute would need to be amended to enable a prosecution in such circumstances.[43]

Yet worryingly in *Commonwealth v. Cass*[44] the court successfully construed a statute as including the fetus in its definition of person. In *Cass*, the court held that a third party could be prosecuted for negligently killing a viable fetus despite the fact that the defendant was unaware of the pregnant status of the woman. Massachusetts instituted a vehicular homicide statute in 1976[45] and in *Cass* the Supreme Judicial Court decided by a 4-3 majority that a viable fetus constituted a person within the meaning of the statute on the basis that ordinary usage of the term 'person' includes the viable fetus.

The *Cass* decision was duly criticized, not only on the ground that such a perception of popular usage was incorrect, but also on the ground that the court was in effect prospectively amending the relevant statute.[46] The majority were keen to align the tort law, which endorsed wrongful death litigation, and the criminal law. Yet the law does not demand that the criminal and civil systems exist on the same principles; quite the contrary.[47] Thus, in *State v. Amaro*[48] Amaro crashed his car into a woman who was nine months pregnant. As a result of the crash her baby was stillborn. The state's charge of vehicular homicide was upheld at first instance, but dismissed by the Supreme Court of Rhode Island. This is despite the fact that the viable fetus is deemed a person for purposes of *civil* law suits in Rhode Island. Freely noted that it is a general principle of statutory interpretation that the courts should '... interpret the term "person" less expansively in statutes which are penal rather than remedial in nature'.[49] Hence the fact that a viable fetus is statutorily defined as a fetus for the purposes of civil law should not make it a person in criminal law.

Just as the courts might interpret the term 'person' to incorporate the fetus in homicide cases, so too it can use existing statutes to protect the fetus from harm. Such ability enables the court to protect the fetus during pregnancy rather than simply imposing penalties upon birth after the damage has resulted in the death or injury of the neonate. For example, in the 1996 case of *Whitner v. State*[50] the Supreme Court of South Carolina held that a viable fetus is a 'child' for purposes of a child-abuse statute, and that a mother might be charged and found guilty of criminal child neglect for harm caused to her fetus through her use of crack cocaine in the final stages of pregnancy.

A Fifth Category: Legislate to Override the Common Law Born Alive Rule

States declaring that a fetus becomes a person at some point other than birth can use the common law to effect the prosecution of those harming it. In such cases, the fetus has legal rights equal to other persons. However, to construe a statute as including the fetus within its definition of person, when it does not expressly do so, has been subject to constitutional criticisms, as evidenced in the aftermath of *Cass*.[51] Similarly, enacting a statute that incorporates the fetus within the definition of 'person' is complex because of the difficulties in adjudicating between the fetus and pregnant woman when each supposedly has equal rights. Another method to protect the fetus is to recognize that it is not yet a person, but to make it a crime to bring about its death.[52]

Such statutes may protect the fetus from conception, but more commonly protect it from viability. Viability is important, first because it is at this point that the fetus is deemed to be able to survive independently of the pregnant woman were it to be given such a chance, and second, because viability is given so much significance in the Supreme Court decision *Roe v. Wade*.[53] Thus, by 1990, 17 states had codified the crime of murder of an unborn child, but 13 of these only criminalize from the onset of fetal viability.[54] However this was not the case in *State v. Merril*[55] where the defendant shot a woman who was 28 days pregnant, and who died with the loss of the fetus. Merril was charged with the murder of both the woman and unborn child under a Minnesota statute including the unborn child as a potential victim in its statutory definition of murder. The defendant argued that this statute conflicted with *Roe*, for it equates the first trimester fetus with a person. The court held that the purpose of *Roe* was to protect the woman's choice to abort, not to allow third parties to destroy the fetus. Hence Minnesota's statute was upheld.

A similar result occurred in a 1994 case, *People v. Davis*.[56] California's Penal Code section 187(a) provides that 'Murder is the unlawful killing of a human being, or a fetus, with malice aforethought'. The case involved the shooting of Maria Flores, who was between 23 and 35 weeks pregnant, in an armed robbery. The fetus was stillborn as a direct result of the attack and the defendant was charged with assaulting and robbing Flores and murdering the fetus. Section 187(a) makes no requirement of viability, but the court at first instance nevertheless held that viability was a prerequisite to prosecution. Because an expert opinion defined the chance of fetal survival at this stage to be merely possible and not probable, the charge of murder of the fetus could not lead to prosecution. The Supreme Court of California agreed with the Court of Appeal that viability was not a prerequisite to conviction, contrary to prior Californian decisions, but that prosecution in this case would offend due process.[57] Therefore future cases in California should proceed on the basis that prosecution for killing of the fetus will not depend on viability.

'Feticide statutes' escape the born alive rule altogether. In some cases the pregnant woman is expressly excluded from liability. However, where this is not the case, such statutes remain problematic because of the necessary conflict of rights.

Conclusion

The legislative process involves careful scrutiny of any bill to ensure that it is constitutional. The Constitution ensures against vagueness, protects individuals from cruel and unusual punishment, and protects liberty, privacy and autonomy. As a result it is very difficult to enact new legislation criminalizing pregnant women, though there have been notable successes. An alternative route is to take existing laws meant to protect children from death or harm and apply them to the fetus or the fetus born alive. However, this too has proved problematic in terms of human rights. Though we do not have a constitution in England and Wales, the common law, the Human Rights Act 1998 and the European Convention for the Protection of Human Rights and Fundamental Freedom protect privacy, due process and prevent uncertainty in law. The born alive rule was accepted in *Attorney-General's Reference (No. 3 of 1994)*[58] with the effect that liability for murder or manslaughter may ensue irrespective of whether the relevant injury is inflicted pre-natally. It is suggested that though it would be possible to apply this concept to recent mothers who harmed or killed the fetus born alive, it is neither theoretically advisable (on the basis of Chapters 1 and 2), legally advisable (on the basis of this chapter and Chapter 4) or the option of maximum utility (Chapters 4 and 6).

Notes

1   In England and Wales the Congenital Disabilities (Civil Liability) Act 1976, s. 4(2)(a) states that '"born" means born alive (the moment of a child's birth being when it first has a life separate from its mother)...' In the USA, states have defined the point at which the fetus becomes a baby in various ways. For example California looks for an independent heartbeat (see *People v. Chavez*, 77 Cal. App. 2d at 625, 176 P.2d at 94 (1992)) whereas Texas requires physical expulsion from the uterus (see *Wallace v. Texas*, 7 Tex. Crim. 570 at 573, 3 S.W. 201 at 206 (1880)).

2   *Attorney General's Reference (No. 3 of 1994)* [1996] 2 All E.R. 10 (hereafter A-G's Ref. C.A.); [1997] 3 All E.R. 936 (hereafter A-G's Ref. H.L.).

3   Hereafter, 'third parties' are taken to refer to people other than the pregnant woman.

4   Sir E. Coke, (1680) 3 *Co. Inst.* 50.

5   J. Temkin, 'Pre-Natal Injury, Homicide and the Draft Criminal Code' (1986) 45(3) *Cambridge Law Journal* 414.

6   J. Temkin, *ibid.,* 418.

7   Offences Against the Person Act 1861, Section 58 '... whosoever with intent to procure the miscarriage of any woman ... shall unlawfully administer to her or cause to be taken by her any poison or other noxious thing, or shall unlawfully use any instrument or other means whatsoever with the like intent shall be guilty of an offence.'

8   *Kong Cheuk Kwan v. The Queen* (1985) 82 Cr. App. R. 18 P.C. where the Privy Council held that *R v. Caldwell* [1982] A.C. 341 applies to involuntary manslaughter.

9   J. Temkin, *op. cit.,* 423.

10   *R v. Kwok Chak Ming (No. 1)* [1963] H.K.L.R. 226 in which a third party stabbed a pregnant woman, directly causing the death of the child which was born alive. Note that the Court of Appeal and the House of Lords in A-G's Ref. *op.cit.,* did not accord with aspects of this case, particularly with the introduction of negligence to the born alive rule. See Chapter 4 p. 57.

11   A-G's Ref H.L. per Mustill LJ at 949. See Chapter 4 p. 59.

12   *R v. West* (1848) 2 Car & Kir 784, 175 E.R. 329. The defendant was later acquitted. The headnote reads: 'If a person, intending to procure abortion, does an act which causes a child to be born so much earlier than the natural time, that it is born in a state much less capable of living, and afterwards dies, in consequence of its exposure to the external world, the person who, by this misconduct, so brings the child into the world and puts it thereby in a situation in which it cannot live, is guilty of murder, and the mere existence of a possibility that something might have been done to prevent the death, would not render it less murder.'

13   *R v Senior* (1832) 1 Mood CC 346, 168 E.R. 1298. The headnote reads: 'Giving a child, whilst in the act of being born, a mortal wound in the head, as soon as the head appears, and before the child has breathed, will, if the child is afterwards born alive, and dies thereof, and there is malice, be murder.'

14   J. Temkin, *ibid.,* 420 says of *R v Senior*: 'The decision ... is authority for no more than that a defendant who has fulfilled all the requirements of the offence of manslaughter will be liable for it even if the relevant injury was inflicted before the birth of the child.'

15   *R v. Kwok Chak Ming, op. cit.*

16   J. Temkin, *op. cit.,* 421.

17   England and Wales have statutes that criminalize actions that harm the fetus, but do so without giving the fetus human status. In the United States, many statutes define the fetus as a person, and it is here that the crucial difference lies. See M.L. Kime, 'The Born Alive Rule Dies a Timely Death' (1995) 30 *Tulsa Law Journal* 539 who noted that the born alive rule has been overruled and held to be antiquated in Oklahoma, Massachusetts and South Carolina.

18   For example where many states require that the appropriate *mens rea* is directed at the fetus or child born alive, a Mississippi statute states that *mens rea* must be established in relation to the pregnant woman: '... the wilful killing of an unborn, quick child, by any injury to the mother of such child, which would be murder if it resulted in the death of the mother, shall be manslaughter.' MISS. CODE ANN. No. 97-3-337 (1972).

19   A state-by-state breakdown of criminal prosecutions is provided by the University of South Carolina at http://hadm.sph.sc.edu/Students/KBelew/fetalab.htm.

20   *Williams v. State,* 316 Md. 677, 561 A.2d 216 (1989) Court of Appeals of Maryland. This case involves the application of 'transferred malice', a concept examined in Chapter 4 p. 57.

21   *State v. Ashley,* 670 So. 2d 1087 (Fla. 1996).

22   *Alaska v. Grubbs,* No. 4FA S89 415 Criminal, slip op. (Sup. Ct. Aug. 25, 1989).

23   Child Abuse During Pregnancy Prevention Act, S. 1444 101th Cong., 1st Sess. (1980). See D.E. Johnsen, 'From Driving to Drugs: Governmental Regulation of Pregnant Women's Lives After *Webster'* (1989) 138 *University of Pennsylvania Law Review* 179 at 221.

24   *Florida v. Johnson,* No. E89-1765 (Fla. Dist. Ct. App., 5th Dist. 1989); *Florida v. Black,* No. 89-5325, slip op. (Fla. Cir., Ct., Jan. 3m 1990) and *Florida v. Hudson,* No. K88-3435-CFA, slip op. (Fla. Cir. Ct. July 26, 1989).

25   In *Georgia v. Coney,* No. 14/403-404 (Super. Ct. of Crisp County filed Nov. 6, 1989) a woman was indicted for distribution of cocaine to her child as also occurred in *People v. K.H.,* No. 89.2931.FY (Mich. Dist. Ct., Muskegon County, Nov. 13 1989) and *Michigan v. Cox,* No. 9053535FH (Cir. Ct. for Jackson County filed Jan. 30, 1990).

26   *Michigan v. Hardy,* No. 12845, slip op. (Mich. Ct. App. April 1, 1991). See also *Massachusetts v. Pellegrini,* No. 87970 (Super. Ct. filed Aug. 21, 1989) and *Michigan v. Bremer,* No. 90-1313-FY (Dist. Ct. Muskegon County), where charges of supplying illicit substances to a minor were dismissed on the ground that that relevant statute was not intended to apply to this scenario.

27   *North Carolina v. Inzar,* Nos 90CRS6960, 90CRS6961 (N.C. Super. Ct. Robeson Cty, Apr. 9, 1991).

28   *Connecticut v. Baez,* No. CR089-010-4414, slip op. (Conn. Super. Ct. filed July 31, 1989). Similarly, in *Illinois v. Green,* No. 88-CM-8256 (Cir. Ct. filed May 8, 1989) a woman was charged with manslaughter and delivery of a controlled substance when her two-day old child died and both mother and child were found to have cocaine in their blood stream. However, the grand jury refused to indict.

29   See for example, *Florida v. Jerez,* No. K89-16257 (Monroe County CT. Jan. 11, 1990); *Nevada v. Bloxham,* No. RJC-36887 (Reno Justice Ct. filed Feb. 1990); *Nevada v. Peters,* No. 90-241 (Sperks Justice Ct. filed Feb. 22, 1990) where women were charged with child abuse after their new-borns tested positive for illicit drugs. In *Kentucky v. Welsh,*

No. 90-CR-006 (Cir. Ct. Boyd County May 25, 1990) a woman addicted to Percadin was convicted of criminal child abuse following the birth of her impaired child. However many such cases have failed on the basis that the relevant statute was not intended to apply to pregnant women. See for example *People v. Morabito*, 580 N.Y.S. 2d 843 (1992); *Reyes v. People*, C.A. 75 Cal. App. 3d, 214, (1977); *Wyoming v. Osmus* S.C., 73 Wyo. 183, 276 P. 2d 469 (1954); *Florida v. Gethers*, 585 So. 2d 1140 (Fla. Dist. Ct. App. 1991).

30   The American Civil Liberties Union (ACLU) is a strong pro-choice group committed to protecting pregnant women from prosecution for crimes against the fetus and child born alive. See L. Rubenstein, 'Prosecuting Maternal Substance Abusers: An Unjustified and Ineffective Policy' (1991) Spring (9) *Yale Law and Policy Review* 130 at 160. Examples of cases where mothers are prosecuted for neglect are: *In re Baby X*, 97 Mich. App. 111, 116, 293 N.W.2d 736, 739 (1980); *In re Smith*, 128 Misc. 2d 976, 979, 492 N.Y.S.2d 331, 334 (Fam. Ct. Monroe County 1985); *In re Ruiz*, 27 Ohio Misc. 2d 31,35,500 N.E. 2d935, 939 (C..P. 1986).

31   G.J. Annas, 'The Impact Of Medical Technology On The Pregnant Woman's Right To Privacy', *American Journal of Law & Medicine* 13 (1987), 213 at 230: 'Child neglect covers a wide variety of activities, but generally involves failure to provide certain things, like clothing, food, housing or medical attention, to the child. Such laws *do not*, however, require parents to provide "optimal" clothing, food, housing or medical attention to their children, and do not even forbid taking risks with children, such as engaging in dangerous sports, or affirmatively injuring children in the form of punishment to teach them a lesson. Even if we can define fetal neglect, we are left with the inherently sexist application of the law.'

32   *D v. Berkshire County Council* [1987] 1 All E.R. 20 (Div. Ct.); 27 (C.A.) and 33 (H.L.). See Chapter 4 p. 71.

33   See A. Ferriman, Health Correspondent, 'Drugs in Pregnancy Under Legal Spotlight: Lords Consider Action Against Addict Mothers', *The Observer*, 5 October 1986, 5 col. 1 and I. Young, 'The Unborn Child and Criminal Proceedings' (1986) December *The Law Society's Gazette*, 3808 discussed in Chapter 4 p. 72.

34   *California v. Stewart*, No. M508197, slip op. (Cal. Mun. Ct., San Diego, Feb. 26, 1987).

35   *Liparota v. U.S.* 435 U.S. 419, 247 (1985).

36   See for example the Florida case of *Lowe v. State* 450 AO. 2d 1191, 1193 (Fla. Dist. Ct. App. 1984) which involved a charge of fetal battery. Here the court ruled that where the term 'fetus' is omitted from the relevant statute, the legislature did not intend fetuses to be protected by the Act.

37   *Ohio v. Andrews* No. JU 68459 (Ohio C.P., Stark County June 19, 1989). Similarly see *Ohio v. Gray*, No. CR88-7406, slip op. (Ohio C.P., Lucas County July 13, 1989) and *Reyes v. Superior Court*, 75 Cal. App. 3d 214, 141 Cal. Rptr. 9122 (Cal. Ct. App. 1977).

38   *Hughes v. State*, 868 P.2d 730 (Okla. Crim. App. 1994) holding that the third party could be charged with two counts of murder having caused the death of both pregnant woman and fetus.

39   This position is criticized in Chapter 1 p. 13.

40   *People v. Chavez*, 77 Cal. App. 2d 621, 176 P.2d 922 (1992).

41   *Hollis v. Commonwealth*, 652 S.W.2d 61 (Ky 1983).

42   KRS No. 507.020.

43   M.A. Miller, 'Criminal Law – Murder – Intentional Killing of Viable Fetus Not Murder – *Hollis v. Commonwealth*' (1984) 11(1) *Northern Kentucky Law Review* 213. Miller argued that the fetus is a person and should be protected as such. See also E. Griffin, 'Viability and Fetal Life in State Criminal Abortion Laws' (1981) 72(1) *Journal of Criminal Law and Criminology* 324.

44   *Commonwealth v. Cass*, 392 Mass. 799 467 N.E. 2d 1324 (1984). Another non-codified state to criminalize killing of the unborn is South Carolina, in *State v. Horne*, 282 S.C. 444, 319 S.E.2d 703 (1984).

45 G.L. c.90 No. 24G(b), enacted, St. 1976, c.227.
46 J. H. Henn, 'Case and Statute Comments: Criminal Law – Vehicular Homicide of a Viable Fetus – Judicial Statutory Amendment' (1986) 70 *Massachusetts Law Review*, 201 at 201.
47 The court's supposition that the viable fetus was synonymous with a 'person' was based on the civil case of *Mone v. Greyhound Lines, Inc.* 386 Mass. 354 (1975), where a viable fetus was deemed a person for purposes of wrongful death statutes. Justice Wilkins, dissenting, distinguished this case on the basis of its civil, as opposed to criminal application, but the court went on to say that the original statute had left the word 'person' undefined precisely so that the courts could later fill the void in a manner consistent with public opinion.
48 *State v. Amaro*, 448 A.2d 1257 (R.I. 1982).
49 Sutherland, *Statutes and Statutory Construction* (C. Sands: USA, 1972), Nos 59.01-59.03 at 1 – 13. As referred to by M.B. Freely 'Criminal Law and Procedure: Fetus not a Person Within Meaning of Rhode Island Vehicular Homicide Statute' (1983) 17 *Suffolk University Law Review* 405 at 407.
50 *Whitner v. State,* 1996 WL 393164 (S.C. 1996). Cornelia Whitner was charged with criminal child neglect under South Carolina Code No. 20-7-50. See A.M. Capron, 'Punishing Mothers', *Hastings Center Report* 28(1) (1998), 31 for commentary.
51 *Commonwealth v. Cass, op. cit..*
52 For example New York has a statute punishing feticide as manslaughter. See N.Y.REV.STAT. pt. IV, Ch. 1, tit. 2 section 8-9 (1829). See also CAL. PENAL CODE No. 187 (West Supp. 1986); FLA.STAT.ANN. No. 782.09 (West Cum. Supp. 1975); ILL.ANN.STAT. ch. 38 No. 9-1.1 (Smith-Hurd Supp. 1985); IOWA CODE ANN. No. 707.7 (West 1979). These statutes impose criminal sanctions for 'murder' of a viable (or third trimester) fetus by third parties. The act must be committed with intent to kill the fetus or the pregnant woman.
53 *Roe v. Wade* 410 U.S. 113 (1973). See Chapter 5 p. 97 for commentary.
54 See *State v. Merril*, 450 N.W.2d 318 (1990) Supreme Court of Minnesota, at 321. Arizona, Indiana and Minnesota impose criminal liability for causing the death of the unborn at any stage. See ARIZ.REV.STAT.ANN No. 13-1103(A)(5) (1989) and IND.CODE ANN. No. 3542-1-6 (Burns 1985).
55 *State v. Merril, ibid.*
56 *People v. Davis,* 7 Cal.4th 797, 30 Cal.Rptr.2d 50, 872 P.2d 591 (1994) Supreme Court of California.
57 See Chapter 5, which deals with this and other constitutional issues regarding the extensions of the born alive rule in American law.
58 *A-G's Ref. H.L. op.cit.*

Chapter 4

Crimes Against the Fetus Born Alive in England and Wales

It is a common law principle in England and Wales that a crime can only be committed against a living person.[1] Therefore the fetus cannot be the victim of murder or other common law crimes. Because the fetus lives symbiotically with the pregnant woman, many harms to the fetus will also harm the woman who *is* a person in being and thus able to pursue a criminal case against any third party who harms her. Therefore the fetus gains cursory legal protection vicariously. The fetus is further safeguarded through statute. Historically, the criminal law has afforded greater protection to the fetus than is currently the case. Section 58 of the Offences Against the Person Act 1861[2] prohibited the pregnant woman or third parties from committing any abortion whatsoever, punishable on conviction by life imprisonment. The Infant Life Preservation Act 1929[3] marked a step away from protection of the fetus as an entity of equal value and gave preference to the health of the pregnant woman when abortion was necessary to save her life. At the same time it emphasized the importance of the viable fetus as it neared fulfilment of its potential for human life,[4] though there is debate as to whether the Act was intended to sanction all abortions prior to 28 weeks or simply to safeguard the fetus during the birthing process.[5] The Abortion Act 1967, as amended by the Human Fertilisation and Embryology Act 1990,[6] liberalized abortion law even further and represents the current legal position.

Once the child is born alive it becomes a 'person' in law and is protected by the criminal common law. If injury occurs *in utero* but live birth follows and the resulting person dies of those injuries, the third party causing them may be liable for the death of the person, even though it was a non-person when the injury was sustained. Person 'A' who injures a fetus that dies *in utero* commits a different crime from person 'B' who injures a fetus that is born alive and subsequently dies. In the Scottish case, *McCluskey v. The Lord Advocate*[7] it was held that a child damaged in the womb by a third person's reckless driving could not be the victim of the offence of death by reckless driving, because the child was still born: it never achieved personhood. In *R v. Tait*[8] a man was convicted under section 16 of the Offences Against the Person Act 1861[9] when he threatened a pregnant woman that he would return to kill her and her (currently unborn) 'baby' should she inform the police of his recent burglary. However, the Court of

Appeal reversed the decision because, though the threat might be construed as existing against the child once born alive (which would come under the ambit of the Offences Against the Person Act),[10] it could also have meant that the defendant threatened to cause miscarriage of the fetus. The latter is not a threat against a third person within the meaning of section 16. As the jury was misdirected about the relevant import of the words, the conviction was unsafe.

In civil law a claim arises where the negligent act of a third party injures a fetus under the Congenital Disabilities (Civil Liability) Act 1976.[11] Liability under the Act does not create a duty of care owed to the non-person fetus, but imposes liability to the disabled child only if the perpetrator had been 'liable in tort to the parent, or would, if sued in due time, have been so'.[12] Unlike civil liability in the US,[13] actions against the mother are expressly excluded. The Law Commission worried that the alternative position might give rise to her liability for failing to stop smoking, drinking alcohol, taking illicit drugs or otherwise failing to act as a reasonable pregnant woman.[14] As Fortin[15] stated, on general negligence principles the mother could not owe a duty of care to a non-entity and should not therefore be sued for pre-natal negligence. However, the Law Commission's view was accepted that a pregnant woman who injures the fetus (later born alive) in a road traffic accident should be liable due to the presence of compulsory third party insurance.[16]

To date the criminal born alive rule has applied to third parties. Application of the rule to criminalize the mother of a child which is born alive and suffers injury or death due to her actions in pregnancy has potential to reverse the historical trend that has gradually increased maternal rights in pregnancy. The *Attorney-General's Reference (No 3 of 1994)*[17] might be applied in future so as to effect this change and this chapter examines the law in England and Wales to assess the likelihood of such a possibility. In doing so, aspects of civil law are discussed to judge its potential impact on the central criminal law doctrines under discussion.

The facts behind the *A-G's Ref.* involved the respondent stabbing his girlfriend whom he knew to be pregnant. He originally pleaded guilty to wounding her with intent to cause grievous bodily harm, and at this point no injury of the fetus was detected. However, the child was born prematurely because the knife had in fact penetrated the abdomen of the fetus, reducing the new-born's life-expectancy by 50 per cent. The knife wound was repaired by surgery, but the child died 120 days after birth, from a lung condition caused by the premature birth. The Attorney-General referred two questions to the Court of Appeal.[18] The first concerned the appropriate *mens rea* for murder and manslaughter where injury was deliberately inflicted, with regards to either a child *in utero* or to a pregnant woman who later gives birth to a live child, which then dies as a result of the injury. The second asked whether the fact that the injury was to the pregnant woman rather than the fetus itself could negate any such liability for murder or manslaughter.[19]

The Court of Appeal's somewhat controversial judgement was tempered by the House of Lords, but it is useful to examine both stages in order to gauge the impetus for change of the currently restrictive policy regarding the rights of the child damaged *in utero* and born alive. Crucially, both the Court of Appeal and the House of Lords accepted the born alive rule. Arguably this was unnecessary[20] and the House of Lords' did so most reluctantly. Nevertheless it is now a feature of the common law and nothing in the formulation of the rule guards against its application to recent mothers.

The *Attorney-General's Reference (No. 3 of 1994)*: The Court of Appeal Decision

The Court of Appeal held that, depending on intent, murder or manslaughter is the appropriate charge following the deliberate unlawful injury of the fetus born alive and dying as a result of those injuries. Taylor LCJ considered the words of Coke and Hale,[21] and decided that the majority of commentators favoured Coke's analysis of the law. Therefore, provided the fetus is born alive and becomes a person in being, the fact that it was not a person in being at the time of the injury is no bar to liability.[22] The *mens rea* and *actus reus* do not have to coincide. Hence if A attacks a pregnant woman and has the required *mens rea* to injure or kill the child born alive, and death results, then he will be guilty of causing that death; if A wishes to blow up a children's nursery and sets the timing device six years prior to the detonation, he will not be able to plead in his defence that the children were not conceived at the time of the *actus reus*.[23] Though the decision dealt only with the application of the born alive rule to third parties, the same legal reasoning could be employed to secure the conviction of women whose actions in pregnancy cause the death of the child born alive.

Having accepted that a child born alive could be the victim of a murder even though the injury occurred when it was not a person in being, Taylor LCJ considered the other elements of the *actus reus* for murder, namely:

> ... (1) that the defendant did an act; (2) that the act was deliberate and not accidental; (3) that the act was unlawful; (4) that the act was a substantial cause of a death; (5) that the death was of a person in being; (6) that death resulted within a year and a day.[24]

Numbers (1) and (2) are merely evidential; of (3) Taylor LCJ held that any injury to the fetus must first concern an unlawful touching of the pregnant woman and so this element is satisfied;[25] the fourth would have caused problems in a society with less advanced technology, but is no longer a problem today; (5) and (6) were not contended ((6) being no longer applicable).

Far more problematic is Taylor LCJ's seventh element of murder, the *mens rea*: '(7) that at the time of doing the act the defendant intended either to kill or to cause really serious bodily injury to the victim or, subject to the extent of the doctrine of transferred malice, to some other person.'[26]

In *R v. Kwok Chak Ming (No. 1)*,[27] a third party stabbed a pregnant woman after which a child was born alive and died as a result of its injuries. The Hong Kong Court of Appeal held that if the jury found that the third party had been aware that the mother was pregnant at the time of the offence, a murder conviction would be appropriate. Taylor LCJ disagreed with this introduction of negligence into the concept of transferred malice. Instead, he saw two ways in which the *mens rea* could be satisfied, both of which received substantial criticism in the House of Lords for building on old fictions.

The first is by satisfying the jury that the defendant intended to kill or cause really serious bodily harm to the fetus and the intention is directed at a child capable of becoming a person in being at a later date. The second is by satisfying the jury that the defendant intended to kill or cause really serious bodily injury to the pregnant woman, by the doctrine of transferred malice.[28] The Court was keen to use the doctrine of transferred malice rather than using terms of *mens rea* directed at the fetus itself, even if the defendant intended to hurt the fetus only and not the pregnant woman. Taylor LCJ held that as the fetus is a part of the pregnant woman in the eyes of the law,[29] any intention to kill or harm it is also intention to kill or harm the pregnant woman. The House of Lords did not concur and felt that Taylor LCJ was seeking to stretch the ambits of the doctrine of transferred malice too far.

The doctrine of transferred malice has evolved from two rules of criminal law. The first states that if a defendant causes the *actus reus* by a different means to that which he intended, he is nevertheless liable for that action. Hence a defendant who stabs his victim with the intention of killing him, but merely injures him, so causing him to fall on the knife and die, is guilty of murder. The second rule states that if a defendant is mistaken as to the identity of his victim, whom he kills, he is still guilty of murder.[30] These rules form the doctrine of transferred malice, by which, provided the *mens rea* for an offence is present, the fact that the *actus reus* is transferred to another victim does not prevent liability. 'A' firing his gun at 'B', missing him and hitting 'C' is liable for 'C''s murder, but 'D' firing a gun at 'E', missing him and damaging a nearby property is not liable for criminal damage.[31]

The doctrine has been accepted by the Law Commission, which has proposed a statutory provision to codify it.[32] However, others are less enthusiastic about the concept. Ashworth, for example, argued that the doctrine could be abolished and replaced with either liability for the attempted crime, or liability for the actual crime based on recklessness. Though this may result in a lighter sentence than seems appropriate, he argued that subjective liability is appropriate and should reflect the intentional act rather than a chance result.[33] The House of Lords disagreed with this part of the Court of Appeal's judgement and refused to stretch the ambits of the doctrine. However, unlike Ashworth, they recognized the legal validity of the doctrine provided the definition is not extended.

The reasoning of the Court of Appeal is as follows. Since the victim is not a person in being at the time of the injury, it follows that malice towards it is impossible. Therefore malice can only be directed at the pregnant woman. Yet even if the malice is in fact directed at the fetus with no malice toward the pregnant woman, the doctrine still operates according to Taylor LCJ, because the fetus is a part of the pregnant woman and any malice towards it must necessarily also be directed at the woman. So what in the final analysis is transferred? According to Taylor LCJ, malice is transferred from the pregnant woman to the fetus and then to the child, should it be born alive. Yet the scenarios recognized by Ashworth, and by Clarkson and Keating, involve transfer of malice from the intended victim to a mistaken or accidental victim. In the Court of Appeal's decision, there is apparently only one victim (the pregnant woman including her appendage) until live birth occurs when transfer is effected from the real victim (the mother including her fetus) to the child alone. Yet it is a long-standing rule that transferred malice is only possible when the *mens rea* exists and the *actus reus* remains the same for the mistaken victim as it would have been for the intended victim had the plan not gone amiss.

Hence, the *actus reus* of the mistaken and intended crimes do not match: the *actus reus* of stabbing a pregnant woman is different to that of causing the death of a child; also, the mistaken and intended victim exist at different times where they are usually envisaged to exist contemporaneously. It was further argued that in terms of causation, the birth and death of the baby are so far removed from the stabbing to prevent transferral of malice.[34] Of the three objections, Taylor LCJ briefly dismissed the first and third, concentrating on the second. He argued that in any case of transferred malice, there could be no transfer until the victim is affected. He used the example of 'D' poisoning baby food and placing it on the shelves, claiming that it would be unjust if 'D' were only guilty of murder if a child so affected by the product was born and living an independent existence from the mother at the date when the poison was put in the food.[35] Bailin criticized this reasoning, for no matter when the food was poisoned, the act resulting in harm occurs when the child is in being; not when it is a non-entity. Further he argued that 'there is something distinctly odd about reliance on transferred malice when the actual victim is the intended one'.[36] It is quite clear that Taylor LCJ's reliance on transferred malice lacks a sound basis, as the House of Lords later confirmed.

The questions posed in the Reference were answered by the Court of Appeal holding that murder or manslaughter could be committed following the deliberate infliction of unlawful injury to either a child *in utero* or to a pregnant woman where the child was subsequently born alive, enjoyed an existence independent of its mother and thereafter died, provided that the injuries inflicted while *in utero* caused or contributed subsequently to the death. Because the fetus was considered by Taylor LCJ to be an appendage of the pregnant woman, any assault on it is as unlawful as such an assault on the pregnant woman. Further, there is no requirement that the person who dies should be a person in being at the time of the act causing eventual death. In answer to the second referred question, it was held that the requisite intent to be proved in a case of murder in these circumstances is an intention to kill or cause really serious bodily injury to the mother, since the fetus before birth is regarded as an integral part of the mother. This decision represents a worryingly liberal approach to the born alive rule, which was widely construed. Fortunately, the House of Lords narrowed the ambit of the decision.

Murder or Manslaughter? The *Attorney-General's Reference (No. 3 of 1994)* in the House of Lords

Taylor LCJ held that the fetus was part of the pregnant woman but the House of Lords disagreed. Because the organisms are distinct, intent to cause really serious bodily injury to the pregnant woman is not synonymous with the same intent towards the fetus or future child. Further, Lord Mustill held that the double transfer of malice from woman to fetus to child was extending the ambit of the doctrine too far.[37]

Lord Mustill began by considering the appropriateness of a murder charge. He outlined five rules relating to murder; the malice aforethought rule, of which he was critical but accepted its place in the criminal law;[38] the doctrine of transferred malice, which he accepted on a narrow interpretation;[39] the rule that the fetus does not have the status of a person until birth and therefore cannot be the victim of a crime of violence;[40] the exception to the coincidence of *actus reus* and *mens rea* rule;[41] and the 'born alive' rule[42] as outlined by Coke. Lord Mustill recognized that the latter rule is not universally supported, but he cited pre-Homicide Act acceptance[43] and, unlike Temkin,[44] views the later cases of *West* and *Senior*[45] as supportive of the rule.

Lord Mustill recognized that by amalgamating and building upon these five rules, it would be conceivable (though ultimately undesirable) to criminalize the act of the third party in the Reference, as murder. He develops a theoretical extension in the following stages:

> If D struck X intending to cause her serious harm, and the blow, in fact, caused her death, that would be murder (rule 1). If she had been nursing a baby Y, which was accidentally struck by the blow and consequently died, that would also be murder (rules 1 and 2). So, also, if an evil-doer had intended to cause harm but not death to X by giving her a poisoned substance and the substance was, in fact, passed on by X to the baby, which consumed it and died as a result (rules 1, 2

and 3). Again it would have been murder if the fetus had been injured *in utero* and had succumbed to the wound after being born alive (rules 1, 2, 4 and 5). It is only a short step to make a new rule, adding together the malice towards the mother, the contemporaneous starting of a train of events, and the coming to fruition of those events in the death of the baby after being born alive.[46]

However, Lord Mustill rejected this line of reasoning on the basis that it 'piles up old fictions'. The original reasoning behind the rule that intent to cause grievous bodily harm will found a conviction for murder no longer applies. It may be that it represents an element of the felony murder rule that was abolished by the Homicide Act 1957 and if so, it has even less justification. However, in *R v. Cunningham*[47] the concept is reaffirmed in the House of Lords, so to abolish it would be a fundamental move indeed. Hence Lord Mustill was content to recognize the lack of merit in the rule, and guard against its extension. Thus, the House of Lords held that on the basis of the narrow set of facts before the court, murder would be an inappropriate charge.

With regard to manslaughter, the Court of Appeal held that such a charge would be appropriate where the defendant intended to cause harm to the pregnant woman short of grievous bodily harm. Taylor LCJ applied the same reasoning as he applied to the charge of murder, with the exception of the differences in intent. As Lord Mustill did not agree with the Court of Appeal's reasoning on murder, neither could he do so in relation to manslaughter. However, the House of Lords held that such a defendant *could* be convicted of unlawful act manslaughter provided that a sober and reasonable person would have considered that such an attack would harm a child if it were later born alive and if causation were proved.

Lord Hope asserted that such a defendant has the *mens rea* needed for a charge of assault on the pregnant woman, which is an unlawful and dangerous act[48] likely to endanger another person. This is a narrow margin for prosecution and formulation of the direction to the jury would be complicated. Yet, however narrow, it presents the opportunity for prosecution and therefore an affirmative answer to the question put to the Attorney-General. Further, as Lord Hope later added, the risk need not merely be in relation to the future child; it can be in relation to anyone and does not even rely on knowledge of pregnancy.

Lord Hope cited *R v. Mitchell*,[49] where the appellant hit a man in a queue, and the man fell against an old lady, who in turn fell, broke her leg and later died of a pulmonary embolism. The appellant was convicted of manslaughter despite a complete lack of physical contact between himself and the old lady. Hence, the following questions must be affirmatively answered before prosecution for unlawful act manslaughter can succeed: '(1) whether the act was done intentionally, (2) whether it was unlawful, (3) whether it was also dangerous because it was likely to cause harm to somebody and (4) whether that unlawful and dangerous act caused the death.'[50]

As Lord Mustill pointed out, consistency between murder and manslaughter is too much to hope for, but the result here is substantial justice.[51] Lord Hope recognized however that the response to this Reference will not cover every case in which a child is born alive and then dies as a result of a criminal act committed whilst it was *in utero*.[52] Even on the House of Lords' narrow interpretation of the born alive rule, there lies the potential application so as to achieve a murder prosecution against women whose actions whilst pregnant cause the death of the child born alive. However, acts and omissions of the pregnant woman that prove harmful to the fetus born alive are more likely to involve recklessness than intention. Therefore, as has proved the case in the USA,[53] actions against recent mothers whose behaviour in pregnancy causes the death of the fetus born alive are more likely to be founded in manslaughter than murder.

Following the *A-G's Reference*, unlawful act or constructive manslaughter is one such potential means. Use of illicit substances might constitute the unlawful act, and the 'constructive' nature of this type of manslaughter means that the pregnant woman need not foresee the death of the child in order to be guilty of the offence. In fact, provided a sober and reasonable person would have considered that the unlawful act would cause injury to a child if it were later born alive and if causation were proved, it is not even a requirement that the woman knew at the time of the act that she was pregnant. The unlawful act in question might be intentionally or recklessly committed and it is merely required that the reasonable man would foresee resulting injury, though not necessarily serious injury and certainly not death.[54]

A manslaughter charge might also be brought where a pregnant woman was grossly negligent as to the death or serious injury of the child once it was born alive. This type of manslaughter is not dependent on the committal of an unlawful act, and could potentially apply to women causing death to the child born alive through alcohol use, for example. Gross negligence manslaughter was revitalized following the 1995 House of Lords decision in *R v. Adomako*.[55] There an anaesthetist negligently failed to notice that a tube had become disconnected, causing a patient to die. It was alleged by the prosecution that his negligence amounted to gross negligence, which Lord Mackay formulated as follows:

> ...the ordinary principles of the law of negligence apply to ascertain whether or not the defendant has been in breach of a duty of care towards the victim who has died. If such a breach of duty is established the next question is whether that breach of duty caused the death of the victim. If so, the jury must go on to consider whether the breach of the duty should be characterised as gross negligence and therefore as a crime. This will depend on the seriousness of the breach of duty ... in all the circumstances in which the defendant was placed.

This definition is somewhat contentious because it imports into criminal law, the tort law concept of negligence. It seems unlikely, for example, that the

House of Lords sought to import the narrower tortious liability in relation to omissions into the criminal law. Thus, the rule that the pregnant woman does not owe a civil duty of care to the child born alive[56] does not necessarily preclude judgement that she is guilty of gross negligence manslaughter if death of the child ensues.

Alternatively, a manslaughter charge could be brought following *Kong Cheuk Kwan v. The Queen*,[57] if there was an obvious and serious risk of causing physical injury to the child when it was born which the defendant either went ahead and disregarded, or failed to consider.[58] This is a more likely cause of action than gross negligence manslaughter, not merely because it is unnecessary to show that a civil duty of care exists, but because the standard of health promotion in England and Wales is such that the major contributors to fetal ill-health would potentially be viewed as 'obvious' risks. Thus, even if the pregnant woman did not know that she was putting the child born alive at risk of personal injury, she might be guilty of the offence provided the risk was obvious.[59] This has worrying connotations if applied to pregnant women whose addictions or poor standard of education cause them to fall short of the standard of the reasonable man.

Thus, murder and particularly manslaughter charges could potentially be applied to women who cause the death of the child born alive through their acts or omissions whilst pregnant. In Chapter 3 it was demonstrated that the US courts have gone further still and extended liability so as to criminalize acts of the pregnant woman causing *injury* to the fetus born alive. The next section examines civil law approaches to the adjudication of materno-fetal conflicts of interest. Though civil and criminal law are quite distinct, the judicial commitment to maternal autonomy in the civil law context is relevant to the anticipated judicial commitment in criminal law.

English Civil Law Approaches

A number of recent medical and family law decisions have raised concern for maternal autonomy. In these cases medical intervention is imposed on the woman ostensibly because she has lost the capacity to consent, but arguably to protect the (often full-term) fetus. As the fetus is not a person in law, the woman's right to withhold consent should not be breached in deference to the interests of the non-person fetus. A parallel can be drawn between these cases and cases of criminalization for acts pertaining to the fetus, because in both scenarios the arguably competent choices of the pregnant woman are undermined. In Chapter 2, a fundamental difference was drawn between the state duty to act positively to an individual's benefit, and the duty not to interfere with his competent choices. The latter was heralded as the stronger right.

This section draws examples from case law where this right has arguably been breached in the context of court-authorized Caesarean section operations. The practice became relatively common in the USA[60] before a case reached the British courts for the first time, in 1992. In most cases, Caesarean sections are authorized on the basis that the woman is deemed temporarily or permanently incompetent.[61] This means that the woman is said to be legally incapable of making the relevant decision. Worryingly, however, the mere fact that the woman is unwilling to submit to a procedure when the life of the fetus is at stake is sometimes viewed as innately irrational and thereby a measure of her incompetence. Before considering the cases in more detail, it is useful to look at the doctrine of informed consent, which provides, amongst other things, that every competent individual has the right to refuse treatment.

Medical Consent

In English law, the competent patient must consent to any treatment proposed by the physician before treatment can lawfully commence.[62] There are three aspects to 'informed', 'voluntary' or 'real' consent, as it is sometimes called. The first refers to the freedom of the consent. Hence any physical force applied by the physician without voluntary consent may constitute a battery in English tort and criminal law. The second aspect involves supplying the patient with sufficient information and failure to do this may lead to a successful negligence claim.[63] The third, which is of greatest concern to this debate, is whether or not consent was actually given and when the courts should ignore the requirement of consent and order the physician to proceed with treatment regardless of its absence or express declination. Hence the patient has not only a right to consent, but also a right to withhold consent.

There are various exceptions to the rule that a patient must consent to treatment. Examples include emergencies (where the patient is presented to the physician in a state whereby he is unable to give consent due to the severity of his condition), the therapeutic privilege (though not set down in law, it is generally accepted that a physician may misrepresent information to the patient in order to avoid excessive harm, where it is in the best interests of the patient to do so), youth (where those under the age of sixteen might not be able to give or withhold consent and a guardian's consent is substituted where it is in the child's best interests)[64] and mental incapacity (where the physician, or a guardian, acts on behalf of a mentally incompetent patient in his best interests). In these cases the welfare of the patient is said to overcome his interest in self-determination and the requirement of consent is waived.

For those who have the capacity to make a decision, there exists in law a right to refuse medical treatment. Hence, in England it has been held in *Airedale National Health Service Trust v. Bland*[65] that a capable adult may refuse treatment, even if his health or life will decline as a result. In *Re C (Adult; refusal of medical treatment)*[66] this was confirmed, and Thorpe J laid down a threefold test in order to determine an adult individual's capacity to make an informed decision regarding medical consent. According to the test, a competent individual should be able to comprehend and retain information regarding treatment; to believe the information; and to make a choice by balancing the information.

However, where a fetus is also at stake the situation is apparently more complex. For in this situation, refusal to consent harms not only the adult but also the fetus, an entity that the state has a legitimate interest in protecting (as argued in Chapter 1). Yet in law the fetus is not a person, hence the adult's right to refuse treatment is not in principle diluted in any way. In practice, however, a different theme has emerged. A number of pregnant women, usually in emergency situations and suffering the pain and emotional turmoil associated with labour have been forced to undergo medical treatment despite their express withholding of consent.

Court-authorized Caesarean Sections

In *Re T (adult: refusal of medical treatment)*[67] a woman was held to have been unduly influenced and to have had insufficient information when she signed a form withholding consent to a blood transfusion. The court held that the transfusion, which was administered despite the signed statement, was lawful whilst affirming that in normal circumstances a competent individual has the right to refuse treatment even if death will result. However, Donaldson MR made an interesting qualification, stating that a possible exception to the general rule might occur where refusal would cause the death of a viable fetus.[68] It is difficult to see why in law this should be the case. However the law has recently created a distinction between the right to give consent to medical treatment and the right to withhold it. This occurred in a very limited sphere, but it is possible that Donaldson MR conceived of a similar application in relation to pregnant women who withhold their consent to medical treatment that would save the life of the viable fetus. Where *children* require treatment in their best interests, proxy consent may be required from their guardian. However where the child is 16 or over, section 8(1) of the Family Law Reform Act 1969 states that they may give consent on the same basis as if they were adults.[69] So too under the *Gillick*[70] ruling, a child under the age of 16 may be able to give consent if the doctor judges him to be of sufficient maturity in relation to the particular decision. However, under recent case law, though children may *give* consent on the same basis as adults, they may not always *withhold* consent if treatment is in their best interests, parental consent is obtained, and the child unreasonably withholds consent.[71] It is possible that Donaldson MR had in mind a similar exception to the rule that competent individuals may always withhold consent, to be applied in the case of women carrying a viable fetus.

Re S (adult refusal of medical treatment)[72] was the first in a line of court-authorized Caesarean section operation cases reported in 1992. There the attending surgeon believed that both woman and fetus would die unless the Caesarean was hurriedly performed, for the baby was well overdue. 'S', a 'Born Again Christian', refused the operation on religious grounds. However, the High Court judge, Sir Stephen Brown, in a 20-minute hearing, authorized the Caesarean to proceed on the ground that it was necessary to save the lives of both 'S' and the fetus. Yet Teff[73] denied that the decision in *Re S* was reached in order to prevent injury to the pregnant woman, and contended that the protection of the fetus was the all-important element. This, he noted, raises the objection that the conferral of judicial status on the fetus was expressly denied in *Paton v. BPAS*,[74] *Re F (in utero)*,[75] *C v. S*[76] and *Rance v. Mid-Downs Health Authority*.[77] In *Re S* there is little consideration of these cases. Instead there is an over-reliance on US precedents.[78] Commentators such as Teff and Morgan were also concerned that the decision might lead to forced medical treatment to prevent not just death, but harm to the fetus (and potential child).[79]

Re S did herald an increase of cases where the decisions of pregnant women were overruled. Due perhaps to the extensive academic criticism of *Re S,* cases turned on proof that the woman was temporarily or permanently incompetent. In two further cases, *Norfolk and Norwich v. W*[80] and *Rochdale v. Choudhary*[81] courts granted orders permitting Caesarean sections against the will of the pregnant women. In the latter case, medical opinion was that both pregnant woman and fetus would die within an hour unless a Caesarean section was performed. The woman refused to give consent because a previous Caesarean had resulted in back ache and prolonged pain. The consultant obstetrician believed that the woman was fully competent, but Johnson J, in a 2-minute hearing, applied the test presented in *Re C* and held that she was incompetent to make a decision due to the pain and emotional stress associated with labour. This decision stretches the ambits of the *Re C* test and received some criticism as a result.[82] It is a rare event that labour is not accompanied by pain and emotional stress and it is worrying in the extreme that consent can be overridden on this basis.

Clearly, the pregnant woman's autonomy suffers a serious breach in this case. Morgan contended that cases of pregnant women who strongly believe in a religion or principle that is likely to cause the death of the viable fetus are likely to be rare. He stated that the corresponding damage to reproductive choice and patient autonomy, should this policy be perpetuated, is immense.[83] Yet these cases show the courts' desire to protect the potential life of the fetus, even when the pregnant woman's beliefs dictate otherwise. It is suggested that if it were only the pregnant woman's life at stake, her competence would be subject to less reflection.[84] Just as the courts are gradually subverting her right to withhold consent to medical intervention, it is possible that they might intervene in other areas of the pregnant woman's life to protect the fetus from her harmful acts and omissions.

The court-authorized Caesarean sections outlined in the above sections were all heard at extremely short notice and a decision was urgently required if the lives of woman and fetus were to be saved. The urgency of the situation has often precluded the possibility of legal representation for the pregnant woman.[85] Such a course of action is now subject to potential criticism under the Human Rights Act 1998, which is protective of due process.[86] In 1994, the Royal College of Obstetricians and Gynaecologists issued guidance in an attempt to guide practitioners through the potential legal consequences of action.[87] The guidelines confirm that every competent patient has the right to withhold consent[88] and that the interests of the fetus are 'subordinated to the rights of pregnant women'.[89] In a summary of the legal position it was stated:

> Although obligations to the foetus increase with its growth *in utero*, UK law does not grant it any legal status. This comes from the moment of birth. The law does not limit a woman's freedom because she is pregnant. Her bodily integrity cannot be invaded on behalf of her foetus without her consent. The foetus has no remedy against injuries caused by her.[90]

Hence, only in the event that the presumption of capacity is clearly rebutted, should the practitioner override a pregnant woman's decision.[91] The guidelines were supplemented in 1996[92] reiterating that practitioners should not intervene on behalf of the fetus if the pregnant woman lawfully withholds consent, 'notwithstanding the controversial judgement of Sir Stephen Brown P. in *Re S*, in which he authorised a Caesarean section despite the patient's refusal of consent'.[93] However, guidance on the crucial issue of how to determine the capacity of a pregnant woman to make a decision is not contained therein. Where a woman has a long-term incapacity and comes under the ambits of the Mental Health Act 1983, the task is relatively simple (though the incapacity in the context of the refusal to consent must be relevant to the long-term incapacity[94]), but the cases outlined above rarely relied on long-term incapacity and instead sought to show temporary incompetence.

The situation was clarified somewhat in 1997 in *Re MB (medical treatment)*, where the *Re C* test was refined.[95] There a pregnant woman consented to a Caesarean section operation because her baby was in breech position and vaginal delivery would have posed a serious threat to its life and health. However 'MB' suffered from a needle phobia and withdrew her consent at the last moment on two occasions. The High Court then granted a declaration that the operation could proceed lawfully, despite the lack of consent, on the basis that 'MB' lacked capacity to make a decision. An hour later, the Court of Appeal dismissed 'MB''s appeal. It was held, when applying the test outlined in *Re C*, that 'MB' was suffering from temporary incompetence as a result of her needle phobia and the shock, confusion and pain associated with a difficult labour; that the operation was in *her* best interests as handicap or death of the fetus would cause long-term harm to her health; and that the use of force was justifiable if necessary. However, it was also felt that some clarification of the *Re C* test was warranted in relation to pregnant women. Thus Butler-Sloss LJ went on to outline six guidance-principles to be used when considering potential incompetence of pregnant women:

1   Every person is presumed to have the capacity to consent to or to refuse medical treatment unless and until that presumption is rebutted;
2   A competent woman who has the capacity to decide, may, for religious reasons, other reasons, for rational or irrational reasons, or for no reason at all, choose not to have medical intervention, even though the consequence may be the death or serious handicap of the child she bears, or her own death. In that event the courts do not have the jurisdiction to declare medical intervention lawful and the question of her own best interests, objectively considered, do not arise;
3   Irrationality is here used to connote a decision which is so outrageous in its defiance of logic or of accepted moral standards that no sensible person who had applied his mind to the question to be decided could have arrived at it ... ;
4   A person lacks capacity if some impairment ... of mental functioning renders the person unable to make a decision whether to consent or to refuse treatment ... ;
5   ... '[T]emporary factors' ... (confusion, shock, pain or drugs) may completely erode capacity but ... such factors must operate to such a degree that the ability to decide is absent;
6   Another such influence may be panic induced by fear. Again careful scrutiny of the evidence is necessary because fear of an operation may be a rational reason for refusal to undergo it. Fear may also, however, paralyse the will and thus destroy the capacity to make a decision.[96]

Hence, rather than the threefold test (of ability to comprehend, believe and weigh up the information) outlined by Thorpe J in *Re C*, the test takes on two distinct parts: comprehension and the weighing up of the relevant information. This represents an admirable attempt at defining a controversial area of law. However, it is rare that any birth is not accompanied by at least one element of confusion, shock, pain, drugs or fear. Further, the rationality of the woman's objection, though not in itself amounting to incompetence, may be indicative of it. Consequently, any woman who disagrees with the practitioners as to the best course of action regarding the birth of her child is in danger of being labelled irrational, and so incompetent when the fear and pain of labour are taken into account. It seems that despite the assertion that capable patients retain the right to withhold consent, and that the pregnant status of the woman is not a concern in law, it will not be unduly hard to make a case for incapacity whenever a woman is in labour.[97]

Though the court in *Re MB* sought to give added protection to pregnant women's autonomy, the test remains vague and as a result, autonomy is afforded little more protection than before the case. To get the appropriate balance between paternalism and patient autonomy is no easy matter, but, as is argued in Chapter 2, procedural rather than substantive autonomy should be sought and protected. On this basis an individual can be procedurally autonomous even if irrational. When considering an individual's competence to make a decision, it would therefore be preferable to consider his decision in the context of his life rather than in the context of objective rationality. It may be irrational to refuse a blood transfusion, and in the pain and emotional turmoil of labour this may be viewed as negating a person's capacity to make the decision. However, in the light of that individual's religious, cultural, political or moral beliefs and evidence of their practice, an objective view of irrationality should not be taken as proof of incompetence. Though time is often of the essence in these cases, and a full investigation into an individual's life practices will rarely prove possible, some enquiry should be made, and the rationality of the decision viewed in context.[98]

If it is possible to claim that an otherwise competent woman has temporarily lost her ability to give consent due to the emotional and painful process of labour, how much easier it is to withdraw a woman's autonomy rights when she suffers a drug addiction. In *Metropolitan Borough Council v. DB*[99] the 17-year old, crack-cocaine addicted 'DB' did not seek ante-natal care because she feared doctors. Having suffered an eclamptic fit at 33 weeks she saw a doctor who described her as 'simple'. She was admitted to hospital, discharged herself but returned when she was told that the lives of herself and the fetus were in danger. The hospital applied to the High Court, which granted an order that she be given the necessary treatment and reasonable force be used to facilitate this. Whether it was her 'simplicity', her age, her addiction or a combination of the three that resulted in the order is not entirely clear.

A 1998 Court of Appeal case, *R v. Collins & Ors, ex parte S (No. 2)*[100] confirmed the right of competent pregnant women to refuse treatment, regardless of the viable status of the fetus. This affirmation was, for the first time in a line of cases, part of the *ratio* of the decision. Following this, in *R v. Merton Borough Council and Ors, ex parte Sutherland*[101] the applicant applied for judicial review of her detention under section 2 of the Mental Health Act 1983 and subsequent Caesarean section operation performed against her will. 'S'[102] only sought ante-natal care in the eighth month of pregnancy by which time she was suffering from pre-eclampsia which posed a risk to her own life and that of the fetus. 'S' was admitted to a hospital under section 2 of the Mental Health Act 1983[103] and then transferred to a second hospital. The hospital applied *ex parte* for a declaration to authorize her treatment and reasonable force where necessary. It did so without 'S''s knowledge and without any attempt to get legal representation for her. Hogg J authorized the operation, which went ahead though 'S' remained adamant in her desire for a natural birth. After the Caesarean section was carried out, the section 2 detention was terminated and 'S' applied for judicial review of the original detention, her admission to hospital, detention in the hospital and the circumstances of the hearing where she claimed that she had been denied a fair trial. Leave was granted due to the importance of the case, despite the application being out of time and it was ordered that the judicial review regarding the hospital's decisions should be held in conjunction with the appeal from Hogg J.

The subsequent hearing was *St. George's Healthcare National Health Service Trust v. S and R v. Collins and Others, Ex parte S*.[104] The Court of Appeal reversed the judgement of Hogg J in the Family Division, who had ordered that 'S''s mental incapacity should lead to the negation of the consent requirement.[105] The Court of Appeal also allowed 'S' to seek relief through judicial review of the decision of the social worker and hospital trusts involved. Despite the irrationality of 'S''s decision, the Court held that it is within her rights to insist on medical treatment that would normally be available to her, and similarly to refuse it. The admission to hospital of 'S' and her continued detainment were both held to be unlawful. Further, it was held that section 2 of the Mental Health Act 1983 should only be used to assess a mental disorder. It should not be used to detain a person whose thinking is perceived to be unusual or irrational.[106] In this case there was no evidence that 'S' was being detained to assess a mental condition or indeed to treat it.[107] 'S' was detained so that her physical condition could be treated which was wrong. Even if a person is correctly detained under the Mental Health Act, the court stated that medical procedures should not be carried out against her will if they are unconnected to that detention unless she has a diminished capacity to consent.

On 30 July 1998 guidelines were handed down in open court[108] in order to aid hospital authorities where a Caesarean section is in the therapeutic interests of the pregnant woman and her capacity to give or withhold consent is questionable. The advice comprises a repetition and expansion of the *Re MB* guidance. In summary the guidance states that:

- Competent patients can accept or refuse treatment and application to the High Court to refute this is pointless in this instance.
- Where a patient is incompetent his best interests are paramount. Advance directives, given prior to the temporary or long-term capacity, should usually be heeded.
- Concern over the patient's capacity should be identified at the earliest opportunity (preferably before the situation amounts to an emergency).
- The opportunity for legal representation should be made (through the individual's own solicitors or the Official Solicitor[109]).
- Any hearing should be *inter partes*. Sufficient information should be made available to the judge.
- The above guidelines may not prove viable in an emergency situation.

Hence, it seems that commitment to reproductive autonomy rights is at last receiving attention and support. However, the preceding trend of protecting the fetus from the harmful conduct of the pregnant woman forms a worrying precedent in the light of the US example outlined in the preceding chapter. A further problem is that the majority of the court-authorized Caesarean cases listed above involved *emergency* situations where time was of the essence. In emergencies, the guidelines issued in *St. George's* may be forsaken in order to eradicate unnecessary delay in the attempt to save the lives of mother and fetus. In some cases the pregnant woman may avoid ante-natal care until she is near to full term, in which case medical practitioners have little opportunity to assess her mental state prior to the situation escalating into an emergency. Further, the risk always remains that practitioners keen to evade the unnecessary death of a full-term fetus (or simply unaware of the woman's desire for a natural birth) will wait for the situation to become an emergency before taking the case to the High Court, so evading the *St. George's* guidance.

If judicial commitment to maternal autonomy slips in relation to court-authorized Caesarean section operations, it could adversely affect the woman's rights and freedoms in other aspects of pregnancy. Though the criminal and civil law are separate, the rationale of protecting the full-term fetus by ordering medical intervention could be translated to effect similar protection of the fetus from actions of the pregnant woman, using criminal law. As Morgan states:

> There is no slippery slope more perilous than that which is falsely supposed not to be slippery ... if enforced medical regimes are countenanced, the occasionally perceived need for non-therapeutic Caesarean section, hospital detention or inter uterine transfer might trigger demands for court ordered pre-natal screening, fetal surgery and restriction on diet, athletic and sexual recreations of pregnant women. ... If non-consensual Caesarean can be described as doing the mother no harm then it is difficult to imagine how other possible interventions could be refused.[110]

A Resolution of the European Parliament was passed on 8 July 1988, calling for a charter to protect childbirth rights, ranging from appropriate care in pregnancy to freedom from unwanted intervention. England and Wales have yet to respond. The Human Rights Act was ratified on 9th November 1998 and came into force in October 2000. Potentially it will speed up and reduce the cost of enforcing rights that previously came under the ambit of the European Convention on Human Rights. Article 9 protects freedom of thought, conscience and religion including the right to 'manifest his religion or belief, in worship, teaching, practice and observance'. In future, this might give rise to claims if women are forced to undergo Caesarean section operations in contravention of their religious beliefs. Article 14[111] prohibits discrimination; however, it only relates to the exercise of rights protected by the Convention and is not freestanding. Even so, the prohibition of discrimination applies to any status (presumably including pregnancy) and the list contained therein is not closed. Article 6 protects the right to a fair trial, which has been an issue arising in a number of the court-authorized Caesarean section cases. Incorporation of these rights into the law of England and Wales will potentially afford added protection to the autonomy and privacy of pregnant women. Human rights issues are examined in detail in Chapter 5.

Re D

A woman refusing to undergo a Caesarean section operation in order to save the fetus is a relatively rare occurrence when compared to the number of women taking drugs, smoking or otherwise conducting themselves in a manner incompatible with fetal health or life. In the family law context, a worrying precedent was created in *D v. Berkshire County Council.*[112] In making a care order, the court took into consideration the mother's actions during pregnancy which lead to the child being born with drug-withdrawal symptoms. Wagstaffe[113] criticized the decision. Child care and supervision orders are governed by the Children Act 1989 section 31(2).[114] As a child is defined as a person under the age of 18[115] and a fetus is not a person,[116] then arguably impairment to a fetus (rather than a child), cannot satisfy section 31. Hence, a fetus damaged as a result of the pregnant woman's drug dependency cannot be the subject of a care order at birth, unless the woman continues to harm him in some other manner. Though in civil law a child injured whilst *in utero* can bring an action against a third party wrongdoer[117] despite the fact that he had no legal standing at the time of injury, the purpose of this law is to redress past wrongs. Wagstaffe argued that the same could not be said of the child protection order which exists to protect the child from present or future harm, not to redress old injuries. Consequently, he claimed that it is inappropriate to apply section 31 in the context of a fetus born alive and suffering as a result of past, non-continuing injuries.

Yet the House of Lords came to a different conclusion in *D v. Berkshire County Council,*[118] where the harmful behaviour of a pregnant woman was redressed once the child was born alive. It was held that when considering whether to make a care order under section 1(2)(a) of the Children and Young Persons Act 1969 (which has now been superseded by the Children Act 1989) in respect of a baby born with drug withdrawal symptoms, the juvenile court could properly consider events and circumstances prior to the baby's birth.[119] This demonstrates a willingness of the courts at the highest level to condemn maternal treatment of the unborn child and to (inappropriately) redress past wrongs through a care order.[120]

The media speculated that maternal negligence during pregnancy, such as smoking or drinking alcohol, might result in the child being taken into care.[121] Though such fears are arguably unfounded due to the strict limitations set in *Re D*, there were concerns that the *criminal* law might be extended. For example, Young[122] feared that, using the same logic, criminal proceedings may be taken against the mother or even others as aiders and abettors. He gave two examples; the first is section 27 of the Offences Against the Person Act 1861, which states that endangering the life or health of a child under the age of two is a crime.[123] By a simple application of the civil law principle contained in *Re D*,[124] smoking or drinking by the pregnant woman that results in loss of life or permanent injury to the health of the fetus could arguably result in the committal of this offence. The second example is section 1 of the Children and Young Persons Act 1933, which criminalizes assault, neglect and abandonment of any child under the age of sixteen.[125] The inclusion of neglect in this section could potentially be used to criminalize omissions by the pregnant woman, such as failing to heed the doctor's advice.

Professor Freeman said of *Re D*: 'The implications of the Lords' judgement go far beyond what we can imagine. It would open the way for cases like the Stewart case to be brought here in Britain.'[126] The Californian case *California v. Stewart*,[127] which is discussed in Chapter 3,[128] involved a pregnant woman who was criminalized for failing to follow the physician's recommendations. Though it was eventually overturned, the case triggered similar cases across the USA. California now has a far harsher policy regarding pregnant women who harm their fetus, as shown in *People v. Davis*.[129]

Re D occurred under the ambit of the Children and Young Persons Act 1969, which has since been replaced with the Children Act 1989. Wagstaffe[130] therefore questions whether *Re D* is still good law. The emphasis under the Children Act is on harm suffered at the time of the application rather than any harm suffered before that date. Consequently, it is possible that *Re D* could be distinguished on this basis.[131]

Conclusion

Though the law in England and Wales is relatively settled where the fetus is injured and dies *in utero*, it remains unsettled where the fetus is born alive and dies, or survives to lead an impaired existence as a result of those injuries. The *Attorney-General's Reference (No. 3 of 1994)* provides some guidance in the case of a child dying of injuries sustained *in utero* caused by a third party. However, this still leaves the problem of what remedy is open to the child merely impaired by such injuries, and it also leaves uncertain whether the pregnant woman can be held criminally liable for death or injury caused to the fetus born alive.

The *A-G's Ref.* involved a third party, and on the particular facts the House of Lords confined the appropriate homicide charge to manslaughter. Nevertheless the potential remains for application of the rule to recent mothers. This is particularly so in the light of the English civil courts' failure to adequately protect the pregnant woman's autonomy despite the law's adherence to the principle that the fetus is not a person in being until birth.

The case of *St. George's Healthcare National Health Service Trust v. S*[132] affirmed a commitment to maternal autonomy in the civil court, and expanded upon the guidance set out in *Re MB*.[133] Where possible, practitioners should ascertain the wishes of the pregnant woman prior to labour in order to assess her mental condition without the added turmoil usually associated with childbirth. However, where practitioners are faced with an emergency situation, as they were in the majority of the court-authorized Caesarean section cases outlined in this chapter, deviation from the *St. George's* guidelines is anticipated. In *Re MB* it was noted that the irrational and emotional state almost always associated with labour might constitute evidence of temporarily impaired capacity. Hence, it seems that in any emergency situation, the possibility of overriding a woman's wishes remains. Where a woman is of a cultural, religious or moral belief that may conflict with the interests of the fetus, it seems that she is best advised to create an advance directive in as formal a manner as possible. This way her refusal to consent is more likely to be heeded and her positive requests for certain types of treatment will receive consideration.

The commitment of the English civil law to pregnant women's autonomy has been less than satisfactory over the past seven years, though *St. George's* marks a step towards rectification. It remains to be seen whether the criminal law will be kept within its currently narrow ambits or be subject to extension as evidenced in the USA. The Human Rights Act 1998 has potential to impact on both civil and criminal law. It is hoped that the often vague rights contained therein will be interpreted in a manner protective of reproductive autonomy. Article 5 protects liberty and security, but contains exceptions that might be used to criminalize pregnant women who use drugs or alcohol.[134] Article 8[135] protects the right to respect for private and family life. However, Article 8(2) states that:

> There shall be no interference by a public authority with the exercise of this right except such as is in accordance with the law and is necessary in a democratic society in the interests of national security, public safety or the economic well-being of the country, for the prevention of disorder or crime, for the protection of health or morals, or for the protection of the rights and freedoms of others.

Thus, it might be argued that the pregnant woman's autonomy can be legitimately curbed on the basis that the resulting harm is sufficiently damaging to 'health' (of the fetus born alive) or 'morals' (depending on the moral rather than legal status of the fetus); that it offends the 'rights and freedoms' of the resulting child; or even that it creates 'disorder' (in view of the fact that fetal alcohol syndrome and other effects of maternal substance use have been said to create a propensity toward crime and social disorder).[136] Thus an application of the Human Rights Act 1998 may herald increased protection of maternal autonomy, but also carries the potential for extended criminalization. The rights contained in the US Constitution are similarly open to interpretation and are examined in the next chapter along with other relevant Articles of the Human Rights Act. This chapter has demonstrated that taking into consideration civil law principles, criminal law cases and the potential interpretations of the Human Rights Act 1998, there exists the potential for extended criminalization of pregnant women who harm or kill the fetus born alive.

Notes

1   *Attorney-General's Reference (No 3 of 1994)* [1997] 3 All E.R. 936.
2   Offences Against the Person Act 1861, Section 58: 'Every woman, being with child, who, with intent to procure her own miscarriage, shall unlawfully administer to herself any poison or other noxious thing, or shall unlawfully use any instrument or other means whatsoever with the like intent, and whosoever, with intent to procure the miscarriage of any woman, whether she be or not with child, shall unlawfully administer to her or cause to be taken by her any poison or other noxious thing, or shall unlawfully use any instrument or other means whatsoever with the like intent, shall be guilty of felony, and being convicted thereof shall be liable to be kept in penal servitude for life.'
3   Infant Life Preservation Act 1929, Section 1(1): 'Subject as hereinafter in this subsection provided, any person who, with intent to destroy the life of a child capable of being born alive, by any wilful act causes a child to die before it has an existence independent of its mother, shall be guilty of felony, to wit, of child destruction, and shall be liable on conviction thereof on indictment to penal servitude for life. Provided that no person shall be found guilty of an offence under this section unless it is proved that the act which caused the death of the child was not done in good faith for the purposes only of preserving the life of the mother.'
4   Infant Life Preservation Act 1929, Section 1(2): 'For the purposes of this Act, evidence that a woman had at any material time been pregnant for a period of twenty-eight weeks or more shall be prima facie proof that she was at that time pregnant of a child capable of being born alive.'
5   See K. Norrie 'Abortion in Great Britain: One Act, Two Laws' (1985) 3 *Criminal Law Review* 475.
6   Abortion Act 1967, Section 1(1) (as amended by the Human Fertilisation and Embryology Act 1990, Section 37) 'Subject to the provisions of this section, a person shall not be guilty of an offence under the law relating to abortion when a pregnancy is terminated by a registered medical practitioner if two registered medical practitioners are of the opinion, formed in good faith (a) that the pregnancy has not exceeded its twenty-fourth week and that the continuance of the pregnancy would involve risk, greater than if the pregnancy were terminated, of injury to the physical or mental health of the pregnant woman or any existing children of her family; or (b) that the termination is necessary to prevent grave permanent injury to the physical or mental health of the pregnant woman; or (c) that the continuance of the pregnancy would involve risk to the life of the pregnant woman, greater than if the pregnancy were terminated; or (d) that there is a substantial risk that if the child were born it would suffer from such physical or mental abnormalities as to be seriously handicapped.'
7   *McCluskey v. The Lord Advocate* [1989] RTR 182.

8 *R v. Tait* [1989] 3 WLR 891. See J. Wood, 'Recent Judicial Decisions: Threat to Kill', *Police Journal* April (1990), 170.

9 As amended by the Criminal Law Act 1977 to read: 'A person who without lawful excuse makes to another a threat, intending that that other would fear it would be carried out, to kill that other or a third party shall be guilty of an offence and liable on conviction on indictment to imprisonment for a term not exceeding ten years.'

10 See *Rex v. Shephard* [1919] 2 K.B. 125 where the father was convicted of soliciting to murder under the Offences Against the Person Act 1861, Section 4 when he instructed the mother to kill the child as soon as it was born.

11 Congenital Disabilities (Civil Liability) Act 1976 Section 1(1): 'If a child is born disabled as a result of ... an occurrence before its birth ... and a person (other than the child's own mother) is under this section answerable to the child in respect of the occurrence, the child's disabilities are to be regarded as damage resulting from the wrongful act of that person and actionable according at the suit of the child.' Note that the actions of the pregnant woman are expressly excluded, but that this does not prevent *criminal* liability should the law extend in this direction.

12 Congenital Disabilities (Civil Liability) Act 1976, Section 1(3) which also states that: 'it is no answer that there could not have been such liability because the parent suffered no actionable injury, if there was a breach of legal duty which, accompanied by injury, would have given rise to the liability.'

13 According to US civil law, the fetus does not have a legal personality until birth. However, a legal fiction can be created in limited circumstances, whereby it is said that once the child is born it is retrospectively given a legal personality whilst it was *in utero*. This is true in property law. Until *Dietrich v. Northampton* 138 Mass. 14 (1884), this was not the case regarding recovery in tort for fetal injury. For these purposes, the fetus had no right of recovery until birth. In 1946 the case of *Bonbretz v. Kotz* 65 F. Supp. 138 (D.D.C. 1946) established that a child born alive can recover in tort for the negligent infliction of pre-natal injury by a third party. The right does not belong to the fetus, but to the child born alive, hence it is not important when in gestation the injury occurred. Liability is a matter of causation rather than establishing a duty of care to the child born alive. In *Renslow v. Mennonite Hospital* 67 Ill. 2d 348, 367 N.E.2d 1250 (1977) a woman recovered for injuries sustained prior to conception of the injured child following her rhesus-negative blood becoming sensitized by rhesus-positive blood in a transfusion. In *Grodin v. Grodin* 102 Mich. App. 396, 301 N.W. 2d 869 (1980), the law giving parental immunity to actions in tort by their children gave way in Michigan and allowed recovery for substance abuse whilst *in utero*. In this case, the negligent use of the antibiotic tetracycline during pregnancy resulted in the discolouration of the child's teeth. There is some criticism of the case (see J. Kahn, 'Of Woman's First Disobedience: Forsaking a Duty of Care to her Fetus – Is This a Mother's Crime?' (1987) 53(767) *Brooklyn Law Review* 807 at 828) on the ground that it misinterprets the parental immunity doctrine, which existed in order to preserve the family unit. However, due to changing values the doctrine has gradually been eroded. This is especially so where the parents are insured (as is similarly the case in England and Wales where a claim by the child is actionable against the mother only in road traffic cases). Kahn criticized *Grodin,* which defines the standard of care of the pregnant woman as matching the standard owed by third parties. This implies a duty and standard of care for her own body that potentially begins long before conception. This arguably breaches her constitutional rights to privacy and autonomy.
   In the USA, civil law alternatives are usually utilized once the child has been born in order to prevent further harm to the child. To this end, Florida provides for a responsible relative or other person to be appointed as a Guardian Advocate for any child likely to need medical attention (FLA. SESS. LAWSERV. ch, 89-345, No. 415.5082 (West 1898)). A number of states have introduced legislation providing that children born with drug dependencies may be labelled 'neglected' and protection (or

legal remedies) supplied as a result (See Chapter 3 p. 45). Case examples include *In re Baby X* 97 Mich. App. 111, 291 N.W.2d 736 (1980), *In re Ruiz* 500 N.E. 2d 935. Ohio (1986), *In re Troy D* 215 Cal. App. 3d 889 (1989). These cases recognized the fetal right to be born sound of body and limb and that pre-natal conduct defeating this constituted neglect. Indiana and Nevada identify children born with illicit drug or alcohol addictions as 'in need of services'. (See IND. CODE ANN. No. 31-6-4-3.1 (Burns 1987); NEV. REV. STAT. ANN. No. 432B.330 (Michie 1989); OKLA. STAT. ANN. tit. 10 No. 1101 (West 1989).)

14 Law Commission Report (Law Comm. No. 60) *Injuries to Unborn Children,* (Cmnd 5709: London, 1974), at para. 54-65.

15 J. Fortin, 'Legal Protection for the Unborn Child' (1988) 51 *Modern Law Review* 54 at 78.

16 Congenital Disabilities (Civil Liability) Act 1976, Section 2. See for example, C. Dyer, 'Boy Wins Damages after Injury *In Utero*', *British Medical Journal* (1992) 304, 1400.

17 *Attorney-General's Reference (No. 3 of 1994)* [1996] 2 All E.R. 10, (hereafter cited as *A-G's Ref. C.A.*) [1997] 3 All E.R. 936 (hereafter cited as *A-G's Ref. H.L.*).

18 Referred under the Criminal Justice Act 1972, Section 36(1).

19 *A-G's Ref. C.A.,* per Taylor LCJ *op. cit.,* at 12. '1. Subject to proof by the prosecution of the requisite intent in either case: whether the crimes of murder or manslaughter can be committed where unlawful injury is deliberately inflicted: (i) to a child *in utero*, (ii) to a mother carrying a child *in utero*, where the child is subsequently born alive, enjoys an existence independent of the mother, thereafter dies and the injuries inflicted while *in utero* either caused or made a substantial contribution to the death.
2. Whether the fact that the death of the child is caused solely as a consequence of injury to the mother rather than as a consequence of direct injury to the foetus can negative any liability for murder or manslaughter in the circumstances set out in question 1.'

20 See J. Temkin, 'Pre-Natal Injury, Homicide and the Draft Criminal Code' (1986) 45(3) *Cambridge Law Journal* 414, discussed in Chapter 3 p. 42.

21 See Chapter 3 p. 41. Coke formed the view that an unlawful injury to a fetus which is later born alive constitutes an offence of murder or manslaughter depending on *mens rea* and causation. Hale disagreed.

22 *A-G's Ref. C.A., ibid.,* 17.

23 The latter example is provided by J. Feinberg, *Harm to Others: The Moral Limits of the Criminal Law* (Oxford University Press: New York and Oxford, 1987), 97.

24 *A-G's Ref. C.A., op. cit.,* 16.

25 Counsel for the defence, Mr. Hawkesworth, argued that to cause an injury to the fetus is not in itself unlawful, only becoming so if the injury falls into the categories of the various statutory offences. Taylor LCJ circumvented this supposition by arguing that injury to the fetus will always involve injury to the pregnant woman. This left open the possibility that as technology advances (particularly in the field of assisted reproduction) a fetus outside its mother will be relatively unprotected by law.

26 *A-G's Ref. C.A., op. cit.,* 16.

27 *R v. Kwok Chak Ming (No. 1)* [1963] H.K.L.R. 226. See Chapter 3 p. 42.

28 *A-G's Ref. C.A., op. cit.,* 17.

29 This point was overruled by the House of Lords. See p. 59. It assumes that the fetus is a mere appendage of the pregnant woman. See J. Keown, 'Homicide, Fetuses and Appendages' [1996] 55 *Cambridge Law Journal* 207.

30 See C.M.V. Clarkson and H.M. Keating, *Criminal Law: Text and Materials* 4th Edition (Sweet and Maxwell: London, 1998), 250.

31 Clarkson and Keating, *ibid.,* 251. Authority for 'A''s liability is *R v. Latimer* (1886) 17 Q.B.D. 369 in which Latimer attempted to hit 'A', missed and struck 'B', cutting his face. Latimer's intent to hit 'A' was enough to convict him of the offence when he mistakenly hit 'B'. Authority for 'D''s liability is *R v. Pembilton* (1974) 12 Cox 607.

Note that though 'D''s liability for criminal damage cannot be attained through transfer of malice, he may be liable for recklessly damaging property.

32 Draft Criminal Law Bill 1993, clause 32 (Law Com. No. 218, 1993). See Law Commission website at *http://www.lawcom.gov.uk/*library/menu-reports-htm.

33 A. Ashworth, 'Transferred Malice and Punishment for Unforeseen Consequences', in P. Glazebrook (Ed.) *Reshaping the Criminal Law* (Stevens: London, 1978), 84.

34 *A-G's Ref. C.A., op. cit.,* 18. These three arguments were put forward by counsel for the defence.

35 *A-G's Ref. C.A., ibid.,* 19.

36 A. Bailin, 'Born To Die' (1996) 146(3) *New Law Journal* 1696 at 1697. See also M. Seneviratne, 'Pre-natal Injury and Transferred Malice: The Invented Other' (1996) 59 *Modern Law Review* 884 at 888 for critical review of Taylor LCJ's use of the doctrine of transferred malice.

37 *A-G's Ref. H.L.*, *op. cit.* See generally Editorial, 'Stabbing Foetus who is Born Alive then Dies can be Manslaughter but not Murder' *The Police Journal* 71(1) (1998), 89.

38 *A-G's Ref. H.L. ibid.,* 941. The cited authority for this proposition is *R v. Vickers* [1957] 2 All E.R. 741. Lord Mustill criticized the intellectual basis of the grievous bodily harm rule (or the 'malice aforethought rule'), whilst recognizing that it is firmly embedded in the criminal law as a result of *R v. Cunningham* [1982] A.C. 566.

39 *A-G's Ref. H.L.*, *ibid.* The cited authority for this proposition is *R v. Pembilton, op. cit.* Lord Mustill later says in criticism of the Court of Appeal's definition of the concept: '... the harking back to a concept of general malice, which amounts to no more than this, that a wrongful act displays a malevolence which can be attached to any adverse consequence, has long been out of date. And to speak of a particular malice which is "transferred" simply disguises the problem by idiomatic language. The defendant's malice is directed at one objective, and when after the event the court treats it as directed at another object it is not recognizing a "transfer" but creating a new malice which never existed before. ... Like many of its kind [the concept of transferred malice] is useful enough to yield rough justice, in particular cases, and it can sensibly be retained notwithstanding its lack of any sound intellectual basis. But it is another matter to build a new rule upon it.' *Ibid.* 948.

40 *A-G's Ref. H.L.*, *ibid.* 941. The cited authority for this proposition is Sir Edward Coke 3 *Co. Inst* (1680) 50. This proposition was acknowledged in the Court of Appeal, the focus being on the difference between the fetus killed in the womb and the child born and later dying as a result of a pre-natal injury.

41 *A-G's Ref. H.L.*, *ibid.* 942. The cited authority for this proposition is *R v. Church* [1965] 2 All E.R. 72. This rule states that the lapse of time between the act and the death of the victim does not prevent the act from amounting to murder provided that there is a causal link between the two.

42 *A-G's Ref. H.L.*, *ibid.* See also 949. The cited authority for this proposition is Coke, *op. cit.*

43 *A-G's Ref. H.L.*, *ibid.* Lord Mustill cites the Fourth Report of the Commissioners on Criminal Law (1839), *British Parliamentary Papers* (1839) vol 19, pp 235, 266 and the Second Report of the Commissioners for Revising and Consolidating Criminal Law (1846), *British Parliamentary Papers* (1846) vol. 24, pp 107, 127. Note Temkin's *infra* objection that after the Homicide Act 1957, Section 1 abolished the felony murder rule, much of the rationale behind Coke's rule is lost.

44 J. Temkin, *op.cit.* See Chapter 3 p. 42.

45 *R. v. West* (1848) 2 Car & Kir 784, 175 E.R. 329. *R v Senior* (1832) 1 Mood CC 346, 168 E.R. 1298.

46 *A-G's Ref. H.L.*, *op. cit.,* 143.

47 *R v. Cunningham* [1982] A.C. 566.

48 Lord Hope quoted Edmund Davies J in *R v. Church* [1965] 2 All E.R. 72 at 76 who said: 'For such a verdict [guilty of manslaughter] inexorably to follow, the unlawful act

must be such as all sober and reasonable people would inevitably recognize must subject *the other person* to, at least, the risk of some harm resulting therefrom, albeit not serious harm.' (Emphasis inserted by Lord Hope). *A-G's Ref. H.L., op. cit.*, 957.

49   *A-G's Ref. H.L., ibid.*, 957. *R v. Mitchell* [1983] 2 All E.R. 427.

50   *A-G's Ref. H.L., ibid.*, 960 per Lord Hope.

51   *A-G's Ref. H.L., ibid.*, 951.

52   *A-G's Ref. H.L., ibid.*, 952.

53   See Chapter 3 p. 44.

54   *R v. Church* [1965] 1 All E.R. 72, as approved in *DPP v. Newbury* [1977] AC 500.

55   *R v. Adomako* [1995] 1 AC 171.

56   An action in negligence by a child against its mother in respect of damage received *in utero* is not permitted in England and Wales, except in relation to injury caused by the pregnant woman's negligence in a road traffic accident. Congenital Disabilities (Civil Liability) Act 1976 Section 1(1). Note that the law in Scotland remains open on the question of whether a child born alive with injuries sustained *in utero* can sue its mother.

57   *Kong Cheuk Kwan v. The Queen* (1985) 82 Cr. App. R. 18 P.C. where the Privy Council held that *R v. Caldwell* [1982] A.C. 341 applies to involuntary manslaughter. In *Seymour* (1983) 76 Cr App R 21 Watkins LJ stated that: 'It is no longer necessary or helpful to make reference to compensation and negligence.' This was approved in *Kong Cheuk Kwan*. The statement constituted an attempt to move away from gross negligence manslaughter, but the concept seems to have survived: *R v. Ball* (1989) 90 Cr App R 378; *R v. Adomako* [1995] 1 AC 171.

58   *Ex parte Jennings* [1983] 1 AC 624; *R v. Goodfellow* (1986) 83 Cr App R 23.

59   *R v. Seymour* [1983] 2 AC 493.

60   See *Raleigh Fifkin-Paul Memorial Hospital v. Anderson*, 42 N.J. 421, 201 A.2d 537 (1964) where a pregnant Jehovah's Witness was forced to undergo a blood transfusion to save her and the fetus' life. Also see *Jefferson v. Griffin Spalding County Hospital* 247 Ga. 86, 274 S.E.2d 457 (1981). The lives of both woman and fetus were put at risk by the woman's refusal to consent to a Caesarean section operation. The woman's right to withhold consent, even if she should die as a result, was not disputed. However, the fetus was viable and therefore protected under the Juvenile Court Code of Georgia. Custody of the fetus was given to a welfare agency, which consented to the operation. See the Royal College of Obstetricians and Gynaecologists, *A Consideration of the Law and Ethics in Relation to Court Ordered Obstetric Intervention* (London, April 1994), Ethics No. 1., para. 2.2 which reported that court orders had been obtained in 11 different states overriding the woman's refusal to consent to a Caesarean section operation.

61   Though this was not the case in *Re S (adult: refusal of medical treatment)* [1992] 3 W.L.R. 806, 4 All ER 671 examined below and hereafter referred to as *Re S*.

62   *Re C (refusal of medical treatment)* [1994] 1 WLR 290. Subject to the exceptions noted in this section. Hereafter referred to as *Re C*.

63   The test for negligence is outlined in *Bolam v. Friern Hospital Management Committee* [1957] 1 W.L.R. 582, especially at 586 where the 'reasonable doctor' test is outlined. The information a patient needs differs according to the nature of the individual and his illness. Because of this, it is hard for the courts to ensure that patients are sufficiently informed. On the other hand, the courts do concern themselves with disclosure (or lack of disclosure) of risks to the patient as in *Sidaway v. the Board of Governors of Bethlem Royal Hospital and Maudsley Hospital* [1985] 1 All E.R. 643.

64   According to the Family Law Reform Act 1969 (*supra* f.n .69) children of age 16 and over may give consent as if they were adults.

65   *Airedale National Health Service Trust v. Bland* [1993] AC 789, at 860, where Keith LJ said (*obiter*) '... it is unlawful, so as to constitute both a tort and the crime of battery, to administer medical treatment to an adult, who is conscious and of sound mind,

without his consent: In *Re F (Mental Patient: Sterilisation)* [1990] 2 AC 1. Such a person is completely at liberty to decline to undergo treatment, even if the result of his doing so will be that he will die.'

66   *Re C, op. cit.* See E. Roberts, 'Re C and the Boundaries of Autonomy', (1994) 10 *Professional Negligence* 98.

67   *Re T (adult: refusal of medical treatment)* [1992] 4 All E.R. 649 (Hereafter *Re T*).

68   *Re T, ibid.,* at 786. 'An adult patient who ... suffers from no mental incapacity has an absolute right to ... refuse [treatment]. ... The only possible qualification is a case in which the choice may lead to the death of a viable foetus ... when ... the courts will be faced with a novel problem of considerable legal and ethical complexity ...'

69   Family Law Reform Act 1969, Section 8(1): 'The consent of a minor who has attained the age of sixteen years to any ... medical ... treatment which, in the absence of consent, would constitute a trespass to the person, shall be as effective as it would be if he were of full age; and where a minor has by virtue of this section given effective consent to any treatment it shall not be necessary to obtain any consent for it from his parent or guardian ...'

70   *Gillick v. West Norfolk and Wisbeck Area Health Authority* [1986] AC 112, [1985] 3 All E.R. 402.

71   See *Re R* [1992] Fam 11; *Re W (a minor) (medical treatment)* [1992] 4 All E.R. 627, in which Balcombe LJ at 641 stated that Section 8(3) retains the effectiveness of parental consent in some circumstances (notably the right to prevent children from withholding consent to life-saving treatment). The Family Law Reform Act 1969, Section 8(3) states: 'Nothing in this section shall be construed as making ineffective any consent which would have been effective if this section had not been enacted.' This point is contested; S. Boseley and C. Dyer, 'New Heart for Dying Girl who Refused Consent', *The Guardian,* 16 July 1999.

72   *Re S, op. cit.*

73   H. Teff, *Reasonable Care: Legal Perspectives on the Doctor-Patient Relationship* (Clarendon Press: Oxford, 1994) states: 'It therefore appears that in *Re S* the judge must have seen the interests of the unborn child as determinative ... . [T]he terms of the declaration authorising the operation referred to it as being "in the vital interests of the patient and the unborn child she is carrying." (*Re T, op. cit.,* 807)' at 153. 'That the courts are reluctant to take the legal implications of patient autonomy to their logical conclusions, even as regards adult patients who are not deemed incompetent, was graphically demonstrated in *Re S.*' at 154.

74   *Paton v. BPAS* [1979] Q.B. 276.

75   *Re F (in utero)* [1988] 2 All E.R. 193.

76   *C v. S* [1989] Q.B. 135.

77   *Rance v. Mid-Downs Health Authority* [1991] 1 All E.R. 801. See Editorial, 'Abortion – Whether Foetus is a Child Capable of Being Born Alive' (1990) 16(3) *Common Law Bulletin* 820.

78   As expressed by K. DeGama, 'Medical Law: Re S' (1993) 2 *Journal of Social Welfare and Family Law,* 147, at 147. In particular Sir Stephen Brown relied on the US case of *Re AC* (1988) 539 A 2d 204 D.C.: (1990) 573 A 2d 1235. In this case a cancer patient refused to consent to a Caesarean section which would have hastened her death. The court ordered the operation to go ahead as the state has an interest in protecting the life of the viable fetus. Both mother and child died. The health of the pregnant woman has (at least ostensibly) been the greatest consideration in all the court-authorized Caesarean sections in the UK, yet this does not seem to be the case in *Re AC*. The inappropriate reliance upon this authority in *Re S* is perhaps emphasized by the fact that the US decision was eventually overturned.

79   H. Teff, *Reasonable Care, op. cit.,*155. 'The lack of a clearly delineated approach, however understandable, could in theory facilitate coerced medical treatment in less drastic circumstances.'

80   *Norfolk and Norwich v. W* [1997] 1 FCR 269, where the woman refused to
      acknowledge her pregnancy despite being fully dilated. A Caesarean section was
      needed to save the life of the fetus and possibly that of the woman. The consultant
      psychiatrist found that she was not certifiable under the Mental Health Act 1983 but
      may not be able to comprehend the necessity of the operation. Hence, though there was
      no mental disorder, the patient was deemed not to have the necessary competence to
      withhold consent. Johnson J based his decision on the necessity to act for the benefit
      of the woman, but added that 'the reality was that the foetus was a fully formed child,
      capable of normal life if it could only be delivered from the mother.'
81   *Rochdale v. Choudhary* [1997] 1 FCR 274. The judge held that she was unable 'to
      make any valid decision about anything of even the most trivial kind' because of the
      emotional stress and pain of labour.
82   See, for example, M. Stauch, 'Court-Authorised Caesareans and the Principle of
      Patient Autonomy' (1997) 6(1) *Nottingham Law Journal* 74 at 76. S. Fovargue and J.
      Miola, 'Policing Pregnancy: Implications of the Attorney-General's Reference (No. 3
      of 1994)' (1998) 6 *Medical Law Review* 265 at 282 argued that, though Johnson J
      authorized the operation in the best interests of the patient, the patient he referred to
      was in fact the fetus rather than the pregnant woman. This is because the pregnant
      woman had clearly stated that she would rather die than have the operation. C. Wells,
      'On the Outside Looking In: Perspectives on Enforced Caesareans', in S. Sheldon and
      M. Thomson (Eds.) *Feminist Perspectives on Health Care Law* (Cavendish: London,
      1998), at 242 stated her concern that *Rochdale v Choudhary, ibid.*, seemed to be
      adjudicated by the principle: 'if you are refusing, you must be incompetent'.
83   D. Morgan, 'Whatever Happened to Consent?' (1992) 142 *New Law Journal* 1448, at
      1448: '... the price which we must be prepared to pay for protecting the integrity and
      autonomy of all competent adults is the rare, occasional risk of death or serious injury
      to an unborn fetus or to the woman herself.'
84   See J. Bales, 'Woman Challenges Hospital's Right to Impose Caesarean', *The Times,*
      23 September 1996, 6, col. 1. Also B. Hewson, 'Mother Knows Best' (1992) 142 *New
      Law Journal* 1538, 1545-6, 1550 and B. Hewson, 'When "No" Means "Yes"' (1992)
      89 *Law Society Gazette* 1148.
85   See C. Dyer, 'Birth of a Dilemma', *The Guardian,* 11 March 1997, 17.
86   The Human Rights Act 1998, Article 6 protects the right to a fair trial.
87   Royal College of Obstetricians and Gynaecologists (RCOG), *A Consideration of the
      Law and Ethics in Relation to Court Ordered Obstetric Intervention*, (London, April
      1994) Ethics No. 1.
88   RCOG, *ibid.*, para. 3.6.1.
89   RCOG, *ibid.*, para. 3.7.3.
90   RCOG, *ibid.*, para. 3.10.
91   RCOG, *ibid.*, para 5.12: 'We conclude that it is inappropriate, and unlikely to be
      helpful or necessary, to invoke judicial intervention to overrule an informed and
      competent woman's refusal of a proposed medical treatment, even though her refusal
      might place her life and that of her fetus at risk.'
92   Royal College of Obstetricians and Gynaecologists (RCOG), *Supplement to A
      Consideration of the Law and Ethics in Relation to Court-Authorised Obstetric
      Intervention* (London, December 1996).
93   RCOG, *ibid.*, para. 3.3.
94   As seen in *R v. Merton Borough Council and Ors, ex parte Sutherland* [10th July 1997]
      I.L.R. Document Number C800046.
95   *Re MB (medical treatment)* [1997] FLR 427 (Hereafter, *Re MB).* See also *Re L (An
      Adult: Non-Consensual Treatment)* [1997] 1 FLR 609. (Reported in (1997) 17 *Family
      Law* 148). Concerning *Re MB* see P. Hargrove 'Case Note: Re MB (Medical
      Treatment)' (1997) 27(2) *Family Law* 514; J. Herring, 'Caesarean Sections, Phobians
      and Foetal Rights' [1997] 56 *Cambridge Law Journal* 509; R. Bailey-Harris, 'Re MB

(Medical Treatment) (1997) 27(2) *Family Law* 542; B. Hewson, 'How to Escape the Surgeon's Knife' (1997) 147 *New Law Journal* 752; S. Michalowski, 'Court-Ordered Caesarean Sections – The End of a Trend?' (1999) 62(1) *Modern Law Review* 115.

96 Per Butler-Sloss LJ *Re MB ibid.*, 436. See Editorial, 'Medical Treatment – Legality of Treatment Without Consent' (1997) 147 *New Law Journal* 600 for quotation. For discussion of these principles, see P. De Cruz 'Caesarean Sections, Consent and the Courts' (1998) 10 *Practitioners' Child Law Bulletin* 8 and Editorial, 'Consent: Adult, Refusal of Consent, Capacity' (1997) 5(3) *Medical Law Review* 317.

97 This is a view expressed by a number of commentators; see for example, J. Harrington, 'Privileging the Medical Norm: Liberalism, Self-Determination and the Refusal of Medical Treatment' (1996) 16 *Legal Studies* 348.

98 This view is also argued by M. Stauch, *op.cit.*, 79: 'To say that an irrational choice may be upheld is ambiguous, so far as giving effect to patient autonomy is concerned, for such choice may or may not be autonomous. What should instead be required is that the choice 'fits' in the general scheme of the patient's life, (though there is no need for the scheme itself to be "rational", whatever that might mean).' Stauch notes that the courts in *Re MB* were bound by *Sidaway v. Governors of Bethlem Royal Hospital* [1985] 1 All ER 643 and therefore any changes to the test in *Re C* would have to be made by the House of Lords.

99 *Metropolitan Borough Council v. DB* [1997] 1 FLR 767, case note in *Childright* (1997) 138, 21.

100 *R v. Collins & Ors, ex parte S (No. 2)* [1998] 2 FLR 728.

101 *R v. Merton Borough Council and Ors, ex parte Sutherland* [10th July 1997] I.L.R. Document Number C800046.

102 When the case reached the Court of Appeal the name was changed and the aggrieved woman was referred to as 'S'.

103 The Mental Health Act 1983, Section 2 reads: '(2) An application for admission for assessment may be made in respect of a patient on the grounds that – (a) he is suffering from mental disorder of a nature or degree which warrants the detention of the patient in a hospital for assessment (or for assessment followed by medical treatment) for at least a limited period; and (b) he ought to be so detained in the interests of his own health or safety or with a view to the protection of other persons.'

104 *St. George's Healthcare National Health Service Trust v. S and R v. Collins and Others, Ex parte S* [1998] 2 FLR 728; *The Times Law Reports*, 8 May 1998, 45. Hereafter cited as '*St. George's*'. For analysis see R. Duce, "Bizarre" Conduct Not Good Reason for Caesarean', *The Times* 8 May 1998, 6 col. 1; R. Bailey-Harris, 'Pregnancy, Autonomy and Refusal of Medical Treatment' (1997) 114 *Law Quarterly Review* 550; A.R. Maclean, 'Caesarean Sections, Competence and the Illusion of Autonomy' (1999) 1 *Web Journal of Current Legal Issues*.

105 *St. George's, ibid., 754* per Judge LJ.

106 *St. George's, ibid.,* 746-753 per Judge LJ.

107 Note that the *Draft Mental Health Bill*, Cm. 5538-I (London: The Stationery Office, 2002) proposes changes to the definition of 'mental disorder' and seeks to get rid of the treatability requirement that currently exists under the Mental Health Act 1983. This would substantially extend the powers of doctors to detain people on grounds of mental health. See Chapter 6 p. 123.

108 *St. George's, op. cit.,* 758.

109 B. Hewson, 'Who's Afraid of the Official Solicitor?' (1997) 141(1) *Solicitor's Journal* 198, is critical of the increased role of the Official Solicitor (who is usually utilized in cases involving children, coma patients or the mentally ill) to facilitate the forced Caesarean sections of pregnant woman against their will.

110 D. Morgan, 'Whatever Happened to Consent?' (1992) 142 *New Law Journal* 1448, at 1448.

111 The Human Rights Act 1998, Article 14 states: 'The enjoyment of the rights and freedoms set forth in this Convention shall be secured without discrimination on any

ground such as sex, race, colour, language, religion, political or other opinion, national or social origin, association with a national minority, property, birth or other status.'

112	*D v. Berkshire County Council* [1987] 1 All E.R. 20 (Div. Court); 27 (C.A.); and 33 (H.L.). Hereafter referred to as *Re D.*

113	See C. Wagstaffe, 'Harming the Unborn Child – The Foetus and the Threshold Criteria' (1998) 28 *Family Law* 160 at 160.

114	Children Act 1989, s. 31(2). A court may only make a care or supervision order if it is satisfied-
(a) that the child concerned is suffering or is likely to suffer significant harm; and
(b) that the harm, or likelihood of harm, is attributable to –
(i) the care given to the child, or likely to be given to him if the order were not made, not being what it would be reasonable to expect a parent to give him; or
(ii) the child's being beyond parental control.

115	Children Act 1989, s. 105.

116	*Paton v. British Pregnancy Advisory Service Trustees* [1979] 1 QB 276; 'The foetus cannot in English law, in my view, have a right of its own at least until it is born and has a separate existence from its mother. This permeates the whole of the civil law of this country.' Per Sir George Baker P at 279; *Re F (in utero)* [1988] 2 All E.R. 193; *C v. S* [1989] Q.B. 135; *Rance v. Mid-Downs Health Authority* [1991] 1 All E.R. 801. See also the Scottish case of *Kelly v. Kelly* [1997] 2 FLR 828.

117	Congenital Disabilities (Civil Liability) Act 1976.

118	*Re D, op.cit.*.

119	It was also important that the mother continued to take drugs after the birth.

120	See S.P. De Cruz, 'Protecting the Unborn Child: Re D' (1987) 17 *Family Law* 207; N. Martin, 'Recent Cases: D (a minor) v. Berkshire C. C.' (1987) May *Journal of Social Welfare* 182; B. Bainham, 'Protecting the Unborn – New Rights in Gestation?' (1987) 50 *Modern Law Review* 361; J. Fortin, 'Legal Protection for the Unborn Child' (1988) 51 *Modern Law Review* 54.

121	See for example, A. Frerriman, Health Correspondent, 'Drugs in Pregnancy Under Legal Spotlight: Lords Consider Action Against Addict Mothers', *The Observer*, 5 October 1986, 5 col. 1.

122	I.M. Young, 'The Unborn Child and Criminal Proceedings' (1986) December *Law Society's Gazette,* 3808.

123	I.M. Young, *ibid.*, 3809. The Offences Against the Person Act 1861, section 27 states that: 'whosoever shall unlawfully ... expose any child, being under the age of two years old, whereby the life of such child shall be endangered or the health of such child shall have been or shall be likely to be permanently injured, shall be guilty of a misdemeanour, and being convicted thereof shall be liable ... to imprisonment ... for any term not exceeding five years.'

124	*Re D, op. cit.*

125	*Re D, ibid.* The Children and Young Persons Act 1933, Section 1 states that: 'if any person who has attained the age of 16 years and has the custody, charge, or care of any child or any young person under that age, wilfully assaults, ill-treats, neglects, abandons, or exposes him, or causes or procures him to be assaulted, ill-treated, neglected, abandoned, or exposed, in a manner likely to cause him unnecessary suffering or injury to health (including injury or loss of sight, or hearing, or limb, or organ of the body, and any mental derangement) that person shall be guilty of an offence ...'

126	Professor M. Freeman of University College, London as quoted by A. Frerriman, *op. cit.*,1.

127	*California v. Stewart,* No. M508197, slip op. (Cal. Mun. Ct., San Diego, Feb. 26, 1987).

128	Chapter 3 p. 46.

129	*People v. Davis,* 7 Cal. 4th 797, 30 Cal. Rptr. 2d 50, 872 P. 2d 591. In Davis it was held that under Penal Code section 187, the unlawful killing of a seven to eight-week fetus constituted murder. This makes California's homicide law the harshest in the United States. See K. B. Folger, 'When Does Life Begin ... or End? The California Supreme Court Redefines Fetal Murder in *People v. Davis*' (1994) 29 *University of San Francisco Law Review* 237.

130 Wagstaffe, *op. cit.*, at 161.

131 Wagstaffe, *ibid.*, 162 refers to the case of *Re M (a minor) (care order: threshold conditions)* [1994] 2 FLR 77, in which *Re D* was referred to with approval, though the question of whether to consider the woman's conduct whilst pregnant did not arise. It was, however, held that a care order is only appropriate where the child is suffering (or likely to suffer) significant harm *at the date of the application.*

132 *St. George's, op. cit.*

133 *Re MB, op. cit.*

134 Discussed in Chapter 5 p. 96.

135 Human Rights Act 1998, Article 8(1): 'Everyone has the right to respect for his private and family life, his home and his correspondence.' Also discussed in Chapter 5.

136 See for example, M.D. Bellew, 'Fetal Alcohol Syndrome, Fetal Alcohol Effect and Genetic Influence on Alcoholism', *Capital Concerns (Kentucky Capital Litigation Resource Center – a Branch of the Kentucky Department of Public Advocacy)* 6 (1991), 1 at 6. In *Harris v. Vasquez*, 913 F.2d 606 (9th Cir. 1990), FAS was raised as a mitigator.

Criticism of the United States' Extensions of the Law

It has been argued that a policy of criminalization in England and Wales would upset the currently maintained balance between maternal and fetal rights and interests. To the author's knowledge, no medical or public health organization supports extended criminalization.[1] In fact it is strongly opposed. Part of their reasoning is that criminal justice and human rights considerations operate against a policy of extended criminalization. These issues are discussed in this chapter.

Criminal Justice Theory

Chapters 1 and 2 proffered theoretical considerations that countered a policy of extended criminalization. This section briefly examines the appropriate functions of the criminal law in order to determine whether criminalization is advantageous in social and economic terms.

The criminal law does not merely set out acceptable standards of behaviour within society but it stigmatizes those found in breach and imposes punishment upon them. What conduct is defined as criminal is something that evolves with public perceptions of politics, religion and morality.[2] On general principles, a person is found guilty of a crime if he has caused harm and is blameworthy.[3] He is blameworthy if he has the required mental commitment to the crime, provided there is no justification or excuse for his actions.[4] Though there are many theories as to what conduct ought to be considered criminal, there is not the scope in this book to cover them in depth. Packer[5] suggested six criteria:

1   The conduct is prominent in most people's view of socially threatening behaviour, and is not condoned by any significant segment of society.
2   Subjecting it to the criminal sanction is not inconsistent with the goals of punishment.
3   Suppressing it will not inhibit socially desirable conduct.
4   It may be dealt with through even-handed and non-discriminatory enforcement.
5   Controlling it through the criminal process will not expose that process to severe qualitative or quantitative strains.

6   There are no reasonable alternatives to the criminal sanction for dealing
    with it.

When each of these criteria is applied to the case for criminalization of
pregnant women for acts and omissions harming the fetus born alive, only
the first supports it.

As was seen in the Introduction, it is true that such conduct is regarded by
most as socially threatening behaviour. Depending on the extent of their use,
both legal and illegal substances have been shown to cause considerable
harm to the fetus with lasting ill-effects to the child born alive. This in turn
causes large expense to society who must provide for the care and treatment
of the child. Criteria one also states that there should not be a large segment
of society that condones the behaviour. Many believe that pregnancy should
not be a precursor to the inhibition of rights that previously went unfettered.
If alcohol is legal prior to conception, it should also be legal after
conception. Yet, Packer is not here addressing the suitability of punishment,
but merely whether the behaviour is condoned by a large segment of society.
It is likely that this question would be answered in the negative and therefore
the first of Packer's criteria is fulfilled.[6]

The second criterion states that 'subjecting it to the criminal sanction is
not inconsistent with the goals of punishment'. Unfortunately, only a sparse
analysis of the goals of punishment can be given here. Thus, the advantages
of criminalization may include specific and general deterrence,
incapacitation, reform and retribution. The call for deterrence through
criminalization is acknowledged, but it is suggested that criminal sanctions
do little to further the goal in this instance. This is largely due to the fact that
addiction is notoriously hard to deter. If the prospective harm to the fetus and
child born alive, or the fact that the child may be taken into care cannot stop
a mother engaging in a particular activity, the criminal law is unlikely to
offer any additional deterrence. The very nature of addiction makes it
extremely difficult for the woman to objectively weigh the potential
consequences. Whether it concerns cigarettes, alcohol or heroin, it may be
beyond her power to give up without help. Though prison can provide a
positive environment for fighting an addiction, so too do education and
treatment and with better and more lasting effect.

Deterrence may be general, but can also be specific. Criminalizing the
use of certain substances whilst pregnant may actually prevent women
continuing the habit and thereby arrest the harm to the fetus. However, the
disproportionality and discrimination here arguably defeat the benefits of
specific deterrence. In fact, criminalization is more likely to deter the
woman from medical treatment (and thereby from detection) than it is from
engaging in the prohibited activity. Damage to the fetus is all the more
likely to result where the woman feels alienated and unable to turn to the
medical profession. Empowerment through a recognition of her right to
freedom from unwanted intervention and positive steps to improve

education and treatment are more likely to aid both fetus and pregnant woman.

Preventing recurrence of the offence is also associated with the goal of incapacitation.[7] In *United States v. Vaughn*[8] a pregnant woman was found guilty of second degree theft and was jailed for a disproportionate term to ensure that her cocaine use would do no further damage to the fetus. The case received extensive criticism on grounds of disproportionality and unfairness.[9] Prisons are often ill equipped to cater for pregnant women.[10] Drugs and alcohol are not altogether eliminated from prison life, and smoking is usually permitted. Steverson[11] argued that the overcrowding, and the lack of specialist pre-natal care, correct nutrition and exercise make prison in the USA an unsuitable environment for the pregnant woman and fetus. An additional problem is that, according to a 1991 US report on drug use in prison, over half of the women in federal prisons were convicted on drug charges.[12] The report drew attention to the fact that substance abuse is prolific in American prisons.[13] Prisons specially equipped to deal with pregnant women are few in number,[14] which often results in the prisoner being moved far from her home, or as occurred in 1997 in England,[15] in having the child removed at birth due to lack of facilities at the woman's institution.

The goal of incapacitation is also served by policies seeking to prevent further pregnancies in women who have previously harmed a fetus born alive. In the USA the contraceptive implant, Norplant, has been offered to substance-using women as a sentencing alternative to imprisonment. Norplant is a long-lasting contraceptive injected into the arm, offered in this context in an attempt to prevent the conception and birth of more damaged children. For example, in *People v. Zaring*[16] Judge Howard Broadman allowed a child abuser to choose Norplant as part of her sentence to prevent future fetal and child abuse.[17] The case was eventually overturned, but the legality of the condition was not discussed. It is worrying that the courts have resorted to such measures without statutory authority. Bills seeking to implement such sentencing alternatives are also subject to human rights criticisms.[18]

When a child is born suffering as a result of a woman's activity during pregnancy, some understandably call for retribution.[19] Yet this goal is arguably rendered inappropriate when the behaviour in question results from an addiction, which might be characterized as a medical disease. This is especially so when she has sought help and been turned away as is often the case in the USA where places on treatment courses are limited and tend to exclude the pregnant due to the complexity of treatment. Further, as there is a distinct correlation between criminalization, race[20] and poverty,[21] it is arguably inappropriate to seek retribution for what results directly from inequality. As Blank said:

> Criminal sanctions against a handful of pregnant substance abusers is inexpensive compared to the more humane but extensive interventions [such as

treatment and education programmes], and it also meets the American need to blame someone – preferably a poor woman with a socially condemned lifestyle.[22]

Murphy[23] argued that retribution is only morally relevant between equals. Where inequality results in different values, the inequality should be tackled rather than the values themselves. This is not to say that other rationales for punishment are not applicable even where inequality thrives, but that the harsh value of retribution is reserved for those occasions where those individuals who share a set of values have strayed sufficiently to merit punishment.[24] A measure of retribution is already achieved where the criminal law applies indiscriminately to punish illicit drug use. It therefore seems that in the case of extended criminalization, the goals of retribution and deterrence are not sufficiently poignant to override the autonomy of pregnant women.

Finally, of rehabilitation or reform, the harmful activity often results from a medical condition (such as depression, drug addiction or alcoholism) and it is submitted that the medical profession rather than prison system is better equipped to aid the woman. Of those activities that do not cause enough harm to the pregnant woman to warrant medical intervention, but which still harm the fetus (such as smoking tobacco, inappropriate diet and failure to exercise) punishment is wholly inappropriate due to its discriminatory nature. Some commentators, considered in Chapter 6, propose that there are circumstances in which treatment should be mandated. Where this is the case, the woman's autonomy is not respected. Nevertheless, where a crime is persistently committed, less severe sentences have failed to reform, and empowerment, education and voluntary treatment have failed, this course of action might be reserved as a last resort. The emphasis, however, must remain on the pregnant woman rather than the fetus. Mandated treatment must not be used as a punishment but as a means of aiding addicted individuals. Neither should it be reserved for pregnant addicts, but used as a sentencing tool for all addicts that the health system has failed to reach.

Packer's third criterion demands that 'suppressing it will not inhibit socially desirable conduct'. Suppressing the woman's right to smoke or drink alcohol will inhibit her autonomy. Where the addiction involves an illicit substance, criminal sanctions over and above those applied when the individual is not pregnant are equally damaging. Empowerment, achieved through a commitment to autonomy, education and treatment is likely to aid both mother and child where criminal sanctions frighten her from the doctor and those who can help her fight the addiction.

The fourth criterion, '[i]t may be dealt with through even-handed and non-discriminatory enforcement', is evidently lacking in a policy of extended criminalization. Activities that are normally considered legally acceptable are made criminal purely on the basis that the woman is pregnant. This occurs regardless of the fact that the father of the fetus can also contribute to ill-effects suffered after birth[25] as can the environment, genetics and a host of unknown factors.

Criterion five states that 'controlling it through the criminal process will not expose that process to severe qualitative and quantitative strains'. Criminalizing women for their actions and omissions whilst pregnant may open the floodgates posing a serious threat to the family unit. Problems of detection also exist: in the USA some states have imposed legislation mandating reporting by the medical profession of any suspected case of maternal substance use in pregnancy.[26] This leads to a deep mistrust of doctors and added complications in the pregnancies of women anxious to avoid them.

The final criterion demands that 'there are no reasonable alternatives to the criminal sanction for dealing with it'. Chapter 6 argues that education and treatment can be realistically used as alternatives to criminalization. Thus, on the basis of Packer's criteria, the case for criminalization is extremely weak. Unfortunately this has not prevented a number of states extending their laws to criminalize pregnant women and recent mothers.

In this context coercive intervention has very little to recommend it, a view that is supported in context by Nelson, who puts forward three goals for criminal law intervention:[27] protection of the child from harm, equity and fairness, and an effective policy. Of the first goal, he argued that though intervention can protect the child from harm, it can also increase that harm if administered in an inept manner. Hence, in certain circumstances it may be in the child's best interests to be with its mother out of jail as opposed to being in foster care. Of his second goal, equity and fairness, criminalization policies single out the lower socio-economic class for punishment and ignore the potential role of the father in causing harm to the fetus born alive. Finally Nelson recommended that in view of the undesirable intrusion of the pregnant woman's autonomy, any coercive intervention must be effective.[28] This is lacking due to the fact that criminalization policies lead women to shun pre-natal care in order to avoid detection.

Coercion should be the last resort and the main thrust of policy must be to prevent the occurrence of drug use in the first instance and to treat and educate those who are addicted. The law should respect the value of each individual's autonomy and constraints should not be placed on individuals unnecessarily. It is theoretically disadvantageous to pursue a policy of extended criminalization, which is self-defeating and backward-looking.

The Elements of Crime

In criminal law the prosecution must show that there was a culpable act (the *actus reus*), a culpable state of mind (*mens rea*) and that the defendant caused the relevant harm. The latter two elements are extremely problematic in the context of pregnant women and recent mothers who harm the fetus born alive.

Mens Rea

In the *Attorney-General's Reference (No. 3 of 1994)*[29] the Court of Appeal and House of Lords differed in their interpretation of the relevant *mens rea* for murder and manslaughter in the case of a third party whose actions cause the death of the fetus born alive. Not surprisingly the matter has caused even greater difficulty when applied to the pregnant woman as one US judge surmised:

> If a legally cognizable duty on the part of mothers were recognized, then a judicially defined standard of conduct would have to be met. It must be asked, by what judicially defined standard would a mother have her every act or omission while pregnant subjected to State scrutiny? By what objective standard could a jury be guided in determining whether a pregnant woman did all that was necessary in order not to breach a legal duty to not interfere with her fetus' separate and independent right to be born whole? In what way would prejudicial and stereotypical beliefs about the reproductive abilities of women be kept from interfering with a jury's determination of whether a particular woman was negligent at any point during her pregnancy?[30]

The relevant standard imposed for a particular crime may be objective or subjective. Both are problematic when applied to the pregnant woman and recent mother. Shaw[31] suggested an objective test. Even in early pregnancy when the law protects the woman's right to seek abortion, Shaw suggested that pre-natal duties should include regular pre-natal check-ups, a balanced diet, weight control, 'judicious use of medications, tobacco, and caffeine' and abstinence from alcohol and illicit drugs.[32] In mid-pregnancy the woman must decide irrevocably whether or not to elect for abortion and once the decision has been made to continue the pregnancy, the 'reasonable' pregnant woman should increase the care of her fetus. After viability, the state interest in the fetus becomes compelling and any 'unreasonable' behaviour is viewed by Shaw with corresponding harshness.[33]

Dobson and Eby[34] are of the view that an objective standard is unlikely to work rationally and fairly, firstly because some women may not be able to meet the standards for financial or medical reasons and secondly because creation of a reasonable standard of care for pregnant women is impractical when taking into account the potential variations according to each woman's situation. As McNulty[35] pointed out, any 'reasonableness' standard must take account not only of fetal health, but also maternal health. The reasonableness of an action is therefore dependent on the health and status of the woman and fetus which may necessitate a higher standard for ill women, and similarly so for poorer women, to maintain a certain level of fetal welfare.

Alternatively, on the basis of a subjective standard a state may punish women who intentionally or wilfully create a substantial risk of serious injury to the fetus, without justification.[36] However Dobson and Eby[37] found that the subjective standard is problematic, largely because the very nature of addiction involves some loss of control and autonomy. Further, it makes women liable for activities even when no harm results, or when medical complications arise that are beyond the control of the woman. Field[38] suggested that there should be a strong presumption against criminalization, but that the presumption should be rebuttable where the benefit to the potential child would far outweigh the harm to the pregnant woman. However, this is not an adequate legal solution, for there is little guidance as to what level of harm is acceptable for the woman to suffer and what is unacceptable for the fetus. Thus, the required *mens rea* causes considerable problems for states that wish to criminalize her harmful behaviour.

Causation

As medical science progresses, health professionals can state with increasing certainty what caused the injury or death of the neonate. Yet there still exists a host of unknown factors in fetal health and much is left to educated guesswork. Where the particular crime is one of strict liability then a crime has been committed merely by engaging in the outlawed activity. Where a causal link between an act and the injury or death to the neonate must be established, the matter is more complex.

As seen in Chapter 3, each state has a degree of control over the protection to be afforded to the fetus, provided it does not offend the Constitution as interpreted in *Roe v Wade*[39] and subsequent decisions. Consequently, across America fetuses are protected to different degrees at different stages in gestation. Some states enact statutes requiring that for the purposes of a particular law, a fetus has the rights of a person, or rights equal to a person's. For example, California's Penal Code Section 187(a) provides that 'murder is the unlawful killing of a human being, or a fetus, with malice aforethought'. In *People v. Davis*[40] a pregnant woman was shot during an armed robbery, and her pre-viable fetus was still-born as a direct result. The defendant was successfully prosecuted for robbery and assault of the pregnant woman and murder of the fetus.[41]

Davis concerned the crime of a third party, but where similar Codes are also applied to pregnant women, causational issues arise. If the woman's actions are criminalized from conception, then her knowledge of pregnancy may or may not affect her culpability. If lack of knowledge of pregnancy is no bar to criminalization then, as Shaw[42] suggested, all fertile women should accordingly plan their activities from the mid-point of their menstrual cycle, in case they should become pregnant.

Many women who engage in a potentially harmful activity give birth to a healthy child.[43] One of the most commonly documented causes of maternal substance use resulting in damage to the neonate is consumption of alcohol. Yet, even in a pregnant woman who consumes 18 units of alcoholic drink per day, the chances of the child being born with Fetal Alcohol Syndrome are estimated at only 30-33 per cent.[44] This is because a number of genetic factors as well as the nutrition and other activities of the pregnant woman affect the outcome. In terms of causation it is hard to say which factor actually caused the ill-effects, and in terms of justice it is unfair to criminalize those whose genes or social deprivation determine the adverse effects of their alcohol consumption.

Causation is particularly problematic where criminalization depends on the illegality of the substance used in pregnancy. For example, in *Texas v. Rodden*,[45] the charges against a cocaine-using pregnant woman for injuring a child were dropped because the woman was also legally taking methadone, which could have caused the ill-effects to the child. As Paltrow stated:

> Prosecutions of pregnant women cannot rationally be limited to illegal conduct because many legal behaviours cause damage to developing babies. Women who are diabetic or obese, women with cancer or epilepsy who need drugs that could harm the fetus, and women who are too poor to eat adequately or to get pre-natal care could all be characterized as fetal abusers.[46]

Where medical tests are performed to determine whether or not there is alcohol or another drug in the bloodstream of a new-born, the results will only show traces if the activity were continued into the last trimester, or sometimes even the days preceding birth. It must be shown that the mother's activity caused the harm to the child in order to prosecute her. Yet it is inherently unjust to punish those who engaged in alcohol or illicit drug use in the last stage of pregnancy but not those who cause equal or greater harm with earlier, now undetectable use. The users likely to be detected with such tests are likely to be the addicted individuals whose culpability is questionable due to the fact that addiction is viewed as a medical condition. Those whose social use of the drug may be defined as more culpable are likely to go undetected.

The health of the fetus born alive is dependent upon a multitude of factors, including the stage in gestation in which the substances were imbibed. In many states, viability is a crucial stage for the onset of rights of the fetus, for at this point it could potentially survive outside the womb. Yet harm caused at this stage is relatively small when compared with that caused by substance abuse in the early stages of gestation.[47] If prosecution depends upon the damage occurring at a certain stage in pregnancy, such as after viability, then not only may this be inconsistent with the extent of the harm suffered by the child *in utero*, but it may be impossible to prove exactly when or why the damage occurred. States that criminalize the supply of drugs to a minor through the umbilical cord in the 30-90-second window after birth but before separation from the mother encounter similar problems,[48] for if the woman did not imbibe the substance in the 24 hours preceding birth then the supply of illegal substances in the crucial 30-90 seconds will be lacking and prosecution unattainable.

It may be that the pregnant woman's activities prior to conception, or before she realized that she was pregnant caused the impairment; she may have an infectious disease or a particular genetic condition which she passes on to the fetus born alive. Alternatively, the cause may not lie with the pregnant woman at all; the environment may adversely affect the child *in utero*, as may work hazards, poverty,[49] or paternal activities.[50] It may be that the male partner physically abused the pregnant woman,[51] or perhaps the paternal smoking habit caused injury to the fetus through the pregnant woman's inhalation of second-hand smoke,[52] or that his drug use prior to conception adversely affected the sperm, or even that male infertility treatment is to blame.[53] Merrick recognized that as the male has no legal role in deciding whether or not to abort the fetus, his dilemma is, in certain circumstances, perceivably greater than the woman's.[54]

Many factors harmful to the fetus are as yet undetermined. Of those we are aware of, some can be linked directly with culpable activities of the pregnant woman. However, even in those seemingly clear-cut cases, it is always possible that other factors, beyond the control of the woman, have made a significant contribution to the outcome.

Human Rights Issues

In Chapter 3 it was noted that attempts to extend criminalization to pregnant women and recent mothers have met with constitutional objections both at a common law and legislative level. States utilized case law and statute in an inconsistent manner. Some of the more restrictive chose to criminalize actions against the fetus from conception, others chose to criminalize from viability; some made criminalization dependent on live birth and simply extended the ambits of the born alive rule by statute; others retained the born alive rule in the form currently employed by courts in England and Wales.[55] Attempts to apply laws enacted to protect children from harm once born alive were frequently unsuccessful on the basis that this was not the legislature's intention. Similarly, enacting new statute to protect the fetus born alive encountered constitutional criticism on the ground that maternal human rights would be compromised.

The respective protection to be awarded to the human rights of the pregnant woman and the interests of the fetus is a matter that goes beyond mere legal interpretation. Policy must first dictate an appropriate balance between the two. As Annas stated:

> [T]reating [the pregnant woman and the fetus] separately before birth can only be done by favoring one over the other. Favoring the fetus radically devalues the pregnant woman treating her like an inert incubator, or a culture medium for the fetus. This view makes women unequal; since only they can have children. ... [This] relegates women to performing one function: childbearing. It is one thing

for the physician to view the fetus as a patient; it is another for the state to assume that the fetus' interests are opposed to its mother's, and ... forcing the mother to subrogate her own rights to those of her fetus.[56]

Some grading of rights is necessary, and Chapter 2 proposes a compromise on the basis of autonomy. The woman's 'negative' autonomy is protected so as to enable her to shun unwanted state intervention. Her 'positive' choices, however are curbed in order to afford the fetus a measure of protection. Analysis of the US Constitution demonstrates this point. In relation to the Human Rights Act 1998 predictions are made on the basis of the application of the European Convention on Human Rights.

Vagueness

One disadvantage of using case law to extend the definitions contained in statute is the constitutional criticism on grounds of 'vagueness'. Following *United States v. Harris*[57] there is a constitutional requirement of definiteness which is violated by any criminal statute that fails to give an ordinary man fair notice that his contemplated conduct is outlawed. Further, the Fourteenth Amendment includes a due process clause, which guarantees a person the right to fair notice that the conduct is criminal. Thus a state that attempts to apply a statute meant to protect children or adults, to fetuses or children born alive, may fail under judicial scrutiny because it has not given the defendant fair warning of the criminal nature of her act.[58]

Denison,[59] however, suggested that though extension of the common law might be subject to criticism under the Fourteenth Amendment, a statute could be phrased to outlaw fetal abuse in some circumstances:

> Any person who, under circumstances or conditions likely to produce great bodily harm or death knowingly or with reckless regard for the consequences, causes or permits the person or health of a child *in utero* to be endangered by substance abuse is guilty of criminal fetal abuse.

He went on to recognize that though fetal abuse cases involving illicit substances could be outlawed in this way, the vagueness criteria may still prevent criminalization of licit substance use during pregnancy. Though even in this case, he claimed that vagueness would not necessarily defeat a correctly worded statute. There is precedent to say that an activity can be legal in one context and illegal in another, as with driving under the influence of alcohol, or causing a public nuisance for example. In support, Balisy[60] suggested that the right to use narcotics, tobacco and alcohol are not fundamental rights and therefore, on the principle set down in *California v. Larve*,[61] the state should be able to restrict these lesser supported rights. However, as previously argued, laws against driving under the influence of alcohol are well defined and satisfactorily balance the rights of the individual to pursue the activities of alcohol use and the rights of society to be protected from harm. To limit pregnant women so as to prevent potential harm to fetuses would require disproportional limitations on many aspects of her autonomy. The law would lack certainty due to many pragmatic problems, such as the fact that she may not know she is pregnant when she performs the harmful act, or the lack of medical knowledge about the extent to which various acts and omissions may harm the fetus, or factors beyond her control (such as genetics, environment or poverty).

Thus, even a carefully worded statute might be said to offend the Constitution on the ground of vagueness. This is especially so when the statute criminalizes intentional behaviour that creates a substantial risk of serious injury without justification, but does not state the manner in which that harm must be caused. Because serious injury can be inflicted by a range of acts and omissions (performed by both pregnant women and third parties), a woman might need a substantial degree of knowledge to avoid harming the fetus.[62] As her knowledge of these factors is likely to depend on class, intellectual and financial situation, such an enactment might offend the vagueness prohibition.

Article 7 of the UK Human Rights Act 1998 contains a principle similar to the Fourteenth Amendment.[63] The wording of the US Constitution has been tested in court, (though as seen, a debate continues as to the meaning of the provision), whereas the Human Rights Act is a recent piece of legislation. However, case law on the European Convention of Human Rights is useful in determining the likely response of UK courts. Article 7 protects the principle of legal certainty: the criminal law must be framed clearly so that individuals know what behaviour is proscribed. In *SW v. United Kingdom*[64] a change in the UK common law outlawed rape within marriage. It was held that this change was foreseeable and therefore Article 7 of the European Convention on Human Rights was not violated. On the basis of the US example it could be argued that a change in law to protect the fetus from maternal harm is foreseeable in the UK. However, the likelihood is that Article 7 will operate to prevent criminalization on the grounds outlined above in relation to the US prohibition on vagueness.

Discrimination

The European Union has ruled that discrimination in the work place is sex discrimination. In both *Dekker v. Stichting Vormingscentrum Voor Jonge Volwassen (VJV – Centrum) Plus*,[65] and *Handels – Og Kontorfunktionaerernes Forband I Danmark [acting for Hertz] v. Dansk Arbejdsqiverforening [acting for Aldi Marked K/S]*,[66] the Court held that dismissal or refusal of employment on the ground of pregnancy was direct discrimination under the 1976 Equal Treatment Directive.[67] This represents a major breakthrough, for previously English courts had attempted to equate the pregnant woman with a male counterpart, which had, for obvious reasons, proven limited. These cases show that the courts are keen to place the woman on a par with other workers, regardless of her pregnancy. In England and Wales it might therefore be argued that a law criminalizing pregnant women for their conduct injuring the fetus offends Sections 1, 29 and 39 of the Sex Discrimination Act 1975.

This argument is further supported by an examination of Article 14 of the Human Rights Act 1998,[68] which prohibits discrimination on the ground of status within the context of the Act. Far more extensive is the US Eighth Amendment prohibiting 'cruel and unusual punishment'. In *Robinson v. California*[69] the Supreme Court held that a statute criminalizing addiction to drugs without any affirmative act constituted 'cruel and unusual punishment' on the basis that it criminalized a 'status' or disease. It is argued by some that criminalizing fetal abuse is unconstitutional on similar grounds, because unless states actually criminalize delivery through the umbilical cord (which has proved largely unsuccessful) they are forced to criminalize the drug u*se*, coupled with the pregnant status of the woman.[70] In short, the claim is that *mens rea* is lacking because drug addiction is a medical disease, and the crime only becomes so because of the (pregnant) status of the woman.

Carrying this a step further, some argue that it is the bodily functions of sex, conception and gestation, or even femaleness itself that is being criminalized. They claim that this offends the equal protection clause of the Fourteenth Amendment.[71] However, in the US case, *Michael M v. Superior Court*[72] the court refused to view discrimination based on pregnancy as 'sex discrimination' on the ground that pregnancy is a 'risk' rather than a gender characteristic. Hence the statute in question was not discriminating against the woman on the basis of her sex, but on a correct differentiation between pregnant and non-pregnant women. Therefore differentiation between pregnant and non-pregnant is arguably not discrimination on the basis of sex. Since the activity itself (smoking or using illicit drugs for example) is not protected by the Constitution, some argue that curbing the right of a sector in society to engage in that activity is not necessarily unconstitutional. Despite this authority, Roberts[73] argued that the gradual erosion of the principle in *Roe v Wade*[74] offends the Constitution. Though states cannot prevent women from seeking abortion when they have the private medical insurance or other means to cover the cost, they can prevent access to state-funded abortion. Coupled with the lack of pre-natal care and drug-treatment programmes, this severely limits the choices of under-privileged women, and in particular women of colour. This, she claims, amounts to an invasion of the constitutional rights to autonomy (privacy) and equal protection.

The equal treatment objection to criminalization depends on the extent to which criminal law sanctions are applied. As a huge range of acts and omissions by the pregnant woman potentially affect the fetus, there is scope for interference in almost every aspect of the pregnant woman's life in order to protect it. Law[75] contended that any law governing reproductive issues should be subjected to scrutiny to ensure that '(1) the law has no significant impact in perpetuating either the oppression of women or culturally imposed sex-role constraints on individual freedom or (2) if the law has this impact, it is justified as the best means of serving a compelling state interest'.[76] A central tenet of this work is that criminalization is not the best means of achieving optimal health for the pregnant woman and the fetus born alive. Therefore, arguably the biological differences between men and women do not provide justification for the oppression of their autonomy. As seen above, the European Court of Justice does not share the USA's view that pregnancy alters the woman's status in the eyes of the law.[77] Therefore a policy of extended criminalization is more likely to be viewed as discriminatory in England and Wales.

Liberty, Privacy and Autonomy

Article 5 of the UK Human Rights Act 1998 protects the right to liberty and security. It states that 'Everyone has the right to liberty and security of person' but Article 5 also contains a list of exceptions to the rule. Among these are Article 5(1)(a), 'the lawful detention of a person after conviction by a competent court', and also of pertinence to this chapter, Article 5(1)(e), 'the lawful detention of persons for the prevention of the spreading of infectious diseases, of persons of unsound mind, alcoholics or drug addicts or vagrants'. Though article 5(1)(e) might conceivably be used to extend criminalization, the European Convention on Human Rights has been interpreted so as to protect individuals' liberty from invasions of an 'arbitrary fashion'.[78] This might, for example, prevent a drug-using woman being incarcerated for the duration of her pregnancy in order to protect the fetus. Instead the sentence should be commensurate with the crime. In relation to the European Convention on Human Rights, Article 5(1)(e) has only been used to detain those who 'have to be considered as occasionally dangerous for public safety' or 'their own interests necessitate their detention'.[79]

The Fourteenth Amendment of the US Constitution protects the right to liberty[80] and extended criminalization arguably breaches it in a number of ways. For example, where maternal and fetal rights conflict, a woman may feel that the traumas of abortion are preferable to the criticism and criminalization she might otherwise face,[81] and her liberty is arguably curbed in this way. The slippery slope argument also has force in this context: if women must refrain from using illegal substances in pregnancy, not because they are generally illegal but on the basis that the activity harms the fetus, then other activities that are harmful might be criminalized on the same basis. Cocaine use already constitutes a criminal activity. If the crime is extended on the basis of pregnancy, then why should the rights to drink alcohol, smoke tobacco or omit pre-natal care not be similarly curbed? The potential for increasing control over her life whether the goal is fetal health, or health of the child born alive, becomes increasingly evident.[82]

Historically the right to liberty did not extend to the protection of reproductive rights. In the famous Supreme Court decision in *Buck v. Bell*,[83] Justice Oliver Wendell Holmes authorized an enforced sterilization stating: 'It is better for all the world, if instead of waiting to execute degenerate offspring for crime, or let them starve for their imbecility, society can prevent those who are manifestly unfit from continuing their kind ... . Three generations of imbeciles are enough.'

It is only relatively recently that the Supreme Court has hailed as a constitutional right, the right of liberty in relation to reproductive decisions.[84] The right to liberty underlies rights to privacy and autonomy. In *Griswold v. Connecticut*[85] a statute prohibiting the use of contraception by married couples was struck down on the basis of privacy. The precise content of the right to privacy is unclear; however there is authority to say that child-bearing is one area that is protected by the requirement, as was held by the Supreme Court in *Cleveland Board of Education v. La Fleur*,[86] for example. In the revolutionary case of *Roe v. Wade*[87] the US Supreme Court held that the woman's constitutional right to privacy incorporated her right to seek abortion in certain circumstances. Does this right to privacy protect her from criminalization for acts harming or killing the fetus born alive? The negative answer stems not only from the *Roe* decision but also from the gradual erosion of the principles contained therein.

The Supreme Court ruled that the Fourteenth Amendment of the Constitution protected pregnant women's and fetal rights respectively, on the basis of three trimesters, each of which roughly corresponds to three of the nine months of pregnancy. Justice Blackmun wrote for the majority holding that during the first trimester, the pregnant woman's Fourteenth Amendment constitutional right to privacy encompasses her right to terminate her pregnancy, provided that she can find a physician to carry out the procedure. During the second trimester, abortion can be obtained in the interests of the health of the pregnant woman. However in the third trimester, the state may regulate or prohibit abortion in the interests of fetal life. Justice Blackmun avoided the contentious issue of when life and personhood begin, though he recognized that: '[T]he law has been reluctant to endorse any theory that life, as we recognize it, begins before live birth or to accord legal rights to the unborn except in narrowly defined situations and except when the rights are contingent upon live birth.'[88]

Roe invalidated 46 out of 50 state laws and superseded repeal laws in the remaining four states.[89] The marked dichotomy between the pro-choice and the pro-life movements increased in fervour. Attempts were made to reverse *Roe* by amending the Constitution or by claiming that *Roe* misconstrued the Constitution. Though these attempts have so far failed,[90] the principles contained in *Roe* have been substantially eroded.

Roe represented an attempt to balance the interests of the pregnant woman and the fetus where conflict arises. It limited the state's positive obligation to provide the pregnant woman with access to abortion, so increasing the protection owed to the fetus as it nears fulfilment of its potential for personhood. Equally it perpetuated the negative obligation on the state to refrain from exercising constraint on the woman, particularly in the early stages of pregnancy. Yet, this delicate balance has not been maintained. First, subsequent Supreme Court decisions have eroded the principles contained in *Roe*, enabling constraint of pregnant women in order to protect the fetus from abortion. Second, the decision applies only within the limited context of abortion. Thus states have extended other aspects of the law to achieve protection of the fetus at the expense of the woman's privacy rights.

The erosion of the principles set out in *Roe v Wade* can be seen in a number of Supreme Court decisions. In *Maher v. Roe*[91] the court held that states receiving Medicaid funding were not obliged to fund abortions. In accordance with *Roe v Wade*, abortions were still available but only for those able to afford them. Justice Brennan dissented stating: 'This disparity in funding by the State clearly operates to coerce indigent pregnant women to bear children they would not otherwise choose to have, and just as clearly, this coercion can only operate upon the poor, who are uniquely the victims of this form of financial pressure.'[92]

In *Harris v. McRae*[93] the Supreme Court went further still, upholding the right of states to refuse to fund even medically necessary abortions for recipients of Medicaid funding. *Webster v. Reproductive Health Services*[94] perpetuated this trend. The Supreme Court upheld a Missouri statute that 'prohibited the use of public employees and facilities to perform or assist abortions not necessary to save the mother's life' and prohibited the use of public funds for abortion counselling except where the mother's life is at stake. Women could still obtain a legal abortion, but not if they relied on public funding.[95] It is precisely those women who rely on Medicaid funding who are later refused places on drug-treatment programmes and then made the recipients of prosecution on the ground that they damaged or killed the fetus born alive. Chapter 6 puts forward a case for state-funded treatment and education options. Without this any state limiting abortion will inevitably face the increase of neonates damaged by their mother's harmful addictions.

The implications of *Webster* go further. The case involved the legitimization of Missouri's definition of 'person' as having effect from conception.[96] Where *Roe* avoided the contentious issue of defining when life begins, the 5:4 decision in *Webster* upheld Missouri's wide definition of 'person' and refused to pronounce it unconstitutional. Thus some states have declared for the purposes of certain statutes, that personhood begins before birth.[97] Parness and Pritchard,[98] in support of the interpretation of *Roe* in *Webster*, argued that *Roe* neither precludes nor excludes the possibility of legal personhood status at any stage of gestation and that personhood can therefore be inferred on the fetus through statute, at any point in gestation. Chief Justice Rehnquist, who wrote for the majority in *Webster*, stated that the Missouri provision '... does not by its terms regulate abortion or any other aspect of appellees' medical practice'.[99] However, the dissenting opinion was that the declarations conflicted with the pregnant woman's privacy right to abort that was originally upheld in *Roe*.[100]

The trend of diminishing the impact of *Roe* was continued in *Planned Parenthood v. Casey*,[101] which concerned the constitutionality of a statute, which was upheld despite its restrictive approach to abortion. The statute legalized conditions of spousal notification, a 24-hour waiting period, counselling and public disclosure.

The second means by which the impact of *Roe* has been diminished is by limiting its impact to abortion cases. An obvious implication of *Roe* is that the privacy rights of the pregnant woman outweigh the state interest in fetal health until the third trimester, when that interest becomes 'important and legitimate'[102] or even 'compelling'.[103] This would imply that women should be free from criminal prosecution for acts that harm the fetus born alive, at least when those acts occur in the first two trimesters. However Balisy[104] argued that although abortion is proclaimed in *Roe* as a 'fundamental' right, rights to alcohol and other substances that are harmful to a fetus are not fundamental.[105] If the *fundamental* right to abort can be denied in certain circumstances, as is held in *Roe*, then surely, Balisy argued, the courts can restrict mere *privileges*. Consequently, *Roe* (and the constitutional right to privacy defined therein) does not necessarily prevent criminalization of pregnant women for harming or killing the fetus or fetus born alive. Despite arguments to the contrary in the 1990 Massachusetts Supreme Court case of *Commonwealth v. Pellegrini*,[106] Chapter 3 illustrates instances where courts have upheld the criminalization of recent mothers for harming the fetus born alive.

Privacy also involves the protection of an individual's right to confidentiality. If a fetus is being harmed *in utero*, it is advantageous to the fetus to arrest that harm at the earliest opportunity. Yet to intervene prior to birth may involve physicians reporting cases of suspected or confirmed substance use to the authorities, so enabling the criminal law (or the family law system) to play its role.[107] A criminal statute prohibiting fetal abuse may also require doctors to judge and report the behaviour of pregnant individuals, thereby putting them in an unenviable policing role. In practical terms, such a pregnant woman is likely to avoid the doctor and thereby put the fetus at an increased risk.[108] Alternatively, she may opt for abortion, which offends the goal of protecting fetal life.[109] Instead doctors might be asked to report cases of suspected substance use after a baby has been born. Though this is equally likely to dissuade those who will potentially face criminal sanctions from seeking much needed pre-natal care, and though it fails to curb harm *during* pregnancy, reporting after birth has the advantage that future pregnancies could be closely monitored and the neonate given special protection and treatment. Determining the cause of injury involves testing of the mother, neonate or both, all of which are problematic.[110] In the case of the mother, she can withhold consent to the procedure. In the case of the child, the mother would usually be required to give proxy consent, but where the test is in the child's best interest, a court or statute may declare it lawful.

A state may demand routine testing for drugs but this is both expensive and may lead to drug-using pregnant women avoiding medical care during labour to prevent detection, criminal sanctions and possibly having the child taken from her care. Alternative tests could be reserved for babies who present with symptoms suggestive of maternal drug use or for mothers who have a history of drug use.[111] This then leaves the possibility of removing the baby from its mother where future injury is likely.

Reporting laws place intolerable legal and ethical dilemmas on the doctor. First, it produces an element of uncertainty where doctors must treat two legal entities with conflicting rights. Whether they are dealing in law with one person (the pregnant woman) and one fetus, or two persons (the pregnant woman and the fetus) depends on the state's definition of personhood.[112] Secondly, they may lose the right to uphold patient confidentiality if reporting is required by the law. In constitutional terms, such a breach of patient confidentiality potentially runs contrary to the right to privacy.[113] Finally, testing women and neonates without consent may run contrary to the Fourth Amendment.[114] In the 1990s this was put to the test when the Medical University of South Carolina, serving an under-privileged population with a high proportion of patients from ethnic minorities, instigated a reporting policy. Any pregnant patient who was suspected of using cocaine was subjected to a drug test. At first patients who tested positive were immediately reported to the police.[115] Later a change in policy dictated that women should be offered a place on a drug-treatment programme. The alternative to enrolment and successful completion of the course was reporting to the police and arrest.[116] The Supreme Court held in *Ferguson v. City of Charleston*,[117] that the hospital's drug testing policy was unconstitutional because it violated the Fourth Amendment's bar against unreasonable searches and seizures. Nahas[118] criticized the decision on the basis that it is extremely narrow. It does not prevent testing without consent (providing an appropriate warrant is obtained), it does not prevent the use of treatment as an alternative to notification of the authorities and it does not prevent prosecution of women who harm the fetus born alive through their drug use.

The Fourth Amendment protects, amongst other things, freedom from unwanted bodily intrusion;[119] a right that is further protected by both the common law[120] and the Bill of Rights.[121] Autonomy arguably underpins the rights of parents to control the upbringing and education of their children,[122] and it is possible that this might be extended to uphold their control of unborn children.[123] However, Balisy argued against this view,[124] stating that parental autonomy does not exempt parents from control by the state. In fact it usually creates positive duties owed by parents to their children. Nevertheless, a New York court in *In re Torres*[125] held that drug use by a pregnant woman could not form the sole basis of neglect on the grounds that the potential intrusions into the life of the woman would form an unwarranted violation of her bodily integrity.[126]

Though the US definition of autonomy has wider connotations than the definition accepted in Chapter 2, G. Dworkin's[127] definition seeks to protect individuals' rights to procedural autonomy. State intrusion should be kept to a minimum, and though the fetal potential for life is important, it is suggested that other means of protection are possible and preferable to breaching the autonomy of pregnant women through extended criminalization. Article 8 of the UK Human Rights Act 1998 contains the right to respect for private and family life.[128] Depending on the future interpretation of Article 8, it might herald increased protection for reproductive rights (in the context of forced medical treatment as well as freedom from extended criminalization), but the converse is also possible on the basis of exceptions to the general rule, contained in Article 8(2). Though there has yet to be a case determining the relevance of Article 8 to reproductive autonomy, *NHS Trust A v M; NHS Trust B v H*[129] has bearing on the debate. The case involved the hospital trusts seeking declarations to enable their hospitals to discontinue artificial nutrition and hydration for two patients in a permanent vegetative state. In granting the declarations, Dame Butler-Sloss reconsidered the principles laid down in *Airedale NHS Trust v Bland*[130] in the light of the Human Rights Act 1998. The court accepted that Article 8 protects the right to personal autonomy and that any intrusion into bodily integrity must be justified under Article 8(2).[131] The decision turned on the application of Article 2, which contains a positive obligation to take adequate and appropriate steps to safeguard life. Counsel argued that in this context, Article 8 conflicts with Article 2 and should therefore be balanced against it. As a result it might be argued that the withdrawal of treatment is not justified under Article 8(2). However, the court held that in determining the scope of the Article 2 positive obligation, Article 8 simply provides assistance. The positive obligation is not absolute.[132] Accordingly, where treatment is withheld in the patient's best interests so defined by a responsible body of medical opinion, the state's obligation under Article 2 is discharged.[133]

However, it is suggested that the scope of Article 8(2) could be utilized more successfully in arguments to protect the life and health of the fetus or child born alive. It contains a number of exceptions to the general rule against public interference,[134] including the protection of health or morals and the protection of the rights and freedoms of others. Both of these exceptions could potentially be used to curb pregnant women's autonomy and to defend a policy of criminalization.

Conclusion

There is undoubtedly a crisis relating to impairment of children born alive, caused by maternal conduct in pregnancy. Yet to deal with this through criminalization is, as Holland expressed,[135] the least expensive and also the least effective means by which to tackle the problem. Even for those states where the legal goal is to protect fetal life on an equal basis to person's, the protection afforded to the fetus/potential child through a policy of criminalization of pregnant women is transitory. Even when autonomy and other human rights of the pregnant woman are set aside, the drug-using pregnant woman is likely to avoid the doctor (so risking the health of the fetus) or seek abortion to avoid criminal sanctions. As was recognized in *Commonwealth v. Kemp*:[136]

> (C)riminal prosecution of women for their conduct during pregnancy fosters neither the health of the woman nor her future offspring; indeed, it endangers both. Criminal prosecution cruelly severs the woman from the health care system, thereby increasing the potential for harm to both mother and fetus. Pregnant women threatened by criminal prosecution have already avoided the care of physicians and hospitals to prevent detection.

Though the pregnant woman arguably has a moral responsibility to act in a way commensurate with optimum fetal health, this cannot be translated into law without unduly curbing the human rights of the pregnant woman. The law in England and Wales recognizes that the fetus is not a person. Therefore the human rights of the pregnant woman are necessarily of greater importance than the secondary rights afforded to the fetus. Consequently, though the born alive rule might be justified in its application to third parties who cause the death of a child born alive, it should not be extended to criminalize pregnant women or recent mothers whose activities allegedly injure or kill the child *in utero* or born alive. Such prosecutions are backward-looking and self-defeating.[137] Third parties should be criminalized, but out of recognition of maternal harm, and on the strict grounds currently applied in England and Wales. To equate the fetus with a born person is a dangerous precedent in terms of human rights and the other legal issues considered in this chapter.[138] In both the United States and in England and Wales, instead of extending criminal sanctions, education and treatment are necessary, coupled with tort and family law intervention where needed.

Notes

1   The Center for Reproductive Law & Policy, *Punishing Women for their Behavior During Pregnancy: An Approach That Undermines Women's Health and Children's Interests* (New York: Center for Reproductive Law & Policy, 1996.) Excerpts from Statements by Public Health And Public Advocacy Groups:

American Medical Association: 'Pregnant women will be likely to avoid seeking prenatal or other medical care for fear that their physicians' knowledge of substance abuse or other potentially harmful behavior could result in a jail sentence rather than proper medical treatment.' Board of Trustees Report, Legal Interventions During Pregnancy, 264 *JAMA* 2663, 2667 (1990). ...

American Public Health Association: The APHA 'recommends that no punitive measures be taken against pregnant women who are users of illicit drugs when no other illegal acts, including drug-related offenses, have been committed.' Policy Statement No. 9020, *Illicit Drug Use by Pregnant Women* (reprinted in 81:2 Am. J Pub. Health 253 (1991)).

American Society of Addiction Medicine: 'The imposition of criminal penalties solely because a person suffers from an illness is inappropriate and counterproductive. Criminal prosecution of chemically dependent women will have the overall result of deterring such women from seeking both prenatal care and chemical dependency treatment, thereby increasing, rather than preventing, harm to children and to society as a whole.' Board of Directors, *Public Policy Statement on Chemically Dependent Women and Pregnancy* 47 (Sept. 25, 1989). ...

Center for Substance Abuse Treatment, U.S. Department of Health and Human Services Consensus Panel on Pregnant, Substance-Using Women: 'The Consensus Panel strongly supports the view that the use of alcohol and other drugs by women during pregnancy is a public health issue, not a legal problem.... The panel does not support the criminal prosecution of pregnant, substance-using women. Furthermore, there is no evidence that punitive approaches work.' *Pregnant, Substance-Using Women*, DHHS Pub No. (SMA) 93-1998 (1993). ...

2   Immorality is usually considered a prerequisite for criminal behaviour. Thus H.L. Packer, *The Limits of the Criminal Sanction* (1968) at 264 stated: 'We can sum up the prudential limitations as follows: the criminal sanction should ordinarily be limited to conduct that is viewed, without significant social dissent, as immoral. The calendar of crimes should not be enlarged beyond that point and, as views about morality shift, should be contracted.' Of course, to define morality is as difficult as describing what conduct should be considered criminal. Packer identifies the voice of society as indicative of what is moral, but this is not always the case. As Clarkson and Keating, *Criminal Law: Text and Materials* 4th edn (Sweet and Maxwell: London, 1998), 7 point out, the Race Relations Act would not have been passed if society's opinion were utilized to define morality.

3   Though there are crimes of strict liability, for example certain driving offences.

4   Clarkson and Keating, *op. cit.,* 87.

5   H.L. Packer, *op. cit.*, 296.

6   See M. Curriden, 'Holding Mom Accountable: Roe v. Wade Does Not Prevent Criminal Prosecution of Prenatal Abuse' (1990) March *American Bar Association Journal* 50 where a survey of 15 states revealed that 71 per cent of the public favoured criminalization for pregnant women who injure their fetus born alive through illegal drug use.

7   See Sherman, 'Keeping Baby Safe from Mom', 3 October 1988, 11 *National Law Journal* 1.

8   *United States v. Vaughn* Crim. No. F-2172-88B (D.C. Sup. Ct., Aug. 23, 1988).

9   J. Berrien, 'Pregnancy and Drug Use: The Dangerous and Unequal Use of Punitive Measures' (1990) 2(2) *Yale Journal of Law and Feminism* 239, at 241; also S.A. Garcia, 'Maternal Drug Abuse: Laws and Ethics as Agents of Just Balances and Therapeutic Interventions', *The International Journal of the Addictions* 28(13) (1993), 1311, at 1315.

10   I. Burrell, 'Mother Knows Best, But Who Decides?' *The Independent*, 18 January 2000, Supplement at 11, considering the case of convicted prisoner 'L', who gave birth in a mother and baby unit of the prison, whilst held on remand. The article questions the appropriateness of sentences which impose prison on women with children.

11   J.W. Steverson, 'Stopping Fetal Abuse with No-Pregnancy and Drug Treatment Probation Conditions' (1994) 34(2) *Santa Clara Law Review* 295 at 327. See also Stein and Mistiaen, 'Pregnant in Prison', *Progressive* 18 (1988), 18.

12   C. Marshall (Honourable), 'Plenary Session (Women Prisoners), War on Drugs, 200 Years of the Penitentiary: Criminal, Social and Economic Justice' (1991) 34 *Howard Law Journal* 512, at 513.

13   See E. M. Barry, 'Quality of Prenatal Care for Incarcerated Women Challenged' (1985) Nov./Dec. *Youth Law News* 2. Barry studied three Californian prisons showing that only 44 per cent of prison pregnancies end in live births and that prisons are not by any means free of illicit drugs.

14   E. M. Barry, 'Recent Development: Pregnant Prisoners' (1989) 12 *Harvard Women's Law Journal* 189 at 189.

15   A. Treneman, 'Which of the Two Sides Will be Left Holding the Baby After the Battle of the Bulge?' *The Independent*, 27 September 1997 at 21 col. 1. A judge refused to allow a persistent teenage shoplifter out of prison a fortnight early so that her baby could be born outside prison.

16   *People v. Zaring*, Californian Court of Appeal No. F014606 (22 July 1992). The judge allegedly once ordered a person to wear a T-shirt proclaiming 'I am a felon'.

17   As reported in S.B. Goldberg, 'No Baby, No Jail: Creative Sentencing Has Gone Overboard, a Californian Court Rules' (1992) 78 *American Bar Association Journal* 90. See also S. L. Jebson, 'Conditioning a Woman's Probation on her Using Norplant: New Weapon Against Child Abuse Backfires' (1995) 17(169) *Campbell Law Review* 301, and D.E. Stich, 'Alternative Sentencing or Reproduction Control: Should California Courts Use Norplant to Protect Future Children From Child Abuse and Fetal Abuse?' (1993) 33 *Santa Clara Law Review* 1017.

18   T. Zorpette *et al.*, 'Norplant: Miracle Drug or Threat to Women's Rights?' (1993) 20 *Human Rights* 16 at 16.

19   I.M. Young, 'Punishment, Treatment, Empowerment; Three Approaches to Policy for Pregnant Addicts', in P. Boling (Ed.) *Expecting Trouble: Surrogacy, Fetal Abuse and New Reproductive Technologies* (Boulder: San Francisco, 1995) stated at 110: 'The level of passion directed against pregnant addicts often seems higher than that felt for most ordinary criminals. It is not just anyone who has harmed their baby; it's the child's *mother*. The mother is supposed to be the one who sacrifices herself, who will do anything for her child, who will preserve and nurture it. That's what mothering *means*. The rage directed at pregnant addicts unconsciously recalls the feeling we all had as children – rage toward our mothers who were not always there for us, did not always respond to our needs and desires and sometimes pursued their own purposes and desires. The mother who harms her child is not merely a criminal – she is a monster.' In the UK, for example, in *St. George's Healthcare National Health Service Trust v. S* and *R v. Collins and Others, Ex parte S* [1998] 2 FLR 728 (see Chapter 4 p. 69) a pregnant woman who was forced to undergo a Caesarean section operation achieved judicial review of the court authorization. This was criticized by L. White, 'There is No Right to be Selfish', *The Sunday Times* 23 February 1997, 5: 'That Ms S's daughter was born by caesarean only because her mother was deemed mentally unstable is absurd. What if Ms S had been merely bloody-minded, silly, drugged, uninformed, out to prove a point, or make an ex-boyfriend suffer as she herself intimated? Then the doctors could have done nothing, yet if we were talking puppies Rolf Harris would be there like a shot.'

20   See D.E. Roberts, 'Drug-Addicted Women Who Have Babies' (1990) 26 *Trial* 56 and D.E. Roberts, *Killing the Black Body: Race, Reproduction and the Meaning of Liberty* (Pantheon Books: New York, 1997).

21   For evidence of poverty amongst the vast majority of those potentially targeted for criminalization, see M. McNulty, 'Pregnancy Police: The Health Policy and Legal Implications of Punishing Pregnant Women for Harm to Their Fetuses' (1987) 16 *New York University Review of Law and Social Change* 277, at 292.

22   R.H. Blank, 'Mandating Outpatient Treatment for Pregnant Substance Abusers: Attractive but Unfeasible', *Politics and the Life Sciences* 15(1) (1996), 49 at 50.

23   J. Murphy, 'Marxism and Retribution', in *Retribution, Justice and Therapy* (D. Reidel: The Hague, 1979), 83, as referred to by I.M. Young, *op. cit.,* 114.

24   Public vengeance is described by M. Cohen, 'Moral Aspects of the Criminal Law' (1940) 49 *Yale Law Review* 897 at 1025 as to 'represent the breakdown of human intelligence, as well as good will. It shows perhaps the ugliest phase of our human nature'.

25   See *infra.,* 90.

26   *Supra,* 99.

27   L.J. Nelson, 'Intervention Does More Harm Than Good' (1990) 5(4) *Journal of Interpersonal Violence* 530, at 530.

28   See also L. Rubenstein, 'Prosecuting Maternal Substance Abusers: An Unjustified and Ineffective Policy' (1991) Spring (9) *Yale Law and Policy Review* 130.

29   *Attorney-General's Reference (No. 3 of 1994)* [1997] 3 All E.R. 936. For analysis see Chapter 4 p. 56.

30   *Stallman v. Youngquist,* 531 N.E.2d 355 (Ill. 1988) at 360.

31   M.W. Shaw, 'Conditional Prospective Rights of the Fetus' (1984) 5(1) *The Journal of Legal Medicine* 63.

32   Shaw, *ibid.,* 83.

33   Shaw, *ibid.,* 83-88.

34   T. Dobson and K. Eby, 'Criminal Liability for Substance Abuse During Pregnancy: the Controversy of Maternal Versus Fetal Rights' (1992) 36 *Saint Louis University Law Review,* 655 at 684.

35   M. McNulty, *op. cit.,* 305.

36   As suggested by McNulty, *ibid.,* 308, who criticized the subjective standard on the grounds that it is unlikely to deter or rehabilitate substance-abusing women, and will have the effect of discouraging women from seeking pre-natal care.

37   Dobson and Eby, *op. cit.*

38   M.A. Field, 'Controlling the Woman to Protect the Fetus' (1989) 17 *Law, Medicine and Health Care* 122 at 124.

39   *Roe v. Wade* 410 U.S. 113 (1973).

40   *People v. Davis* Supreme Court of California, 7 Cal.4th 797, 30 Cal.Rptr.2d 50, 872 P.2d 591 (1994).

41   However, in this case it was thought that the defendant could not reasonably have suspected the law to follow this course, and therefore the rule will not apply to the particular case, but to all cases in the future.

42   M.W. Shaw, 'Conditional Prospective Rights of the Fetus' (1984) 5(1) *The Journal of Legal Medicine* 63.

43   See for example, 'Woman in Fetal Alcohol Case Gives Birth to Healthy Infant', *New York Times,* 17 June 1990 at 20, col. 4, where it was reported that a Wyoming woman was charged with child abuse during pregnancy due to her suspected alcohol intake, and the resulting child was allegedly healthy. For analysis of reliability of toxicology tests, see A. English, 'Prenatal Drug Exposure: Grounds for Mandatory Child Abuse Reports' (1990) 11 *Youth Law News* 3.

44   Royal College of Gynaecologists and Obstetricians (England) *Alcohol Consumption in Pregnancy* guidelines viewable at http://www.rcog.org.uk. See also J. Laurance, Health Correspondent, 'Pregnant Women May Drink – In Moderation', *The Times,* 3 March 1997, at 9, reviewing the Royal College's Report. It is stated that more than two small glasses of wine per day (or their equivalent) may harm the fetus. Yet, the *Sunday Times*

reported only the month before that: 'Even indulging in as little as a glass of wine a week produces a detectable rise in lead levels in blood passing through the umbilical cord to the fetus.' In M. Piggott, 'Medical Note', *The Sunday Times,* 9 February 1997, at 18.

45   *Texas v. Rodden,* No. 37365R (Dist. Ct. Tarrant County filed June 1, 1989).

46   L. M. Paltrow, 'When Becoming Pregnant Is a Crime', *Crim. Just. Ethics,* Winter-Spring (1990), 41 at 42.

47   See K. Lichtenburg, 'Gestational Substance Abuse: A Call for Thoughtful Legislative Response' (1990) 65 *Washington Law Review* 377 at 380 where she recognizes that damage caused by cocaine abuse in the first trimester cannot be reversed by ceasing cocaine use.

48   As for example in *Florida v. Johnson* No. E89-1765 (Fla. Dist. Ct. App., 5th Dist. 1989). Johnson was charged with delivery of cocaine to her child through the umbilical cord and sentenced to 15 years probation with a variety of conditions. This was upheld by the appellate court but overturned by the Florida State Supreme Court. See further Chapter 3 p. 45.

49   For example, K. Pollitt, 'Fetal Rights: A New Assault on Feminism', *The Nation,* 26 March 1990, at 409 acknowledged that poverty in pregnancy has a large impact on the health of the neonate. Examples of important factors include poor medical care, lack of education, poor living conditions and inadequate diet.

50   R.E. Little and C.F. Sing, 'Father's Drinking and Infant Birth Weight: Report of an Association', *Teratology* 36 (1987), 59 showed a link between paternal drinking prior to conception and decreased birth-weight of the neonate. Note that in the UK, a civil claim from the child born alive potentially lies against third parties (including the father) under the Congenital Disabilities (Civil Liability) Act 1976.

51   See J. McFarlane, 'Battering During Pregnancy: Tip of an Iceberg Revealed', *Women and Health* 15(3) (1989), 69. McFarlane reported that as many as one in twelve women (in a large metropolitan area) were physically abused during their pregnancy of these 87 per cent had been previously abused, and 29 per cent had not. In a study of 589 postpartum women, physically abused women were four times more likely to deliver a low-weight baby.

52   See for example, Jun Zhang et al., 'A Case-Control Study of Paternal Smoking and Birth Defects, *International Journal of Epidemiology* 21 (1992) 273. Further, it has been shown that where the partner of a pregnant woman smokes, the child is at a 1.4 fold increased risk of sudden infant death syndrome, in E.A. Mitchell and J. Milerad, 'Smoking and Sudden Infant Death Syndrome', in World Health Organisation *Tobacco Free Initiative: International Consultation on Environmental Tobacco Smoke (ETS) and Child Health* (WHO: Geneva, 1999), 105.

53   See F. Cohen, 'Paternal Contributions to Birth Defects', *Nursing Clinics North America* May (1986), 46. Also C.R. Daniels, 'A Million (Missing) Men: A Commentary on Mathieu's Compromise on Pregnancy and Substance Use', *Politics and the Life Sciences* 15(1) (1996), 54. See also S. Connor, Science Correspondent, 'Male Infertility Treatment Linked to Birth Defect', *The Sunday Times,* 23 February 1997, at 9. See generally J.R. Schroedel and P. Peretz, 'A Gender Analysis of Policy Formation: The Case of Fetal Abuse' (1994) 19(2) *Journal of Health Politics, Policy and Law'* 335, who suggested that a patriarchal belief system has led to the woman being blamed for a problem that is the fault of both males and females.

54   J.C. Merrick, 'Paternal Obligations During Pregnancy: Breaking New Ground', *Politics and the Life Sciences* 13(2) (1994), 251 at 252. See also L.M. Paltrow, 'Paternal-Fetal Conflict: An Idea Whose Time Should Never Come', *Politics and the Life Sciences* 13(2) (1994), 253.

55   As applicable only to third parties who injure a fetus born alive and dying of the injuries so caused.

56   G.J. Annas, 'The Impact Of Medical Technology On The Pregnant Woman's Right to Privacy', *American Journal of Law & Medicine* 13 (1987), 213, at 229-230.

57 *United States v. Harris* 347 U.S. 612, 617 (1954).

58 This was recognized in *People v. Hardy* 469 N.W. 2d 50 (Mich. Ct. App. 1991). In *Bouie v. City of Columbia* 378 U.S. 347 (1964), at 353 the Supreme Court held that: 'An unenforceable judicial enlargement of a criminal statute, applied retroactively, operates precisely like an *ex post facto* law, such as Article 1, Section 10 of the Constitution forbids.'

59 J. Denison, 'The Efficacy and Constitutionality of Criminal Punishment for Maternal Substance Abuse' (1991) 64(2) *Southern California Law Review* 1103 at 1121. The quote is loosely based on Section 273a of the California Penal Code.

60 S.S. Balisy 'Maternal Substance Abuse: The Need to Provide Legal Protection for the Fetus' (1987) 60 *Southern California Law Review* 1209.

61 *California v. Larve* 409 U.S. 109 (1972).

62 See M. McNulty, 'Pregnancy Police: The Health Policy and Legal Implications of Punishing Pregnant Women for Harm to Their Fetuses' (1987) 16 *New York University Review of Law and Social Change* 277, at 310. McNulty gave the example of *In re Male R*, 102 Misc. 2d 1, 10 n. 18, 422 N.Y.S.2d 819 (Fam. CT. 1979) where the court refused to hold that a child suffering drug withdrawal was 'actually impaired' within the meaning of the child abuse statute because such a finding would offend the constitutional prohibition of vagueness.

63 Human Rights Act 1998, Article 7(1): 'No punishment without law: 1. No one shall be held guilty of any criminal offence on account of any act or omission which did not constitute a criminal offence under national or international law at the time when it was committed. Nor shall a heavier penalty be imposed than the one that was applicable at the time the criminal offence was committed.'

64 *SW v. United Kingdom* (1995) 21 EHRR 363.

65 *Dekker v. Stichting Vormingscentrum Voor Jonge Volwassen (VJV – Centrum) Plus* Case 177/88 [1991] IRLR 10

66 *Handels – Og Kontorfunktionaerernes Forband I Danmark [acting for Hertz] v. Dansk Arbejdsqiverforening [acting for Aldi Marked K/S]* Case 179/88 [1991] IRLR 31.

67 See N. Bamforth, 'Scrutiny: The Treatment of Pregnancy Under European Community Sex Discrimination Law' (1995) 1(1) *European Public Law* 59 at 60.

68 Human Rights Act 1998, Article 14: 'Prohibition on Discrimination: The enjoyment of the rights and freedoms set forth in this Convention shall be secured without discrimination on any ground such as sex, race, colour, language, religion, political or other opinion, national or social origin, association with a national minority, property, birth or other status.' Note the list is not closed and, if pregnancy is viewed as a 'status', then discrimination on grounds of pregnancy is prohibited.

69 *Robinson v. California* 370 U.S. 660 (1962). Following the case of *Linder v. U.S.* 268 U.S. S, 18 (1925) where the Supreme Court held that drug addiction is a disease that requires medical treatment as opposed to criminalization.

70 See for example B. Cuoma, 'Mens Rea and Status Criminality' (1967) 40 *South Californian Law Review* 463, at 487. However, in *Powell v. Texas* 392 U.S. 514 (1968) the Supreme Court rejected Cuomo's view holding that public drunkenness is an act rather than a status and therefore capable of being a crime. Nevertheless D. Korver in 'The Constitutionality of Punishing Pregnant Substance Abusers under Drug Trafficking Laws: The Criminalization of a Bodily Function' (1991) 32 *Boston College Law Review* 629 at 633 suggests that Powell is not applicable in the case of fetal abuse. At 658: 'Because criminal responsibility can only be imposed for the act of taking drugs during pregnancy, rather than for placental delivery alone, Florida and other states prosecuting pregnant drug addicts under drug trafficking statutes are really punishing the woman for their drug use, coupled with the status of pregnancy.'

71 See *Eisenstadt v. Baird* 405 U.S. 438 (1971) which held that the right of non-married couples to use contraception is protected under the Fourteenth Amendment. Also S. Faludi, *Backlash, The Undeclared War Against American Women* (Crown Publishers:

New York, 1992) reviewed by R.L. Eisenberg, 'An Unlady-Like Response to Legal Conceptions of Women' (1992) 105 *Harvard Law Review* 2104. See also American Civil Liberties Union commentary such as M. Oberman, 'Commentary: The Control of Pregnancy and the Criminalization of Femaleness' (1992) 7 *Berkeley Women's Law Review* 1, at 2: 'The criminal justice system's responses reflect a belief that some of these women should not be having sexual intercourse, others should not be bearing children, still others should not be permitted to parent their children, and still others should not be permitted to terminate their pregnancies.' Oberman was particularly concerned that poor women, younger women and black women are over-represented in the fetal abuse criminal statistics.

72   *Michael M v. Superior Court* 450 U.S. 464 (1981). This is supported by the view of Balisy, *op. cit.*, 1232. Balisy claimed that fetal abuse legislation does not necessarily offend equal protection rights, because they exist to prevent criminalization of one sex's conduct and exempting the conduct of the opposite sex when the same conduct poses similar dangers. In this case, the danger of a man imbibing alcohol is not the same as the danger of a pregnant woman imbibing alcohol, therefore there is no unfairness on equal protection grounds. Balisy noted that should the male's conduct be proved relevant in causing similar harm then it too should be subject to criminal sanctions.

73   D.E. Roberts, 'Punishing Drug Addicts who have Babies: Women of Color, Equality, and the Right of Privacy' (1991) 104 *Harvard Law Review* 1419.

74   *Roe v. Wade* 410 U.S. 113 (1973).

75   S. Law, *Rethinking Sex and the Constitution*, (1984) 132 *U. PA. L. REV.* 955 at 1009.

76   *Ibid.*

77   Note though, that the European Union supports Article 40.3.3 of the Constitution of Ireland and thereby protects the Irish constitutional right to life of the unborn. See D. R. Phelan, 'Right to Life of the Unborn v. Promotion of Trade in Services: The European Court of Justice and the Normative Shaping of the European Union' (1992) 55 *Modern Law Review* 670.

78   *Engel v. Netherlands* (1976) 1 EHRR 647 at para. 58.

79   *Guzzardi v. Italy* (1980) 3 EHRR 333.

80   U.S. CONSTITUTION Amendment 14, Section 1: 'Nor shall any State deprive any person of life, liberty, or property, without due process of law ...' See commentary of M.L. Stearns, 'Maternal Duties During Pregnancy: Toward a Conceptual Framework' (1986) 21(3) *New England Law Review* 595 at 599.

81   For example, in *People v. Morabito*, N.Y., 580 N.Y.S.2d 843 (1992) Martina Greyhound was charged with reckless endangerment for allegedly sniffing paint fumes whilst pregnant. After her arrest, she obtained an abortion and the charges were dropped.

82   This argument is often referred to as the 'slippery slope' argument. Proponents of this view are numerous, see McNulty, *op. cit.*, and M.A. Field, 'Controlling the Woman to Protect the Fetus' (1989) 17 *Legal Journal of Medicine and Health Care* 114 for example.

83   *Buck v. Bell*, 274 U.S. 200 (1927).

84   In *Skinner v. Oklahoma*, 316 U.S. 535, 541 (1942) the Court affirmed the fundamental 'value of reproductive autonomy over a majoritarian decision in favor of sterilization'.

85   *Griswold v. Connecticut* 381 U.S. 479 (1965).

86   *Cleveland Board of Education v. La Fleur* 414 U.S. 632 (1974). See also *Eisenstadt v. Baird* 405 U.S. 438 (1971), where it was held at 453 that the right of privacy 'is the right of the individual, married or single, to be free from unwarranted governmental intrusion into matters so fundamentally affecting a person as the decision whether to bear or beget a child'. Also *Whalen v. Roe* 429 U.S. 589 (1977) at 600 upheld the right to privacy in the context of marriage, procreation, contraception, family relationships, child rearing and education.

87   *Roe v. Wade, op. cit.* Hereafter referred to as *Roe.*
88   *Roe, ibid.,* 161. See also R. Manson and J. Marlot, 'A New Crime, Fetal Neglect: State
      Intervention to Protect the Unborn – Protection at What Cost?' (1987) 24 *California
      Western Law Review* 161 who contended that extension of the criminal law to include
      fetal abuse goes against the rationale of *Roe.*
89   See M.C. Segers and T.A. Byrnes (Eds.) *Abortion Politics in the American States* (M.E.
      Sharp: New York and London, 1995), at 5.
90   For example in *City of Akron v. Akron Center for Reproductive Health Inc.,* 103 S. Ct.
      2481 (1983) it was said at 2487: 'These cases come to us a decade after we held in *Roe
      v. Wade* that the right of privacy, grounded in the concept of personal liberty guaranteed
      by the Constitution encompasses a woman's right to decide whether to terminate her
      pregnancy. Legislative responses to the Court's decision have required us on several
      occasions, and again today, to define the limits of a State's authority to regulate the
      performance of abortions. And arguments continue to be made, in these cases as well,
      that we erred in interpreting the Constitution. Nonetheless, the doctrine of *stare decisis,*
      while perhaps never entirely persuasive on a Constitutional question, is a doctrine that
      demands respect in a society governed by the rule of law. We respect it today, and
      reaffirm *Roe v. Wade.'*
91   *Maher v. Roe* 432 U.S. 464 (1977), *Beal v. Doe,* 432 U.S. 438 (1977).
92   *Ibid.,* at 483.
93   *Harris v. McRae* 448 U.S. 297, 324-26 (1980).
94   *Webster v. Reproductive Health Services,* 109 S.Ct. 3040 (1989).
95   See also *Rust v. Sullivan,* 500 U.S. (1991) where it was affirmed that denial of public
      funding for abortion did not offend the Constitution. For criticism see D.
      Hirschenbaum, 'When CRACK is the Only Choice: The Effect of a Negative Right of
      Privacy on Drug-Addicted Women' (2000) 15 *Berkeley Women's L.J.* 327.
96   The relevant statute, MO. REV. STAT. No. 1.205.1(1)-(2) (1986) pronounces that:
      '[t]he life of each human being begins at conception. ... [u]nborn children have
      protectable interests in life, health, and well-being.' It goes on to state at No. 1.205.2,
      that fetuses should be provided with 'all the rights, privileges, and immunities available
      to other persons, citizens, and residents of this state'.
97   For example *California v. Smith,* 59 Cal. App. 3d 751, 129 Cal. Rptr. 498 (1976) where
      a homicide charge against a man for killing a pre-viable fetus was dropped on the
      ground that *Roe, op. cit.,* only gives personhood status to viable fetuses.
98   J.A. Parness and S.K. Pritchard, 'To Be or Not to Be: Protecting the Unborn's
      Potentiality of Life' (1982) 51(2) *Cincinnati Law Review* 257 at 268.
99   *Webster, op. cit.,* 3050. Chief Justice Rehnquist held that the declaration merely
      expressed the state's preference for childbirth over abortion without in any way
      prohibiting the latter.
100   *Roe, op. cit.,* 4003. Blackmun J, in his dissenting opinion, called the decision: '... an
      implicit invitation to every state to enact more restrictive abortion laws, and to assert
      their interest in potential life as of the moment of conception.' Where *Roe* made
      abortion a privacy right, *Webster* redefined it as a 'liberty interest' thereby diminishing
      the force of the right.
101   *Planned Parenthood v. Casey,* 112 S.Ct. 2791 (1992).
102   *Roe, op. cit.,* 163.
103   *Roe, ibid.,* 163-4.
104   S.S. Balisy, 'Maternal Substance Abuse: The Need to Provide Legal Protection for the
      Fetus' (1987) 60 *Southern California Law Review* 1209 at 1220.
105   A right that is protected by the Constitution.
106   *Commonwealth v. Pellegrini* No. 87970 (Mass. Super. Ct. Plymouth Cty, Oct 15 1990),
      where it was held that: '... because of the intrusion required by this prosecution;
      namely, the state's attempt to reach and deter behavior during pregnancy, [the
      woman's] privacy rights are seriously threatened.'

107   For example, Utah Code Ann. 62A-4a-411 (1997) holds that any person required to report a case of suspected fetal alcohol syndrome or drug dependency, who wilfully fails to do so, is guilty of a misdemeanor. Similarly statutes exist in Minnesota (MINN.STAT. Section 626.556 (1988)); and Oklahoma (OKLA.STAT.ANN. tit. 21 Section 846 (West 1989)).

108   A number of academics and ethics committees hold this view. See for example L. Paltrow, 'Fetal Abuse: Should We Recognize it as a Crime?' (1989) *American Bar Association Journal*, August, 38, who quotes the California Medical Association as stating: 'Prosecution is counterproductive to the public interest as it may discourage a woman from seeking prenatal care or dissuade her from providing accurate information to health-care providers.' There is also statistical evidence. For example, M.L. Poland, M.P. Dombrowski, J.W. Ager, R.J. Sokol, 'Punishing Pregnant Drug Users: Enhancing the Flight From Care' *Drug and Alcohol Dependence* 31 (1993), 199 interviewed 142 low-income postpartum women to ascertain their attitudes to potential effects of a punitive law on the behaviour of substance-using pregnant women. 14.8 per cent admitted using illicit drugs in pregnancy. 'A goodness-of-fit chi-square analysis revealed that subjects believed a punitive law would be a significant deterrent to substance-using gravida seeking prenatal care, drug testing or drug treatment ($P <$ 0.01). Comments indicated that substance-using pregnant women would "go underground" to avoid detection and treatment for fear of incarceration and loss of their children.'

109   See for example, E. Atkins, 'Reporting Fetal Abuse through California's Child Abuse and Neglect Reporting Act' (1992) 21(1) *Southwestern University Law Review* 105. See also K.L. Moss, 'Legal Issues: Drug Testing of Postpartum Women and Newborns as the Basis for Civil and Criminal Proceedings' (1990) 23 *Clearing House Review* 1406.

110   See K.L. Moss, *ibid*. Moss criticized states which enforce such testing and referred at 1406 to a 'serious health and civil liberties crisis' violating privacy, due process and sacrificing a valuable doctor/patient relationship. She argued at 1407 that discrimination against the poor is also at issue: 'The imposition of drug tests is often arbitrary and discriminatory, targeting primarily the poor.' Not only are the drug tests unreliable, but they also fail to help the fetus in any way (though may alert authorities to potential abuse of the child after it is born).

111   See for example, D.E. Roberts, 'Drug-Addicted Women Who Have Babies' (1990) 26 *Trial* 56. T. Dobson and K. Eby, 'Criminal Liability for Substance Abuse During Pregnancy: The Controversy of Maternal Versus Fetal Rights' (1992) 36 *Saint Louis University Law Review*, 655 at 676 gave the example of MINN.STAT. No. 626.5562 subd. 2(c) (Supp. 1989) which alters the definition of child abuse to include pre-natal exposure to controlled substances as evidenced by toxicology tests at birth, and gives immunity to healthcare workers performing the tests without the parent's consent. They say: 'In essence, the scope of the amendments allows the state to identify pregnant drug abusers and to assume full control over the mother in the event she fails to cooperate with a predetermined course of treatment.' At 678.

112   See for example, A. Gillmore, 'Is the Fetus a Patient?' *Canadian Medical Association Journal* 128 (1983), 1472.

113   For criticism of reporting laws see S.A. Garcia, 'Maternal Drug Abuse: Laws and Ethics as Agents of Just Balances and Therapeutic Interventions', *The International Journal of the Addictions* 28(13) (1993), 1311 at 1316 where she notes that by 1991 at least eight states had laws requiring doctors to report cases of illicit drug use in pregnancy.

114   *Ferguson v. City of Charleston S.C.*, 186 F.3d 469, 485-86 (4th Cir. 1999), rev'd, 532 U.S. 67, 121 S. Ct. 1281 (2001). The Fourth Amendment protects '[t]he right of the people to be secure in their persons, houses, papers, and effects against unreasonable searches and seizures'. U.S. CONST. Fourth Amendment.

115   B.M. Nahas, 'Drug Tests, Arrests and Fetuses: A Comment on the US Supreme Court's

Narrow Opinion in *Ferguson v City of Charleston*' (2001) 8 *Cardozo Women's Law Journal* 105 at 108. C. M. Bulger, 'In the Best Interests of the Child? Race and Class Discrimination in Prenatal Drug Use Prosecutions' (1999) 19 *Third World L.J.* 709 at 721: 'The arrests resembled the conduct of a state in a totalitarian regime, with police apprehending some patients within days, or even hours, of giving birth, and hauling them to jail in handcuffs and leg shackles. Police attached handcuffs to three-inch wide leather belts that were wrapped around the women's stomachs. Some women were still bleeding from the delivery; when one complained, she was told to sit on a towel at the jail. Another reported that she was grabbed in a chokehold and forcefully escorted into treatment. One woman who was pregnant at the time of her arrest sat in a jail cell waiting to give birth. Another pregnant woman was transported weekly from the jail to the hospital in handcuffs and leg irons for prenatal care; she was still in handcuffs and leg irons when authorities took her to the hospital in labor. She was kept handcuffed to her bed during the entire delivery.'

116   B. Siegal, 'In the Name of the Children: Get Treatment or Go to Jail, One South Carolina Hospital Tells Drug-Abusing Pregnant Women. Now It Faces a Lawsuit and a Civil-Rights Investigation,' *L.A. Times*, 14 August 1994, at 7; 1994 WL 2332673.

117   *Op. cit.*

118   Nahas, *op. cit.*

119   In *Ingraham v. Wright* 430 U.S. 651 (1977) the Supreme Court upheld the right to bodily integrity in the context of school corporeal punishment on the basis of the Fourth Amendment. J.E.B. Myers, 'Abuse and Neglect of the Unborn: Can the State Intervene?' (1984) 20(1) *Duquesne Law Review* 1, at 58 felt that these rights '... empower a woman to resist governmentally imposed regulation of her conduct during pregnancy'.

120   See *Union Pacific Railway v. Botsford*, 141 U.S. 250 (1891) where it was said at 251: 'No right is held more sacred, or is more carefully guarded ... than the right of every individual to the possession and control of his own person, free from all restraint or interference of others.'

121   See *Griswold v. Connecticut, op. cit.*

122   Several cases support this contention, such as *Pierce v. Society of Sisters*, 268 U.S. 510 (1925) which recognized the rights of parents to teach their children and refrain from sending them to school.

123   See for example, M. McNulty, 'Pregnancy Police: The Health Policy and Legal Implications of Punishing Pregnant Women for Harm to Their Fetuses' (1987) 16 *New York University Review of Law and Social Change* 277, at 315.

124   S.S. Balisy, *op. cit.,* 1232.

125   *In re Torres* No. N-3968/88 (N.Y., Fam. Ct., Bronx County Oct. 7, 1988).

126   *In re Torres, ibid.,* at 6 the court held: '[t]o carry the Law Guardian's argument to its logical extension, the State would be able to supersede a mother's custody rights to her child if she smoked cigarettes during her pregnancy, or ate junk food, or did too much physical labor or did not exercise enough. The list of potential intrusions is long and constitutes entirely unacceptable violations of the bodily integrity of women.'

127   See Chapter 2 p. 27.

128   Human Rights Act 1998, Article 8(1): 'Everyone has the right to respect for his private and family life, his home and his correspondence.'

129   *NHS Trust A v M; NHS Trust B v H* [2001] Lloyd's Rep. Med. 28.

130   *Airedale NHS Trust v Bland* [1993] AC 789.

131   *Peters v The Netherlands* (1994) 77A/B D.R.

132   *Osman v United Kingdom* (1997) 29 EHRR 245, at 305: 'For the court, and having regard to the nature of the right protected by Article 2, a right fundamental in the scheme of the Convention, it is sufficient for an applicant to show that the authorities did not do all that could reasonably be expected of them to avoid a real and immediate risk to life of which they have or ought to have knowledge.'

133 Though a higher test is utilized by the High Court in persistent vegetative state cases whereby the court can reject the medical opinion that withdrawal of treatment is in the best interests of the patient. *Frenchay Healthcare NHS Trust v S* [1994] 2 All E.R. 403.

134 Human Rights Act 1998 Article 8(2): 'There shall be no interference by a public authority with the exercise of this right except such as is in accordance with the law and is necessary in a democratic society in the interests of national security, public safety or the economic well-being of the country, for the prevention of disorder or crime, for the protection of health or morals, or for the protection of the rights and freedoms of others.' See Chapter 4 p. 73.

135 R. Holland, 'Criminal Sanctions for Drug Abuse During Pregnancy: The Antithesis of Fetal Health' (1991) 8 *New York Law School Journal of Human Rights* 415 at 434.

136 *Commonwealth v. Kemp,* 75 Westmoreland L.J. 5, at 11 (Pa. Ct. C.P. 1992) affirmed, 643 A. 2d 705 (Pa. Super. CT. 1994).

137 See for example, G.P. Smith II, 'Fetal Abuse; Culpable Behaviour by Pregnant Women or Parental Immunity?' (1988) 3 *Journal of Law and Health* 223.

138 See J.A. Parness, 'Social Commentary: Values and Legal Personhood' (1981) 83 *West Virginia Law Review* 487 at 498.

Chapter 6

Alternatives to Extended Criminalization

Chapter 1 argues that the fetus does not deserve human rights by virtue of the fact that it merely has *potential* to become a person in law. When it is born and achieves legal personhood the law recognizes some rights retrospectively, but it is put forward that these retrospective rights should not extend to criminalization of recent mothers for acts harming or killing the fetus born alive. This is because such a policy would breach the woman's human rights[1] and upset the carefully maintained balance between the state's maintenance of those rights and its interest in protecting the fetus and resulting child. Chapter 2 recommends that potential conflicts between maternal and fetal interests can be successfully adjudicated by placing greater importance on the negative obligation on the state to withhold interference than the positive duty to intervene on her behalf and to the detriment of the fetus.

There are further endemic moral problems with criminalizing activities harmful to the fetus, when the harm is often a bi-product of poverty, race, ignorance, lack of education, lack of appropriate funding and health problems (with the associated lack of adequate treatment). Pregnant women who harm the fetus, later born alive, are usually from the poorest and least privileged quarters of society.[2] In the USA the lack of a welfare state and the gradual erosion of the principle in *Roe v Wade*[3] have led to a system protective of the rich person's privacy and dismissive of the poor's.[4] On both sides of the Atlantic Ocean an active programme of state-funded treatment and education is necessary to protect the human rights of the pregnant woman and reduce the incidence of fetal harm.

Engaging in activities that are harmful to the individual, the fetus and to society involves an element of culpability. The moral responsibility of women to protect the health of a fetus, especially when they intend to bring it to term, is not disputed. However, the focus here is on the appropriate *legal* response to the ethical dilemma. In some circumstances, the culpability is such that the activity is criminalized. Where this is achieved in a non-discriminatory manner (such as criminalization of the activity, rather than the activity coupled with pregnancy), this is an acceptable means of addressing societal condemnation. In other cases, however, the required degree of culpability may be lacking due to physical or mental illness, or the addictive nature of the substance in question. In those circumstances, society has a duty not merely to condemn but to aid. Having argued vehemently as to what policy should be *avoided* in order to address the problems associated with the harmful acts and omissions of pregnant women, this chapter considers a means of tackling the problem in a manner protective of the pregnant woman's human rights. Education and treatment (and in some cases mandated treatment) are suggested as realistic and potentially effective measures by which to offer aid and protection to mother and fetus.

Education

In the Introduction, the harmful effects that a pregnant woman's activities can have on the fetus and child born alive were illustrated. Though widely recognized as a problem in the USA, the public in the UK are slower to appreciate or document it and the problem is escalating at a more sedate pace. As a result, educational initiatives aimed at pregnant women against the harmful effects of (legal and illegal) drugs have been fewer in number.

In general, pregnant women are keen to know how to optimize the health of the fetus and those healthcare professionals in regular contact with the pregnant woman work hard to promote this.[5] Women who are addicted to legal or illegal substances can still be reached through this medium, but these women have conflicting desires to feed their addiction and protect the fetus. As they are less likely to attend antenatal classes and actively seek guidance, education must be brought to them. In other words, health promotion activities need to target the poorer sectors of society as well as those known or likely to be involved in licit or illicit drug use. For this group, lack of education is a very real problem. Field,[6] commentating on the US system, suggested that many women who damage the fetus through drug use, are ignorant as to the effects of their addiction. Field argued that educational measures could have a positive effect on resources, and prevent the unjust incarceration and stigmatization of pregnant women. However, the educational intervention would have to target the women rather than relying on them to seek guidance.

As Greer[7] suggested, what are needed are state campaigns, increased access to pre-natal information, and specialist support groups. Some such efforts are being made in the US. Various states have mandated educational initiatives aimed at the public and healthcare providers.[8] For example New York City, Columbus, Philadelphia, Kentucky and Washington D.C. require notices in public places where alcohol is sold, warning of the effects of drinking whilst pregnant or trying to conceive, and there have been a number of 'National Fetal Alcohol Syndrome Weeks'.[9]

Unfortunately, education is by no means the easy option. The effect is slow and widespread as opposed to the swift example set by criminalizing individuals. Commitment to education and treatment is likely to cost more than simply incarcerating offending women for the duration of their pregnancy.[10] Persuading individuals to heed education is particularly difficult when they suffer from a harmful addiction. For example, a 1994

English mass media campaign on smoking and pregnancy resulted in no significant changes in the smoking habits among the relevant pregnant women and their partners.[11] However, it is suggested that this may simply be the fault of the particular campaign, for the same paper refers to many successful campaigns and suggests certain criteria which should be employed before a measurable success rate can be achieved.[12]

The UK Health Education Authority Smoking and Pregnancy campaign from 1991-1996 was monitored over four years. The rather disappointing results were reported in 1997.[13] Though a proportion of women who smoked prior to pregnancy gave up either once they intended to become pregnant or during pregnancy,[14] the number of pregnant women who smoke actually rose over the course of the campaign. Thus by 1996 one in three pregnant women reported that they smoked, compared with only one in four in 1992. In general terms, the number of young women who smoke has risen over the study period, and the report indicates that the increase of smoking in pregnancy may be a result of the rise in smoking prevalence in teenage girls and young women.[15] Rather than give up altogether, pregnant women tend to cut down on smoking (40 per cent of pregnant smoking women cut down in 1996).[16] Thus the results indicate that younger women should be targeted in future campaigns, as should partners of pregnant women, as this remains a factor strongly influencing prevalence of smoking in the pregnant. The report also stressed the need for health professionals to receive adequate training and resources to deliver smoking and pregnancy advice. As a result, the Health Education Authority produced an information pack, 'Action on Smoking and Pregnancy' in 1997.[17]

In Europe there is a growing commitment to reducing the impact of smoking. On 22 June 1998 the Council of Ministers adopted the Directive banning tobacco advertising.[18] However, the Directive was opposed both by Germany who took their complaint to the European Court of Justice, and by four UK-based tobacco companies.[19] The companies unsuccessfully contended that the issue of advertising tobacco was within the remit of national law as opposed to that of the European Union.

The UK Report on the Scientific Committee on Tobacco and Health in March 1998 advised that more scientific work was needed to determine the nature of problems caused by smoking in pregnancy to the fetus and child born alive.[20] It added: 'The public should be kept aware of the known hazards of smoking in pregnancy.'[21] The report also advised that paternal smoking around the time of conception could increase the risk of certain cancers in the issue.[22] Educational initiatives to this effect would therefore be advisable, though this element does not appear in the White Paper *Smoking Kills*. The follow-up Scientific Committee on Tobacco and Health Statement, 2001[23] stated that 'Smoking in pregnancy causes adverse outcomes notably miscarriage, reduced birth weight for gestation and perinatal death'.[24] It targeted the pregnant smoker as one of three specialist groups which may require 'intensive support by specialist counsellors'.[25]

Smoking Kills was released in November 1998 in order to implement the European Directive.[26] Paragraph 5 deals exclusively with smoking cessation in pregnant women. It recognized that smoking in pregnancy is harmful to the fetus as it potentially leads to a lower birth-weight and passes on harmful carcinogens.[27] 24 per cent of women smoke in pregnancy and only 33 per cent give up whilst pregnant.[28] The White Paper also recognized that helping pregnant women to stop smoking is cost effective: 'This is because smoking in pregnancy leads to low birthweight babies who may need very costly intensive care treatment. Savings to the NHS can amount to between three and six times the cost of providing help to pregnant women to give up smoking.'[29]

As a result, two initiatives were proposed in the White Paper. The first was to make pregnant smokers the focus of action at local level, especially in the Health Action Zones, which will receive up to £60 million extra funding in all. Part of this will be allocated to smoking cessation.[30] There are few times in a woman's life when the desire to stop smoking is stronger, and therefore this is a particularly good time to encourage it. Follow-up is essential, however, in order to prevent reoccurrence, which is of course, passively harmful to the child as well as the mother.[31] The second initiative involved local NHS action in a national public campaign to change young women's attitudes to smoking. Part of this was tailored to prevention of smoking in pregnancy.[32]

Whether the addiction involves alcohol, tobacco or illegal drugs, the educational directives best serving the pregnant woman and fetus are those that campaign against the addiction before pregnancy actually commences. Therefore the wealth of campaigns that are aimed at the wider population or segments of the population most likely to fall pregnant (which cannot be comprehensively covered in this chapter) are of extreme importance. There is no doubt as to the significant death toll resulting from smoking tobacco. Alcohol and illegal drugs do not have such a significant death toll and therefore receive less attention. Though curbing smoking in pregnancy would aid in the prevention of one of the most common causes of harm to the fetus, drinking and drug abuse need to be made the focus of more educational initiatives.[33]

It is not possible to target all potential (legal or illegal) drug-using pregnant women and some initiatives have focused on women who have used drugs in their first pregnancy. At this stage, though initial educational interventions have evidently failed, there is opportunity to offer the resulting child improved chances of health and happiness by helping the parents, and to prevent reoccurrence if the woman should once again become pregnant. Project T.E.A.M.S.[34] (Training, Education, and Management Skills; Meeting the Needs of Infants Pre-natally Exposed to Drugs) is one such example; it was set up in 1986 and ran for two years in order to increase the skills of professionals dealing with the said infants and parents. Educational initiatives present an opportunity to empower pregnant women and arm them with the necessary resources to combat their addiction. Some of the schemes outlined above include elements of counselling and access to medical care but more organized treatment may be called for to complement education. Such treatment must be both affordable and accessible.

Treatment

Voluntary Treatment

It has been suggested in the preceding chapters that what many women need to combat their problem (and especially those with serious drug addictions), is treatment as opposed to extended criminalization. In the case of tobacco addiction, education may enable a self-help remedy for some pregnant women. In the USA nicotine replacement therapy is available to aid this process.[35] It was not advised in the UK until 2001 when the Scientific Committee on Tobacco and Health recommended that it might be used under medical supervision for pregnant women who smoke heavily and cannot give up without it. There is currently a lack of data as to the effects of nicotine replacement therapy on the developing fetus, leading the Committee to call for a randomized controlled trial on the matter.[36]

Aiding pregnant women with an addiction to a Class A drug is more complicated. Once pregnant, simply withdrawing from the drug in a 'cold turkey' fashion might be harmful to the fetus, as it too suffers withdrawal symptoms. Continuing drug use is also harmful and the fetus successfully carried to term will have to suffer withdrawal at birth. Expert help and treatment is required to aid the mother who wishes her withdrawal to cause the least possible distress to the fetus.

It is argued that the criminal law should operate against pregnant women as it does against any other individual, but activities that are legal for the non-pregnant should not be criminalized for the pregnant. The American College of Obstetricians and Gynaecologists opposes legislation imposing criminal sanctions on women who use drugs in pregnancy, on legal, pragmatic and moral grounds. Nevertheless, such sanctions are utilized in some states.[37] Criminalization has deterrent and retributive aims against women whose activities harm the fetus or child born alive.[38] Yet such policies ultimately lose sight of the fact that the fetus and woman are inextricably linked. What is needed is a policy that focuses on helping both woman and fetus by fighting the harmful addiction. Treatment must be voluntary (unless it is applied in a coercive manner as a non-discriminatory sentencing option) and used in conjunction with education. Where treatment is imposed in an attempt to override refusal to seek medical help during pregnancy, the implications for maternal autonomy are as serious as prosecution.

As with education, treatment is made all the more difficult by virtue of the fact that those who misuse drugs are less likely to seek medical help whilst pregnant. Apathy, guilt, inability to control the addiction and fear that their child will eventually be taken from them because of their behaviour whilst pregnant[39] may all dissuade pregnant women from adequate treatment and so put both the woman and fetus at further risk. Even if the woman opts for treatment, it might take several attempts before success is achieved.[40] Treatment programmes will not reach all those in need (though the same can be said of criminalization policies) and some women will find themselves unable to complete a treatment programme.[41] On the other hand, it may be that the thought of losing or harming the fetus or having the child removed from her after birth due to her inability to care for the child[42] will give the pregnant woman resolve that was lacking prior to pregnancy. Aided by the state, this might represent the ideal opportunity to help her (and the fetus) through treatment.

The Department of Health Report *Why Mothers Die*[43] reported that recreational and regular substance misuse caused five deaths in pregnancy or early motherhood in the given period. The problem that those most likely to misuse drugs are also less likely to seek medical intervention during pregnancy was reiterated:

> It is clear that some women who died had felt inhibited about seeking help. The socially excluded, the very young, or those from some minority ethnic groups did not always appear to have their specific concerns understood. Commissioners and trusts should provide those least likely to use services with the opportunity to gain acceptable professional and social support during their pregnancies.[44]

This bears out the US literature linking poverty and race with inhibition with regard to using medical treatment and accessing medical education. Such groups must be targeted and their inhibitions combated in order to present the women with real choices and adequate help in overcoming their medical and social problems.

The lack of treatment and education undoubtedly result in adverse consequences. McNulty reported that women who do not have access to pre-natal care are three times more likely than mothers who receive adequate care to have babies that die within a year of birth.[45] In the United States, access to pre-natal care is especially low for poor and black women.[46] Many women are uninsured, and even those who are insured are not necessarily covered for pre-natal care.[47] It is often the case that illicit drug-using pregnant women are refused places on drug-treatment programmes because of the problems incumbent with treatment (where the fetus may suffer injury as a result). In one of the most high-profile cases, *Florida v. Johnson*,[48] conviction of the cocaine-addicted African-American pregnant woman occurred after she had been turned away from a treatment programme. Robin-Vergeer[49] extolled the necessity of making more places available and educating women as to their availability, stating that in 1991 only 11 per cent of pregnant addicts received treatment.[50] To this end the American Civil

Liberties Union (ACLU) filed a series of lawsuits against treatment programmes that barred pregnant women.[51] California, in conjunction with their harsh criminalization policy, also demands that drug-treatment programmes give priority to pregnant women.[52] Connecticut and New York have similar policies[53] as do Colorado, Illinois[54] Rhode Island and Washington.[55]

The problems associated with lack of funding to help illicit drug-addicted pregnant women are also perpetuated in relation to alcohol addictions or even to obtaining help for a tobacco addiction. Field[56] recommended that in the United States there should be free pre-natal care for those who cannot afford it. Such pre-natal care also presents an opportunity to impart information and education regarding the health of woman and fetus. In England, the welfare state attempts to lessen the correlation between low-income and ill-health; however the creation of specialist groups to help (illicit or licit) drug-addicted pregnant women to overcome their problems clearly need to be extended.

The fact that women who harm the fetus tend to come from the poorer quarters of society means that criminal law measures will not attack the source of the problem. Punishment will not prevent people from suffering poverty where education and access to treatment can aid the reduction of inequality. McNulty argued that extended criminalization:

> ... would require states to punish economically disadvantaged women for behavior imposed by the state itself through an inadequate patchwork of state health and welfare policies. Improving the currently inadequate maternal-child health care system would promote prenatal health to a far greater degree than would imposing punitive measures. ... The problem of inadequate prenatal care and its consequences cannot be addressed through the criminal law prism of individual culpability. Rather the problem is a systemic one. Resolution will require hard choices about the long-term allocation of scarce resources in society – not token prosecutions that will prove ultimately to be ineffective methods of addressing the problem.[57]

Young[58] stated that criminalization policies discriminate against poor women and in particular poor women from racial minorities. She called for treatment options justified by an 'ethic of care'. This implies that there are different standards of moral responsibility depending on the position of an individual within society. It warrants empathy and understanding as opposed to stark divisions and criminalization. Treatment is the preferred option, and Young made a distinction between treatment that individualizes the woman and treatment that 'develops social solidarity through consciousness-raising and the possibility of collective action'.[59] Therefore if treatment is to work as an option to curb drug abuse in pregnancy, it must not further individualize her. Young criticized the (voluntary and mandatory) programmes, which enforce a strict regime, often with a dress code, discourage friendships or sexual relationships between clients, and carry out random drug testing.[60] As an alternative, Young suggested empowerment through treatment. Education forms a large part of this treatment where individuals are taught to make choices. In short, rather than taking away autonomy, the value should be promoted. Hence medical treatment programmes should be coupled with empowerment strategies, such as discussion groups where drug-using individuals can be made aware of the similar plight of others and help each other through their problems.[61]

In the UK guidance was issued in 1997 on helping drug-using parents,[62] but the issue is notably absent from the high profile Department of Health Drugs Strategy. The Home Secretary is supported by a new Drug Strategy Directorate within the Home Office. A special Health Authority, the National Treatment Agency, was set up in 1995 to oversee the delivery of treatment targets and at a local level Drug Action Teams co-ordinate and apply the strategy. Yet, there are no indications of targets or programmes aimed specifically at the pregnant user. The targets[63] may inadvertently aid pregnant users through the proliferation of treatment centres but are largely concerned with reducing street crime, targeting Class A drugs and aiding those under 25.

The term 'treatment' connotes a number of alternatives for the variety of conditions the pregnant woman may present. The range of activities or omissions that may harm the fetus are diverse. The appropriate treatment may simply involve the payment of additional benefits to enable the woman to abstain from work, attend antenatal classes or follow a specific diet. It might involve counselling to encourage her to combat an addiction, or a drug-treatment programme, or even hospitalization. In the case of an illicit drug habit, she may be characterized as being physically ill, mentally ill or criminal.[64] An explanation of the classifications of the types of illness the pregnant woman might be said to suffer is beyond the scope of this work. However, if she is deemed to have a mental illness then it may be that her ability to consent to treatment (or withhold that consent) is lacking. If the individual is legally incompetent, it might be thought that coercive treatment is the preferable option. Nevertheless, coercion should be resorted to only when the illness requires it, not merely when the woman happens to be pregnant. Coercion should remain a last resort and be applied on the basis of the illness rather than the pregnant status of the individual.

On the cusp between voluntary and mandated treatment, a novel method of tackling the problems associated with drug addiction has been set up in California. The organization is called Children Requiring a Caring Kommunity ('CRACK') and is funded from private donations. Drug-using men and women of child-bearing age enter into a contract under which they are paid to take long-term contraception or undergo sterilization.[65] The aim is 'to offer effective preventive measures to reduce the tragedy of numerous drug affected pregnancies'.[66] A similar initiative was set up in Scotland in 2000.[67] In Scotland the voluntariness of a woman submitting to sterilization for money may be called into question. In the USA the scheme is more dubious still. The scheme targets poor women, and women of colour are over-represented. From 1997 to February 2000, 'CRACK' had 153 participants, all of whom were women. Of these women, approximately 39 per cent were white, 43 per cent African-American, 14 per cent Hispanic and 3 per cent were Native American or bi-racial.[68] The government limits access to safe abortion, limits drug-treatment places and extends a policy of criminal prosecution should the child born alive suffer injury or death as a result of her drug addiction.[69] In short, though a valid attempt to prevent the terrible effects of drug addiction in pregnancy, the programme fails to tackle the social and medical aspects of the problem.

Mandated Treatment

Chapter 5 illustrated that criminalization policies offend human rights and criminal justice objectives and are backward-looking and potentially harmful to both the pregnant woman and the future child. The advantages of education and treatment have been suggested as alternatives. In terms of social use, and many cases of addiction, this method will prove successful over time, though the influences of poverty will unfortunately continue to maintain the significant divergence in the health and education of the poor when compared with the opulent.

One of the primary reasons for the proposal that the law should prevent the subjugation of women's rights during pregnancy is the value of autonomy. Yet there are cases where autonomy is ultimately reduced through addiction. The force of the habit may take precedence over all other concerns, including the individual's personal health and that of the fetus. Therefore there are limited cases where voluntary treatment and education have failed, and enrolment in a treatment centre should be mandated as a sentencing option in criminal law, or as a part of medical treatment (in which case treatment should not be mandated unless the individual lacks the capacity to give or withhold her consent). In either case, the mandated treatment must be formulated so as to place the health and welfare of the addicted individual as of paramount importance. It should not be used as a means of punishment and should not be used merely to protect the fetus. It should only be used on expert medical advice and should be applied indiscriminately to the pregnant and non-pregnant alike.

Yet other commentators have advocated mandated treatment programmes that go far beyond these limited boundaries. In those states where alcohol and other activities are illegal, should harm result to the fetus, mandated treatment is sometimes utilized as a means of protecting the fetus rather than the pregnant woman. It becomes a substitute for imprisonment, with all the incumbent violations of autonomy and privacy. For example, Chan[70] suggested that New York should legislate in order to help combat the problems associated with drug-using pregnant women. Chan advocated giving pregnant women the choice of either treatment or imprisonment. Similarly, a 1989 bill[71] proposed a three-year prison sentence for harm caused to a fetus through both illicit (such as cocaine) and licit (such as alcohol) drug use. The purpose of the bill was to prevent substance abuse and effect rehabilitation. Johnsen[72] was critical of the bill on the ground that the state's interest in reducing the number of impaired new-borns does not rise to the level of a compelling interest supporting the use of special penalties.

Steverson[73] put forward a compromise position of making fetal abuse a crime, but avoiding incarceration wherever possible. This has the advantage of being both prospective and of avoiding a false distinction between currently licit and illicit substances when each harms the fetus in a similar manner. Though treatment and education of pregnant women are necessary to staunch the flow of injured new-borns, Steverson contended that this is not an adequate solution. She suggested that criminalization is needed, but that incarceration should be avoided where possible, giving the woman a choice of incarceration or probation. The terms of the latter would include drug treatment and absence of pregnancy.[74] Yet, this presupposes that the court is unable to determine whether the individual is ill or criminal.

Mathieu[75] recommended community-based out-patient treatment programmes coupled with guaranteed access to pre-natal care, nutritional support and education wherever a drug-using woman (potentially including pregnant alcoholics and cigarette smokers under certain conditions)[76] intends to carry her child to term. However, rather than stressing empowerment and state commitment promoting the autonomy of the pregnant woman, Mathieu believed that the treatment should be imposed where it is not actively sought.[77] Boling[78] was critical of this view stating that: 'we don't need more justifications for blaming and holding accountable pregnant women who use drugs; rather, we need more discussions of public accountability and responsibility for providing the kind of support, especially universal health care and prenatal care.'

Though forcing women to accept treatment does not carry with it the same stigma as criminalization, it remains a coercive response to the problem and should only be used as a general non-discriminatory response to illicit drug addiction. Criticism of Mathieu's proposal is not only based on ideological grounds, but also on grounds of basic resource implication. Chavkin[79] pointed out that medical, public health and support services have been cut in the US, to the extent that many poor, addicted pregnant women simply cannot get treatment. Even were Mathieu's ideas to prove morally acceptable, they would not be possible to implement in the US in the present climate.

It is therefore suggested that the only places for mandated treatment programmes are first those cases where treatment is imposed on expert medical advice, as part of the criminal sentence and regardless of the pregnant status of the individual. For example a criminal offender who is incarcerated may be forced to abstain from drugs during the term of his sentence, and might be given a place on a drug-treatment programme to aid him in this process. Secondly, mandated treatment may be acceptable when a patient is not competent to make an informed choice and it is deemed to be medically in his best interests to be incarcerated and treated under the Mental Health Act 1983. This is the position currently maintained in England and Wales.

However if the planned Mental Health Bill[80] is enacted this position is likely to change. The bill was introduced in response to a loophole in the Mental Health Act 1983 which prevents the detention of individuals unless their condition is therapeutically treatable. Michael Stone of Kent was one of many individuals with a severe, untreatable personality disorder who lived in the community. In 1996 he murdered Lin Russell and her 5-year old daughter, Megan.[81]

The draft bill, which has proved extremely controversial, has raised a number of human rights issues. The Joint Committee on Human Rights[82] is concerned with the proposed definition of 'mental disorder',[83] which could significantly widen the range of people liable to compulsory treatment.[84] The equally wide definition of 'treatment' under the draft bill means that, contrary to existing provisions under the Mental Health Act 1983, a person could be detained even when there is no prospect of any treatment which will actually improve the patient's condition.[85] Coupled with the proposed removal of the provision in the Mental Health Act 1983 expressly preventing detention 'by reason only of promiscuity or other immoral conduct, sexual deviancy or dependence on alcohol or drugs', this is extremely worrying. The exclusion of this term might lead to a breach of both Article 8 (the right to respect for private life) and Article 10 (the right to freedom of expression) of the Human Rights Act 1998 and the European Convention of Human Rights.[86]

Clause 6[87] of the draft bill sets out four relevant conditions to be satisfied before a patient can be compulsorily detained. These conditions, taken with the definitions of mental disorder and treatment, would allow the compulsory detention of an individual in order to protect others, even when they have neither been charged nor convicted of a criminal offence and nothing can be done to alleviate their condition. If 'others' are taken to include the fetus born alive, then compulsory detention under mental health law might be used to enforce treatment or, even when there is no effective treatment available, to prevent access to the harmful substance.

The problems endemic in such a policy are similar to those relating to criminalization, most significant being the potential breaches of human rights.[88] The definition of addiction as a psychiatric illness could lead to the compulsory detention and treatment of alcoholics and drug addicts,[89] not merely when their own health is threatened, but to prevent harm to others. The Mental Health Alliance,[90] a coalition of over 50 organizations, opposed such a move. It will now be introduced to the House of Commons where it is likely to face significant opposition. Should the more controversial aspects of the draft bill prevail, it is not unlikely that the provisions will be exercised to prevent harm to the fetus born alive. With such a civil law precedent in operation, what once seemed a giant leap to criminalization would become a mere step.

Conclusion

The latter chapters have established that further criminalization of pregnant women for causing pre-natal harm to the fetus born alive is not a viable policy. On the basis that the pregnant woman's human rights would be unduly compromised by criminalization, treatment and education have been cited as preferable tools in combating what may begin as a culpable activity, but often extends into a medical condition (such as alcohol or drug addiction) heavily associated with poverty and lack of education. Civil and family law remedies exist where treatment and education fail, though these should be utilized in protection of the child born alive rather than as a means of punishing the woman.

Though education and treatment will fail in many instances, they remain the most forward-looking approaches, respectful of the pregnant woman's rights to freedom from discrimination on the basis of pregnancy. It is hoped that the civil law in the UK affirms its recent commitment to these ideals and refrains from court-authorized medical treatment against the will of the woman unless she clearly lacks capacity to make a decision. It is also hoped that England and Wales will not follow the example set by the US and embark on a policy of criminal prosecution of women who harm their child pre-natally. A means of achieving this, as outlined in Chapter 2, is to leave the woman as free as any other competent person with regards to refusing medical or other interventions, but to curb her rights to demand treatment that may prove harmful to the fetus. Yet, more than this is needed if a firm commitment to autonomy is to be made. The state must actively promote autonomy in pregnancy by arming the woman with education and treatment options. Freedom from unwanted medical intervention and empowerment is likely to bring drug-using pregnant women to the healthcare system, where criminalization drives them away. It will create positive peer pressure and support to combat smoking and excessive alcohol consumption, where criminalization creates only negative stigma. It will provide a caring environment where criminalization presents largely unsuitable conditions for pregnancy and child-birth.

Education and treatment options will differ according to the nature of the pregnant woman's harmful activity. Education can tackle a multitude of problems ranging from diet and exercise advice to Class A drug education and rehabilitation. Likewise, treatment is not always reserved for the illegal addictions or uses and can be well utilized to curb smoking and alcohol consumption. To empower her and actively enforce her freedom of choice, education and treatment must be sufficiently marketed, funded and promoted.

Notes

1   As G.J. Annas, 'The Impact Of Medical Technology On The Pregnant Woman's Right To Privacy', *American Journal of Law & Medicine* 13 (1987), 213 at 230, 'Society can never force a woman to take actions for the sake of the fetus without treating her as something less than a competent adult. Education, service provision, and enhanced opportunities seem most likely to improve the plight of fetuses and pregnant women alike. But if we do not follow the road of equal opportunity and provision of reasonable health care, and if sophisticated methods to monitor the health of fetuses are developed, the rights of women could well become subordinate to the welfare of their fetuses. The result would be a return to oppressive gender-based discrimination.'

2   M. McNulty, 'Pregnancy Police: The Health Policy and Legal Implications of Punishing Pregnant Women for Harm to Their Fetuses' (1987) 16 *New York University Review of Law and Social Change* 277, at 292; D.E. Roberts, 'Punishing Drug Addicts who have Babies: Women of Color, Equality, and the Right of Privacy' (1991) 104 *Harvard Law Review* 1419; D.E. Roberts, *Killing the Black Body: Race, Reproduction and the Theory of Liberty* (Pantheon Books: New York, 1997), chapter 5; L. C. Bower, 'The Trope of the Dark Continent in the Fetal Harm Debate: "Africanism" and the Right to Choice', in P. Boling (Ed.), *Expecting Trouble: Surrogacy, Fetal Abuse and New Reproductive Technologies* (Boulder: San Francisco, 1995) at 142. Chapter 5 p. 87 deals with the issue of discrimination.

3   *Roe v Wade,* 410 U.S. 113 (1973).

4   See for example, D. Hirschenbaum, 'When CRACK is the Only Choice: The Effect of a Negative Right of Privacy on Drug-Addicted Women' (2000) 15 *Berkeley Women's L.J.* 327. 'In Supreme Court decisions over the past twenty years, the right of privacy with respect to childbearing decisions has been limited to such an extent that, essentially, only those women with enough money to purchase the services that fall within the scope of this right are now awarded its full protection.' At 328.

5   The White Paper 'Smoking Kills' (see *infra* f.n. 26) at para 5.11 outlines the importance of the role of midwives, GPs and obstetricians who have regular contact with pregnant women. 'Evidence also shows that pre-natal counselling involving at least ten minutes person-to-person contact and written materials specifically designed for pregnant women, can double quit rates.' At 5.12. Citing University of York NHS Centre for Reviews and Dissemination, *Effectiveness Matters* (York: 1998), Vol. 3, issue 1. They are aided in the task by publications such as *Stopping Smoking Made Easier; Helping Pregnant Smokers Quit, Helping Smokers to Give Up* (COMATAS Ninth Annual Report, DH: HEA Publication, 1996). Note, however, that those who have smoking or other addictive problems are less likely to seek medical care throughout pregnancy. Therefore other campaigning measures are necessary in conjunction with this valuable service.

6   M.A. Field, 'Controlling the Woman to Protect the Fetus' (1989) 17 *Law, Medicine and Health Care* 122 at 124.

7   J.V. Greer, 'The Drug Babies', *Exceptional Children* 56 (1990), 382.

8   For example, DEL. CODE ANN., tit. 16, 190 (1995); MP. REV. STAT. 191.725, 191.727 (1994); R.I. GEN. LAWS 152-3.1 (1994).

9   See S.S. Balisy, 'Maternal Substance Abuse: The Need to Provide Legal Protection for the Fetus' (1987) 60 *Southern California Law Review* 1209 at 1235.

10 However as criminalization has very little effect on curbing the relevant activity, education and treatment are likely to prove more effective and therefore the cheaper

alternative. For example, see Department of Health, *Briefing: The Cost of Smoking to the NHS* (Department of Health: Leeds, 1997).

11 P. Campion, L. Owen, A. McNeill and C. McGuire, 'Evaluation of a Mass Media Campaign on Smoking and Pregnancy', *Addiction* 89 (1994), 1245.

12 Campion et. al. *ibid.,* 145 state that the effects of a campaign are likely to relate to its size and duration, the tone of the message, the motivation of those receiving the message (which is likely to be high in the case of pregnant smokers), and the targeting of a specific rather than general group.

13 K. Bolling and L. Owen, *Smoking and Pregnancy: A Survey of Knowledge, Attitudes and Behaviour* (Health Education Authority: London, 1997).

14 Bolling and Owen, *ibid.*, 2. 'In 1996, 46 per cent of pregnant women reported smoking in the 12 months before they became pregnant, while only 32 per cent reported that they were smoking currently.'

15 Bolling and Owen, *ibid.*, 3.

16 Bolling and Owen, *ibid.*, 4.

17 M. Raw, *Action on Smoking and Pregnancy* (Health Education Authority: London, 1997).

18 Directive 98/43/EC *The Parliament and Council Directive on the Approximation of Member States' Laws, Regulations, and Administrative Provisions on Advertising Tobacco Products.*

19 G. Permanand, 'UK Companies Challenge EU on Tobacco Advertising', *Eurohealth* 4(5) (1998), 37.

20 Department of Health, *Scientific Committee on Tobacco and Health Statement* (Department of Health: London, 20 March 1998) para. 6.4.7.

21 Department of Health, *ibid.*, 6.3.6.

22 Department of Health, *ibid.*, 9.1.

23 Department of Health, *Scientific Committee on Tobacco and Health Statement* (Department of Health: London, 2001).

24 *Ibid.*, para 2.8.

25 *Ibid.*, para. 1.11.

26 Department of Health, *Smoking Kills, A White Paper on Tobacco* (Department of Health: London, 30 November 1998) Cm. 4177.

27 Department of Health, *ibid.*, para. 5.1 citing S.S. Hecht *et al.*, 'Metabolites of the Tobacco-Specific Lung Carcinogen 4-(methylnitrosoamino)-1-(3-pyridyl)-1-butanone (nnk) in the Urine of Newborn Infants', *American Chemistry Society* 216 (1998), 32.

28 Department of Health, *ibid.*, para 5.2 citing K. Foster et. al., *Infant Feeding 1995: Office for National Statistics* (The Stationery Office: London, 1997). See also L. Chatenoud et. al., 'Prevalence of Smoking Among Pregnant Women is Lower in Italy than England', *British Medical Journal* (1999) 318, 1012.

29 Department of Health, *Smoking Kills, ibid.*, para 5.5.

30 Department of Health, *ibid.*, para 5.7.

31 Department of Health, *ibid.*, paras 5.7-5.8.

32 Department of Health, *ibid.*, para 5.9.

33 See Department of Health, *Young Teenagers and Alcohol in 1996 Volume 1* (Department of Health: London, 1997) to illustrate the prevalence of alcohol abuse among the young.

34 S. Edelstein, V. Kropenske, J. Howard, 'Project T.E.A.M.S.', *Social Work* 35(4) (1990), 313.

35 The American Agency for Health Care Policy and Research stated that NRT should be offered to pregnant heavy smokers who cannot stop without it: US Department of Health and Human Services, *Clinical Practice Guideline 18: Smoking Cessation* (US Government Printing Office: Washington DC, 1996).

36 The Department of Health, *Report on the Scientific Committee on Tobacco and Health* (Department of Health: London, 20 March 1998) para 5.13 did not recommend nicotine replacement therapy for pregnant women in the UK. See Department of Health website

at http://www.official-documents.co.uk/documents/doh/tobacco/report.htm. However the Committee changed its position in 2001: The Department of Health, *Scientific Committee on Tobacco and Health Statement* (Department of Health: London, 2001) paras 1.16, 1.17 and 1.20. See http://www.doh.giv.uk/scoth/pdfs/statement2001.pdf.

37 See M. Poland et. al., 'Punishing Pregnant Drug Users: Enhancing the Flight From Care', *Drug and Alcohol Dependence* 31 (1993), 199 at 202.

38 See J.W. Steverson, 'Stopping Fetal Abuse With No-Pregnancy and Drug Treatment Probation Conditions' (1994) 34(2) *Santa Clara Law Review* 295 at 329. Also see Chapter 5, which demonstrates that deterrence and retribution are arguably inappropriate goals in this context.

39 See *D v. Berkshire County Council* [1987] 1 All E.R. 33. Chapter 4 p. 71.

40 The Department of Health, Task Force to Review Services for Drugs *Report of an Independent Review of Drug Treatment in England* (Department of Health: Wetherby, 1996), acknowledged that service purchasers and providers must recognize that some clients need many attempts at treatment before a successful result is obtained.

41 These two criticisms of treatment programmes are made by J.W. Steverson, *op. cit.,* 319-323.

42 This is not to suggest that removal of the child should ever be used as a punishment or that it should occur in any situation where the threat to the child is not serious and ongoing. This is merely to say that the fact that the woman is pregnant and stands to harm the fetus and potentially lose her child is likely to give her strength to combat the problem that did not exist prior to her pregnancy.

43 Department of Health, *Report on Confidential Enquiries into Maternal Deaths in the United Kingdom 1994-1996: Why Mothers Die* (Department of Health: London, 14 December 1998).

44 Department of Health, *ibid.,* 5.

45 Hughes, Johnson, Rosenbaum, Simons, 'The Health of America's Mothers and Children: Trends in Access to Care', *Clearinghouse Review* (1986) 472, at 473 quoting U.S. Department of Health, Education and Welfare, *Health People: The Surgeon General's Report on Health Promotion and Disease Prevention* (1979).

46 M. McNulty, 'Pregnancy Police: The Health Policy and Legal Implications of Punishing Pregnant Women for Harm to Their Fetuses' (1987) 16 *New York University Review of Law and Social Change* 277, at 292-9. Aside from the lack of insurance McNulty argued that: 'Practical difficulties also prevent poor women from obtaining adequate prenatal care, including inadequate coordination of services, problems in securing Medicaid, unpleasant surroundings, long waits for appointments, and inadequate transportation.' At 298.

47 McNulty, *ibid.,* 296 reported that: '36% of all poor women of child-bearing age are completely without insurance, compared to ten percent of all other women.' The National Commission to Prevent Infant Mortality, (USA) *Death Before Life: The Tragedy of Infant Mortality*, Appendix 27-32 (1988) states that in 1987 the private health insurance of five million women of childbearing age did not cover maternity.

48 *Florida v. Johnson*, No. E89-1765 (Fla. Dist. Ct. App., 5th Dist. 1989). The case was eventually overturned. See Chapter 3 p. 45.

49 B. Robin-Vergeer, 'The Problem of the Drug-Exposed Newborn: A Return to Principled Intervention' (1990) 42 *Stanford Law Review* 745.

50 Robin-Vergeer, *ibid.* quoted M. Cronin, M. Ludtke and J. Willwerth, 'Innocent Victim' *Time* (1991) 56.

51 For example, *Elaine W. v. North General Hospital* (NY Super. Ct. Nov. 23 1989). (No index number) involving lawsuits against four private alcohol and drug-treatment programmes in New York City. For commentary see K. Moss, 'Substance Abuse During Pregnancy' (1990) 13 *Harvard Women's Law Journal* 278 at 297.

52 See J. Larson, 'Creating Common Goals for Medical, Legal and Child Protection Communities', in *Drug Exposed Infants and Their Families: Co-ordinating Responses*

of the Legal, Medical and Child Protection System (American Bar Association Center on Children and the Law: Washington D.C., 1990).

53 See I.M. Young, *infra*, fn 54, at 111.

54 See Colorado General Assembly House Bill 1299, 1991 Colo. Sess. Laws H.B. 1299 (setting up a treatment information centre, hotline and grants to local authorities). However, the weakness here is that there is no state mandate. Consequently action can only be initiated from local government or private agencies. The same flaw occurs under Illinois, House Bill No 1128 1991 Ill. Laws H.B. 1128. See T. Dobson and K.K. Eby, 'Criminal Liability for Substance Abuse During Pregnancy: The Controversy of Maternal Versus Fetal Rights' (1992) 36 *Saint Louis University Law Review* 655 at 690 for commentary.

55 J. Steverson, *op. cit.,* 317. Rhode Island and Washington's policies are designed to: '(1) provide early treatment intervention and child care services for parents while they undergo alcohol or drug treatment; (2) mandate that drug treatment programs do not discriminate against pregnant women; and (3) provide increased funding of prenatal services for poor women.'

56 M.A. Field, 'Controlling the Woman to Protect the Fetus' (1989) 17 *Law, Medicine and Health Care* 122, at 124.

57 McNulty, *op. cit.,* 299.

58 I.M. Young, 'Punishment, Treatment, Empowerment; Three Approaches to Policy for Pregnant Addicts', in P. Boling (Ed.), *Expecting Trouble: Surrogacy, Fetal Abuse and New Reproductive Technologies* (Boulder; San Francisco, 1995) at 109. See also K.L. Moss, 'Legal Issues: Drug Testing of Postpartum Women and Newborns as the Basis for Civil and Criminal Proceedings' (1990) 23 *Clearinghouse Review* 1406.

59 Young, *ibid.* 110.

60 Young, *ibid.* 118.

61 The advantages of empowerment were recognized by the Department of Health, *Scientific Committee on Tobacco and Health Statement* (Department of Health, London, 2001) which recommended the group therapy model for pregnant smokers.

62 Department of Health, *Drug Using Parents: Policy Guidelines for Inter-Agency Working* CI(97)18 (Department of Health: London, 1997).

63 The targets are: 'Increase the participation of problem drug users in drug treatment programmes by 55% by 2004 and by 100% by 2008, and increase year on year the proportion of users successfully sustaining or completing treatment programmes. ... Reduce the proportion of people under the age of 25 reporting the use of Class A drugs and reduce frequent use of any illicit drug amongst young people, especially by the most vulnerable young people; Reduce levels of drug related death by 20% by 2004; and implement a national alcohol strategy by 2004.' See http://www.drugs.gov.uk.

64 See S. Garcia, 'Maternal Drug Abuse: Laws and Ethics as Agents of Just Balances and Therapeutic Interventions', *The International Journal of the Addictions* 28(13) (1993), 1311.

65 http://www.cracksterilization.com/cgi-bin/jump. See J.M. Johnson, 'Reproductive Ability for Sale, Do I Hear $200?: Private Cash-for-Contraception Agreements As an Alternative to Maternal Substance Abuse' (2001) 43 *Arizona Law Review* 205.

66 *Ibid.*

67 D. White, 'The Crack Pot; Vet Joins US Militants Who Want to Pay Scots Junkies to Be Sterilised', *Sunday Mail* (Scotland), 6 August 2000, at 19.

68 Children Requiring a Caring Kommunity, *Statistics* http://www.cracksterilization.com/stats/ stats.html.

69 D. Hirchenbaum, 'When CRACK is the Only Choice: The Effect of a Negative Right of Privacy on Drug-Addicted Women' (2000) 15 *Berkeley Women's Law Journal* 327. 'In Supreme Court decisions over the past twenty years, the right of privacy with respect to childbearing decisions has been limited to such an extent that, essentially, only those women with enough money to purchase the services that fall within the scope of this right are now awarded its full protection.' At 328.

70 L. M. Chan, 'S.O.S. From the Womb; A Call for New York Legislation Criminalizing Drug Use During Pregnancy' (1993) 21 *Fordham Urban Law Journal* 199.

71 Presented by Peter Wilson, *Child Abuse During Pregnancy Prevention Act of 1989,* S. 1444 101th Cong., 1st Sess. (1980). See D.E. Johnsen, 'From Driving to Drugs: Governmental Regulation of Pregnant Women's Lives After *Webster'* (1989) 138 *University of Pennsylvania Law Review* 179 at 221.

72 Johnsen, *ibid.*, 212.

73 J.W. Steverson, *op. cit.*

74 The prohibition on pregnancy is subject to criticism on constitutional grounds. In *People v. Zaring,* Californian Court of Appeal No. F014606 July 22 1992, Judge Howard Broadman allowed a child abuser to choose Norplant as part of her sentence to prevent future fetal and child abuse. The case was eventually overturned, but the legality of the condition was not discussed. See Chapter 5 p. 86.

75 D. Mathieu, 'Mandating Treatment for Pregnant Substance Users: A Compromise', *Politics and the Life Sciences* 14(2) (1995), 199 at 205.

76 D. Mathieu, *ibid.*, 205.

77 R. Walton, 'War on Drugs. (200 Years of the Penitentiary: Criminal, Social and Economic Justice)' (1991) 34 *Howard Law Journal* 506 is also of this view. Walton argued that it is undesirable to prosecute pregnant women who are addicted to drugs harmful to the fetus, but recommends that where the woman is not prepared to deal with her addiction, incarceration or forced treatment is appropriate to protect the fetus.

78 P. Boling, 'Mandating Treatment for Pregnant Substance Abusers is the Wrong Focus for Public Discussion', *Politics and the Life Sciences* 15(1) (1996), 51.

79 W. Chavkin, 'Mandatory Treatment for Pregnant Substance Abusers: Irrelevant and Dangerous' *Politics and the Life Sciences* 15(1) (1996), 53.

80 *Draft Mental Health Bill*, Cm. 5538-I (London: The Stationery Office, 2002). For background see Department of Health, *Review of the Mental Health Act: Report of the Expert Committee* (London: Department of Health, 1999 – the 'Richardson Report'); White Paper, *Reforming the Mental Health Act,* Cm 5016 (London: The Stationery Office, December 2000); *Draft Mental Health Bill Consultation Document*, Cm. 5538-III (London: The Stationery Office, 2002); *Draft Mental Health Bill Explanatory Notes*, Cm. 5538-II (London: The Stationery Office, 2002).

81 J. Vasgar and N. Hopkins, 'Jurors Confirm Family Murder Verdict on Michael Stone', *The Guardian,* 5 October 2001.

82 House of Lords / House of Commons, *Joint Committee on Human Rights Twenty-Fifth Report,* Session 2001-2002, HL 181, HC 1294 (London: The Stationery Office, 2002).

83 *Draft Mental Health Bill, op. cit.*, clause 2(6).

84 Joint Committee on Human Rights, *op. cit.*, para 9.

85 The Joint Committee on Human Rights, *ibid.*, paras 13 and 14 stated that though cases from the early 1980s indicated that Article 5.1 of the European Convention on Human Rights is not concerned with the suitability of treatment or conditions of detention (*Ashingdane v. United Kingdom* (1985) 7 EHRR 528; *Winterwerp v. The Netherlands* (1979) 2 EHRR 387), more recent cases have indicated that 'detention initiated lawfully and for a lawful purpose may become unlawful under Article 5 on account of the suitability of the resources which are available for a patient's treatment, the regime to which the patient is subject, and the need to continue to detain the patient to protect him or herself, or the public, from danger'. *Witold Litwa v. Poland*, Eur. Ct. HR, App. No. 31365/96, judgement of 5 October 2000.

86 Joint Committee on Human Rights, *op. cit.,* para 10.

87 Draft Mental Health Bill, *op. cit.,* clause 6:
'(1) that the person is suffering from mental disorder,
(2) that that mental disorder is of such a nature or degree as to warrant the provision of medical treatment to him;
(3) either-

that the person is at substantial risk of causing serious harm to other persons and that it is necessary for the protection of those persons that medical treatment be provided to him, or

in any other case, that –

it is necessary for the health or safety of the patient or the protection of other persons that medical treatment be provided to him, and

that treatment cannot be provided to him unless he is subject to the provisions of the draft bill.'

88   Joint Committee on Human Rights, *op. cit.* Also see A. Travis, 'Human Rights "Risk" in Mental Health Bill', *The Guardian*, 12 November 2002.

89   See Gaby Hinsliff, 'Heavy Drinkers to be Locked Up', *The Observer,* 2 February 2003.

90   The Mental Health Alliance at http://www.mind.org.uk/ (The pages are hosted by Mind). According to J. Carvel and M. White, 'PM Accepts Worries Over Mental Health Law', *The Guardian*, 24 October 2002, the Alliance Chairman Paul Farmer stated: 'We urge the government to seize this chance to pass mental health legislation fit for the 21st century before it is too late. Hundreds of people fear the bill will turn their doctors into jailers, allowing people who have committed no crime to be locked up indefinitely.'

Bibliography

Books and Articles

Abel, E.L. (1998), 'Protecting Fetuses from Certain Harm', *Politics and the Life Sciences*, **17** (2), p.113.

Abel, E.L. and Sokel, R.J. (1987), 'Incidence of Fetal Alcohol Syndrome and Economic Impact of FAS-Related Anomalies', *Drug and Alcohol Dependence*, **19**, p.51.

Alpern, Kenneth D. (ed.) (1992), *The Ethics of Reproductive Technologies*, Oxford and New York: Oxford University Press.

American Medical Association Board of Trustees (1990), 'Legal Intervention During Pregnancy', *Journal of the American Medical Association*, **264** (28), p.2663.

American Medical Association Board of Trustees (1990), *Drug Exposed Infants and Their Families: Co-ordinating Responses of the Legal, Medical and Child Protection System*, Washington DC: American Bar Association Center on Children and the Law.

Anderson, Sir Norman (1978), *Liberty, Law and Justice*, London: Stevens and Sons.

Annas, G.J. (1987), 'The Impact Of Medical Technology On The Pregnant Woman's Right To Privacy', *American Journal of Law & Medicine*, **13**, p.213.

Areen, J., King, P.A., Goldberg, S. and Capron, A.M. (1984), *Law, Science and Medicine*, New York: University Casebook Series.

Ashworth, Andrew (1991), *Principles of Criminal Law*, Oxford: Clarendon Press.

Atkins, E. (1992), 'Reporting Fetal Abuse through California's Child Abuse and Neglect Reporting Act', *Southwestern University Law Review*, **21** (1), p.105.

Bailey-Harris, Rebecca (1997), 'Re MB (Medical Treatment)', *Family Law*, **27** (2), p.542.

Bailey-Harris, Rebecca (1997), 'Pregnancy, Autonomy and Refusal of Medical Treatment', *Law Quarterly Review*, **114**, p.550.

Bailin, Alex (1996), 'Born to Die', *New Law Journal*, **146** (3), p.1696.

Bainham, B. (1987), 'Protecting the Unborn – New Rights in Gestation?', *Modern Law Review*, **50**, p.361.

Bales, Joanna (1996), 'Woman Challenges Hospital's Right to Impose Caesarean', *The Times*, 23 September, 6 col. 1.

Balisy, Sam S. (1987), 'Maternal Substance Abuse: The Need to Provide Legal Protection for the Fetus', *Southern California Law Review*, **60**, p.1209.

Bamforth, Nicholas (1995), 'Scrutiny: The Treatment of Pregnancy under European Community Sex Discrimination Law', *European Public Law*, **1** (1), p.59.

Barber, Rosamond A. (1981), 'Criminal Liability of Physicians: An Encroachment on the Abortion Right', *American Criminal Law Review*, **18**, p.591.

Barron, S.L. and Roberts, D.F. (1995), *Issues in Fetal Medicine*, Proceedings of the 29th Annual Symposium of the Galton Institute, London 1992, New York and London: Macmillan Press Ltd.

Barry, Ellen M. (1985), 'Quality of Prenatal Care for Incarcerated Women Challenged', *Youth Law News*, Nov./Dec., p.1.

Barry, Ellen M. (1989), 'Recent Development: Pregnant Prisoners', *Harvard Women's Law Journal*, **12**, p.189.

Baum Levenbook, Barbara (1992), 'Defender of the Realm: Thomson on Rights', *Law and Philosophy*, **11**, p.449.

Bay, Christian (1958), *The Structure of Freedom*, Stanford, CA: Stanford University Press.

Bayles, Michael (1978), *Principles of Legislation*, Detroit: Reidel Publishers.

Beal, Ron (1984), '"Can I Sue Mommy?" An Analysis of a Woman's Tort Liability for Prenatal Injuries to her Unborn Child Born Alive', *San Diego Law Review*, **21**, p.325.

Beauchamp, T.L. and Childress, J.F. (1989), *Principles of Biomedical Ethics*, New York: Oxford University Press.

Beecham, Linda (1999), 'Tobacco Companies Win Delay on Advertising Ban', *British Medical Journal*, **319**, p.1218.

Bellew, Melissa D. (1990), Kentucky Capital Litigation Resource Center – a Branch of the Kentucky Department of Public Advocacy, 'Fetal Alcohol Syndrome, Fetal Alcohol Effect and Genetic Influence on Alcoholism', *Capital Concerns*, **6**, p.1.

Bennion, Francis (1998), 'Which Sort of Human Rights Act?', *New Law Journal*, **148**, p.488.

Bergman, Frithjof (1977), *On Being Free*, Notre Dame and London: University of Notre Dame Press.

Berlin, Isaiah (1958), *Two Concepts of Liberty,* Oxford: Clarendon Press.

Berliner, Lucy (1990), 'Maternal Substance Abuse and State Intervention', *Journal of Interpersonal Violence*, **5** (4), p.529.

Berrien, Jacqueline (1990), 'Pregnancy and Drug Use: The Dangerous and Unequal Use of Punitive Measures', *Yale Journal of Law and Feminism*, **2** (2), p.239.

Bewley, Susan (1994), 'Legal Frameworks to Prevent Harm In-Utero', *Medical Law International*, **1**, p.277.

Bewley, Susan and Humphrey Ward, R. (eds) (1994), *Ethics in Obstetrics and Gynaecology*, London: RCOG Press.

Billing, L., Erikson, M., Jonsson, B., Steneroth, G. and Zetterstorm, R. (1994), 'The Influence of Environmental Factors on Behavioural Problems in 8-year-old Children Exposed to Amphetamine During Fetal Life', *Child Abuse and Neglect*, **18**, p.3.

Blank, R.H. (1996), 'Mandating Outpatient Treatment for Pregnant Substance Abusers: Attractive but Unfeasible', *Politics and the Life Sciences*, **15** (1), p.49.

Blink, R.H., Boling, Patricia, Chavkin, Wendy, Daniels, C.R., Madden, R.G., Merrick, J.C., Moskowitz, E.H., Patterson, E.G., Andrews, A.B., Peretz, P., Schroedel, J.R., Strickland, R.A., Wexler, D.B., Woliver, L.R. and Mathieu, D. (1996), 'Symposium: Pregnancy and Substance Abuse', *Politics and the Life Sciences*, **15** (1), p.49.

Boling, Patricia (ed.) (1995), *Expecting Trouble: Surrogacy, Fetal Abuse and New Reproductive Technologies*, San Francisco and Boulder: Westview Press.

Boling, Patricia (1996), 'Mandating Treatment for Pregnant Substance Abusers is the Wrong Focus for Public Discussion', *Politics and the Life Sciences*, **15** (1), p.51.

Bolling, K. and Owen, L. (1997), *Smoking and Pregnancy: A Survey of Knowledge, Attitudes and Behaviour*, London: Health Education Authority.

Bondeson, Engelhardt, Spicker and Winship (1983), *Abortion and the Status of the Fetus: Philosophy and Medicine Volume 13, A Collection of Essays*, New York: Reidel.

Bosanquet, Bernard (1951), *The Philosophical Theory of the State*, London: Macmillan Press.

Boseley, S. and Dyer, C. (1999), 'New Heart for Dying Girl who Refused Consent', *The Guardian*, 16 July, p.1.

Bowes, Watson A. and Selegestad, Brad (1981), 'Fetal Versus Maternal Rights: Medical and Legal Perspectives', *Obstetrics and Gynaecology*, **58**, p.209.

Boyce, Nell (1998), 'Bad Dope', *New Scientist*, 25 July, p.16.

Bradley, D.C. (1978), 'A Woman's Right to Choose', *Modern Law Review*, **41**, p.365.

Brazier, Margaret and Lobjoit, Mary (eds) (1991), *Protecting the Vulnerable: Autonomy and Consent in Health Care*, London: Routledge.

Brody, Baruch, A. (1976), *Abortion and the Sanctity of Human Life: A Philosophical View*, Massachusetts: MIT Press.

Brody, Baruch, A. (ed.) (1988), *Moral Theory and Moral Judgments in Medical Ethics*, Dordrecht, Boston and London: Kluwer Academic Publishers.

Bromham, David R., Dalton, Maureen E., Jackson, Jennifer C. and Millican, Peter J.R. (eds) (1992), *Ethics in Reproductive Medicine*, London, Berlin and New York: Springer-Verlag.

Brown, M.T. (2000), 'The Morality of Abortion and the Deprivation of Futures', *Journal of Medical Ethics*, **26**, p.103.

Brown, M.T. (2002), 'A Future Like Ours Revisited', *Journal of Medical Ethics*, 28, p.192.

Brown, M.T. (2002), 'Abortion and the Value of Future. A Reply to: a Defence of the Potential Future of Value Theory', *Journal of Medical Ethics*, **28**, p.202.

Bulger, C.M. (1999), 'In the Best Interests of the Child? Race and Class Discrimination in Prenatal Drug Use Prosecutions', *Third World Law Journal*, **19**, p.709.

Burrell, Ian (2000), 'Mother Knows Best, But Who Decides?', *The Independent*, 18 January, Supplement, p.11.

Byrne, P. (ed.) (1987-88), 'Health, Rights and Resources', *King's College Studies*, London: Oxford University Press.

Campion, P., Owen, L., McNeill, A. and McGuire, C. (1994), 'Evaluation of a Mass Media Campaign on Smoking and Pregnancy', *Addiction*, **89**, p.1245.

Capron, A.M. (1974), 'Informed Consent in Catastrophic Disease Research and Treatment', *The University of Pennsylvania Law Review*, 123, p.356.

Capron, A.M. (1998), 'Punishing Mothers', *Hastings Center Report*, **28** (1), p.31.

Carvel, J. and White, M. (2002), 'PM Accepts Worries Over Mental Health Law', *The Guardian*, 24 October.

Case Note (1983), 'Criminal Law – Person Who Kills Viable Fetus Cannot be Prosecuted Under Statute Which Defines Murder as Causing the Death of Another Person', *Journal of Family Law*, **21**, p.761.

Case Note (1990), 'Abortion – Whether Foetus is 'a Child Capable of Being Born Alive', *Common Law Bulletin*, **16** (3), p.820.

Case Note (1997), 'Re S Application for Judicial Review', *Family Law*, **27** (2), p.640.

Case Note (1997), 'Medical Treatment: A Metropolitan Borough Council v. DB', *Childright*, **138**, p.21.

Cassens Moss, Debra (1987), 'Is Ignoring M.D. Criminal? California Case Raises Questions of Women's Duties During Pregnancy', *American Bar Association Journal*, **73**, p.23, col.1.

Chadwick, Ruth F. (ed.) (1992), *Ethics, Reproduction and Genetic Control*, London and New York: Routledge.

Chapman, Simon (1999), 'Scare Tactics Cut Smoking in Australia to All Time Low', *British Medical Journal*, **318**, p.1508.

Chan, Louise Marlane (1993), 'S.O.S. From the Womb: A Call for New York Legislation Criminalizing Drug Use During Pregnancy', *Fordham Urban Law Journal*, **21**, p.199.

Chard, T. and Richards, M.P.M. (eds) (1992), *Obstetrics in the 1990s: Current Controversies*, Clinics in Developmental Medicine, nos. 123/124, Oxford and New York: Mac Keith Press.

Chasnoff, I.J. (1988), 'Drug Use In Pregnancy: Parameters of Risk', *Pediatric Clinicians of North America*, **35**, p.1403.

Chatenoud, L., Chiaffarino, F., Parazzini, F., Nebzi, G. and Vecchia, C.L. (1999), 'Prevalence of Smoking Among Pregnant Women is Lower in Italy than England', *British Medical Journal*, **318**, p.1012.

Chavkin, W., Allen, M.H. and Oberman, M. (1991), 'Drug Abuse and Pregnancy: Some Questions on Public Policy, Clinical Management, and Maternal and Fetal Rights', *Birth*, **18** (2), p.107.

Chavkin, W. (1996), 'Mandatory Treatment for Pregnant Substance Abusers: Irrelevant and Dangerous', *Politics and the Life Sciences*, **15** (1), p.51.

Clarkson, C.M.V. and Keating, H.M. (1994), *Criminal Law: Text and Materials*, 4th edn, London: Sweet and Maxwell.

Closen, Michael L. and Isaacman, Scott H. (1990), 'Criminally Pregnant: Are AIDS Transmission Laws Encouraging Abortion?', *American Bar Association Journal*, **76**, p.73, col.3.

Clouser, K.D. and Gert, B. (1990), 'A Critique of Principalism', *Journal of Medicine and Philosophy*, **15**, p.219.

Cohen, F. (1986), 'Paternal Contributions to Birth Defects', *Nursing Clinics North America*, May, p.46.

Cohen, L.A. (1980), 'Fetal Viability and Individual Autonomy: Resolving Medical and Legal Standards for Abortion', *UCLA Law Review*, **27**, p.1340.

Cohen, M. (1940), 'Moral Aspects of the Criminal Law', *Yale Law Review*, **49**, p.897.

Coke, Sir Edward (1680), *Co. Inst*, **3**, p.50.

COMATAS (1996), *Stopping Smoking Made Easier; Helping Pregnant Smokers Quit, Helping Smokers to Give Up*, COMATAS Ninth Annual Report, London: HEA Publication; Department of Health.

Commissioner on Criminal Law (1839), Fourth Report, *British Parliamentary Papers*, **19**, p.235.

Commissioners for Revising and Consolidating Criminal Law (1846), Second Report, *British Parliamentary Papers*, **24**, p.107.

Committee on Substance Abuse and Committee on Children with Disabilities (1993), 'Fetal Alcohol Syndrome and Fetal Alcohol Effects', *Pediatrics*, **91** (5), p.1004.

Connor, Steve, Science Correspondent (1997), 'Male Infertility Treatment Linked to Birth Defect', *The Sunday Times*, 23 February, p.9.

Cooper, R.J. (1992), 'Abortion – the New Law', *Journal of Criminal Law*, **56**, p.297.

Council for Science and Society (1984), *Human Procreation: Ethical Aspects of New Technologies*, Report for a Working Party Council for Science and Society, Oxford, New York and Toronto: Oxford University Press.

Cranston, M. (1953), *Freedom, a New Analysis*, London: Longman, Green & Co.

Cronin, M., Ludtke, M. and Willwerth, J. (1991), 'Innocent Victim', *Time*, p.56.

Cuoma, B. (1967), '*Mens Rea* and Status Criminality', *South California Law Review*, **40**, p.463.

Curriden, Mark (1990), 'Holding Mom Accountable: *Roe v. Wade* does not Prevent Criminal Prosecution of Prenatal Abuse', *American Bar Association Journal*, March, p.50.

DeBettencourt, Kathleen B. (1990), 'The Wisdom of Solomon: Cutting the Cord that Harms', *Children Today*, **19** (4), p.17.

Daniels, C.R. (1996), 'A Million (Missing) Men: A Commentary on Mathieu's Compromise on Pregnancy and Substance Use', *Politics and the Life Sciences*, **15** (1), p.54.

DeCruz, Dr S.P. (1987), 'Protecting the Unborn Child: Re D', *Family Law*, **17**, p.207.

DeCruz, Dr S.P. (1998), 'Caesarean Sections, Consent and the Courts', *Practitioners' Child Law Bulletin*, **10** (1), p.8.

DeGama, Katherine (1993), 'Medical Law: Re S', *Journal of Social Welfare and Family Law*, **2**, p.147.

Denison, James (1991), 'The Efficacy and Constitutionality of Criminal Punishment for Maternal Substance Abuse', *Southern California Law Review*, **64**, p.1103.

Department of Health, Department of Health and Social Services, Northern Ireland, The Scottish Office Department of Health, Welsh Office (1998), *Report on Scientific Committee on Tobacco and Health*, London: Department of Health.

Department of Health (1996), Task Force to Review Services for Drugs, *Report of an Independent Review of Drug Treatment in England*, Wetherby: Department of Health.

Department of Health (1997), *Briefing: The Cost of Smoking to the NHS*, Leeds: Department of Health.

Department of Health (1997), *Dying for a Fag Anti-smoking Summit*, Preston: Department of Health.

Department of Health (1997), *Young Teenagers and Alcohol in 1996 Volume 1,* London: Department of Health.

Department of Health (1997), *Drug Using Parents: Policy Guidelines for Inter-Agency Working* CI(97)18, London: Department of Health.

Department of Health (1998), *Report on the Scientific Committee on Tobacco and Health*, London: Department of Health.

Department of Health (1998), *Smoking Kills: A White Paper on Tobacco* Cm 4177, London: Department of Health.

Department of Health (1998), *Why Mothers Die: Report on Confidential Enquiries into Maternal Deaths in the United Kingdom 1994-1996*, London: Department of Health.

Department of Health (1999), *Review of the Mental Health Act: Report of the Expert Committee*, London: Department of Health.

Department of Health (2001), *Scientific Committee on Tobacco and Health Statement*, London: Department of Health.

Department of Social Security (1984), *Report of the Committee of Inquiry in Human Fertilization and Embryology*, London: HMSO.

Devins, Neal (1994), 'Book Review Essay: Through the Looking Glass: What Abortion Teaches Us About American Politics', *Columbian Law Review*, **94**, p.243.

Devlin, Patrick (1965), *The Enforcement of Morals*, Oxford and New York: Oxford University Press.

Diduck, Alison (1993), 'Legislating Ideologies of Motherhood', *Social and Legal Studies*, **2** (4), p.461.

Dobson, Roger (1999), 'Death Rates Higher in Wales', *British Medical Journal*, **318**, p.12.

Dobson, Tracy and Eby, Kimberly K. (1992), 'Criminal Liability for Substance Abuse During Pregnancy: The Controversy of Maternal Versus Fetal Rights', *Saint Louis University Law Review*, **36**, p.655.

Dougherty, Charles J. (1985), 'The Right to Begin Life with Sound Body and Mind: Fetal Patients and Conflicts with Their Mothers', *University of Detroit Law Review*, **63** (7), p.89.

Douglas, Gillian (1991), *Law, Fertility and Reproduction*, London: Sweet and Maxwell.

Douglas, Gillian (1997), 'Re L (Patient: Non-Consensual Treatment)', *Family Law*, **27** (1), p.325.

Dressler, Joshua (1995), *Understanding Criminal Law*, Legal Text Series, USA.

Duce, Richard (1998), '"Bizarre" Conduct Not Good Reason for Caesarean', *The Times*, 8 May, p.6, col.1.

Dworkin, Gerald (1988), *The Theory and Practice of Autonomy*, Cambridge and New York: Cambridge University Press.

Dworkin, Ronald M. (1977), *Taking Rights Seriously*, Avon: The Bath Press.

Dworkin, Ronald M. (1993), *Life's Dominion: An Argument about Abortion and Euthanasia*, London: HarperCollins Publishers.

Dworkin, Ronald M. (ed.) (1977), *The Philosophy of Law*, Oxford Readings in Philosophy, Oxford: Oxford University Press.

Dyer, Clare (1997), 'Birth of a Dilemma', *The Guardian*, 11 March, p.17.

Dyer, Clare (1992), 'Boy Wins Damages after Injury *In Utero*', *British Medical Journal*, **304**, p.1400.

Edelstein, Susan, Kropenske, Vickie and Howard, Judy (1990), 'Project T.E.A.M.S.', *Social Work*, **35** (4), p.313.

Editorial (1989), 'Fetus Illegally Jailed, Inmate's Lawyer Argues', *Washington Times*, 4 August, p.4.

Editorial (1990), 'Abortion – Whether Foetus is a Child Capable of Being Born Alive', *Common Law Bulletin*, **16** (3), p.820.

Editorial (1990), 'Woman in Fetal Alcohol Case Gives Birth to Healthy Infant', *New York Times*, 17 June, p.20, col.4.

Editorial (1997), 'Medical Treatment – Legality of Treatment Without Consent', 147 *New Law Journal*.

Editorial (1997), 'New Zealand: Unborn Children: "Persons" and Maternal Conduct', *Medical Law Review*, **5** (1), p.143.

Editorial (1997), 'Consent: Adult Refusal of Consent, Capacity: Re MB (Medical Treatment)', *Medical Law Review*, **5** (3), p.317.

Editorial (1998), 'Right to Refuse Treatment to Save Foetus: *St. George's Healthcare National Health Service Trust v. S*', *Health Law*, **3** (6), p.8.

Editorial 91998), 'Stabbing Foetus who is Born Alive then Dies can be Manslaughter but not Murder', *The Police Journal*, **71** (1), p.89.

Eisenberg, Rebecca L. (1992), 'An Unlady-Like Response to Legal Conceptions of Women', *Harvard Law Review*, **105**, p.2104.

English, Abigail (1990), 'Prenatal Drug Exposure: Grounds for Mandatory Child Abuse Reports', *Youth Law News*, **11**, p.3.

Epstein, Julia (1995), 'The Pregnant Imagination, Fetal Rights, and Women's Bodies: A Historical Inquiry', *Yale Journal of Law and the Humanities*, **7** (1), p.139.

Faludi, Susan (1991), *Backlash, The Undeclared War Against American Women*, New York: Crown Publishers.

Farr, Kathryn A. (1995), 'Fetal Abuse and the Criminalization of Behaviour During Pregnancy', *Crime and Delinquency*, **41** (2), p.235.

Feinberg, Joel (1987), *Harm to Others: The Moral Limits of the Criminal Law*, vol.3, New York and Oxford: Oxford University Press.

Field, Martha A. (1989), 'Controlling the Woman to Protect the Fetus', *Law Medicine and Health Care*, **17**, p.122.

Finfer, S., Howell, S., Miller, J., Willett, K. and Wilson-MacDonald, J. (1994), 'Managing Patients who Refuse Blood Transfusions: an Ethical Dilemma', *British Medical Journal*, **308**, p.1423.

Florey, C.V., Teylor, D., Bolumar, F., Kaminski, M. and Olsen, J. (eds) (1992), 'EUROMAC – A European Concerted Action; Maternal Alcohol Consumption and its Relation to the Outcome of Pregnancy and Child Development at 18 Months', *International Journal of Epidemiology*, **21**, supplement 1.

Folger, Katherine B. (1994), 'When Does Life Begin ... or End? The California Supreme Court Redefines Fetal Murder in *People v. Davis*', *University of San Francisco Law Review*, **29**, p.237.

Forsythe, Clarke (1987), 'Homicide of the Unborn Child: The Born Alive Rule and Other Legal Anachronisms', *Val. University Law Review*, **21**, p.563.

Fortin, Jane (1988), 'Legal Protection for the Unborn Child', *Modern Law Review*, **51**, p.54.

Foster, K., Lader, D. and Cheesbrough, S. (1997), *Infant Feeding 1995: Office for National Statistics*, London: The Stationery Office.

Fovargue, Sara and Miola, Jose (1998), 'Policing Pregnancy: Implications of Attorney-General's Reference (No. 3 of 1994)', *Medical Law Review*, **6** (3), p.265.

Freeley, Mary Beth (1983), 'Criminal Law and Procedure: Fetus Not a Person Within Meaning of Rhode Island Vehicular Homicide Statute. (Annual Survey of Rhode Island Law for 1981-1982 Term)', *Suffolk University Law Review*, **17**, p.405.

Freeman, M.D.A. (1980), 'Removing Babies at Birth: A Questionable Practice', *Family Law*, **10**, p.131.

Ferriman, Annabel, Health Correspondent (1986), 'Drugs in Pregnancy Under Legal Spotlight: Lords Consider Action Against Addict Mothers', *The Observer*, 5th October, p.5 col.1.

Gannon Shoop, J. (1992), 'News and Trends: States Cannot Punish Pregnant Women for "Fetal Abuse," Courts Say', *Trial*, **28**, p.11.

Garcia, Sandra A. (1993), 'Maternal Drug Abuse: Laws and Ethics as Agents of Just Balances and Therapeutic Interventions', *The International Journal of the Addictions*, **28** (13), p.1311.

Gillmore, Anne (1983), 'Is the Fetus a Patient?', *Canadian Medical Association Journal*, **128**, p.1472.

Gillon, Raanan (1988), 'Pregnancy, Obstetrics and the Moral Status of the Fetus', *Journal of Medical Ethics*, **14**, p.3.

Gillon, Raanan (1991), 'Human Embryos and the Argument from Potential', *Journal of Medical Ethics*, **17**, p.59.

Gillon, Raanan (ed.) (1994), *Principles of Health Care Ethics*, Chichester: John Wiley & Sons.

Gillon, Raanan (2001), 'Is there a "New Ethics of Abortion"', *Journal of Medical Ethics*, **27**, p.5.

Gittler, Josephine and McPherson, Marie (1990), 'Prenatal Substance Abuse', *Children Today*, **19** (4), p.3.

Glazebrook, P. (ed.) (1978), *Reshaping the Criminal Law*, London: Stevens.

Glover, Jonathan (1977), *Causing Death and Saving Lives*, London: Penguin.

Goldberg, Stephanie B. (1992), 'No Baby, No Jail; Creative Sentencing Has Gone Overboard, a Californian Court Rules', *American Bar Association Journal*, **78**, p.90.

Goldman, Rachel B. (1985), 'Criminal Law – Viable Fetus is Person for Purposes of Massachusetts Vehicular Homicide Statute (casenote)', *Suffolk University Law Review*, **19**, p.145.

Goldsmith, Stephan (1990), 'Prosecution to Enhance Treatment', *Children Today*, **19** (4), p.13.

Grace, John (1999), 'Should the Foetus have Rights in Law?', *Medico-Legal Journal*, **67** (2), p.57.

Green, T.H. (1941), *Lectures on the Principles of Political Obligations*, London: Longman Green and Co.

Greer, Jeptha V. (1990), 'The Drug Babies', *Exceptional Children*, **56**, p.382.

Griffin, Eugene (1981), 'Viability and Fetal Life in State Criminal Abortion Laws', *Journal of Criminal Law and Criminology*, **72**, p.324.

Gross, Hyman (1979), *A Theory of Criminal Justice*, New York: Oxford University Press.

Grubb, Andrew (ed.) (1993), *Choices and Decisions in Health Care*, Chichester: John Wiley & Sons.

Hacker, P.M.S. and Raz, J. (eds.) (1977), *Law, Morality and Society: Essays in Honour of H.L.A. Hart*, Oxford: Clarendon Press.

Hall, J.M. (1999), 'Drug Misuse Stems From a Person's Autonomy to Choose', *British Medical Journal*, **318**, p.1142.

Hapler, Thomas (1996), 'Privacy and Autonomy; From Warren and Brendeis to Roe and Cruzen', *The Journal of Medicine and Philosophy*, **21**, p.121.

Hargrove, Patricia (1987), 'Case Note: Re D (a minor)', *Family Law*, **17**, p.202.

Hargrove, Patricia (1997), 'Case Note: Re MB (Medical Treatment)' *Family Law*, **27** (2), p.514.

Harpwood V. (ed.) (1996), *Legal Issues in Obstetrics*, Aldershot: Dartmouth.

Harrington, John (1996), 'Privileging the Medical Norm: Liberalism, Self-Determination and the Refusal of Medical Treatment', *Legal Studies*, **16**, p.348.

Harris, John (1985), *The Value of Life: An Introduction to Medical Ethics*, London, Mass., Melbourne, Henley: Routledge and Kegan Paul.

Harrison, Ivor (1993), 'What is an Addict? An International Perspective', *Medical Law International*, **1**, p.113.

Hart, H.L.A. (1955), 'Are There Any Natural Rights?', *Philosophical Review*, **64**, p.174.

Hart, H.L.A. (1961), *The Concept of Law*, Oxford: Clarendon Press.

Hecht, S.S., Carmella, S.G., Chen, M.L., Salberger, U., Tollner, U. and Lackmann, G.M. (1998), 'Metabolites of the Tobacco-Specific Lung Carcinogen 4-(methylnitrosoamino)-1-(3-pyridyl)-1-butanone (nnk) in the Urine of Newborn Infants', *American Chemistry Society*, **216**, p.32.

Henn, John H. (1986), 'Case and Statute Comments: Criminal Law – Vehicular Homicide of a Viable Fetus – Judicial Statutory Amendment', *Massachusetts Law Review*, **70**, p.201.

Herring, Jonathan (1997), 'Caesarean Sections, Phobians and Foetal Rights', *Cambridge Law Journal*, **56**, p.509.

Hewson, Barbara (1992), 'Mother Knows Best', *New Law Journal*, **142**, p.1538.

Hewson, Barbara (1992), 'When "No" Means "Yes"', *Law Society Gazette*, **89**, p.1148.

Hewson, Barbara (1997), 'Who's Afraid of the Official Solicitor?', *Solicitor's Journal*, **141** (1), p.198.

Hewson, Barbara (1997), 'Enforced Caesareans', *Solicitor's Journal*, **141** (3), p.914.

Hewson, Barbara (1997), 'How to Escape the Surgeon's Knife', *New Law Journal*, **147**, p.752.

Hewson, Barbara (2001), 'Reproductive Autonomy and the Ethics of Abortion', *Journal of Medical Ethics*, **27**, p.110.

Hinsliff, G. (2003), 'Heavy Drinkers to be Locked Up', *The Observer,* 2 February.

Hirchenbaum, D. (2000), 'When CRACK is the Only Choice: The Effect of a Negative Right of Privacy on Drug-Addicted Women', *Berkeley Women's Law Journal*, **15**, p.327.

Hoffman Baruch, Elaine, D'Adamo, Amadeo F. and Seager, Joni (1988), *Embryos, Ethica and Women's Rights: Exploring the New Technologies*, New York and London: Harrington Park Press.

Holland, Robert (1991), 'Criminal Sanctions for Drug Abuse During Pregnancy: the Antithesis of Fetal Health', *New York Law School Journal of Human Rights*, **8**, p.415.

Honderich, Ted (ed.) (1973), *Essays on Freedom of Action*, London: Routledge and Kegan Paul.

Horowitz, Robert (1990), 'A Co-ordinated Public Health and Child Welfare Response to Perinatal Substance Abuse', *Children Today*, **19** (4), p.8.

House of Lords / House of Commons (2002), *Joint Committee on Human Rights Twenty-Fifth Report*, Session 2001-2002, HL 181, HC 1294, London: The Stationery Office.

Hughes, Johnson, Rosenbaum, Simons (1986), 'The Health of America's Mothers and Children: Trends in Access to Care', *Clearinghouse Review*, p.472.

Isaacman, Scott H. (1991), 'Are we Outlawing Motherhood for HIV-Infected Women?', Health Law Symposium, *Loyola University of Chicago Law Journal*, **22**, p.479.

Ivamy, E.R. Hardy (1993), *Mozely and Whiteley's Law Dictionary*, 11th edn, London: Butterworths.

Jareborg, Nils (1988), *Essays in Criminal Law,* Uppeala: Eustins Forlag.

Jebson, S.L. (1995), 'Conditioning a Woman's Probation on her Using Norplant: New Weapon Against Child Abuse Backfires', *Campbell Law Review*, **17** (169), p.301.

Jerrard, Rob (1998), 'Stabbing Foetus who is Born Alive then Dies can be Manslaughter but not Murder', *Police Journal*, **71** (1), p.89.

Johnsen, Dawn E. (1986), 'The Creation of Fetal Rights: Conflicts with Women's Constitutional Rights to Liberty, Privacy, and Equal Protection', *Yale Law Journal*, **95**, p.578.

Johnsen, Dawn E. (1989), 'From Driving to Drugs: Governmental Regulation of Pregnant Women's Lives After *Webster*', *University of Pennsylvania Law Review*, **138**, p.179.

Johnson, J.M. (2001), 'Reproductive Ability for Sale, Do I Hear $ 200?: Private Cash-for-Contraception Agreements As an Alternative to Maternal Substance Abuse', *Arizona Law Review*, **43**, p.205.

Jones, K.L., Smith, D.W., Ulleland, C.N. and Streissguth, A.P. (1973), 'Patterns of Malformation in Offspring of Chronic Alcoholic Mothers', *Lancet* (**i**), p.1267.

Kahn, Judith (1987), 'Of Woman's First Disobedience: Forsaking a Duty of Care to her Fetus – Is This a Mother's Crime?', *Brooklyn Law Review*, **53**, p.807.

Kaplan, J. (1971), 'The Role of the Law in Drug Control', *Duke Law Journal*, **65**, p.1065.

Kennedy, Ian (1988), *Treat Me Right: Essays in Medical Law and Ethics*, Oxford: Clarendon Press.

Keown, John (1996), 'Homicide, Fetuses and Appendages', *Cambridge Law Journal*, **55**, p.207.

Keown, John (1998), 'Homicide By Prenatal Assault Revisited', *Cambridge Law Journal*, **57** (2), p.241.e

Kime, Mary Lynn (1995), 'The Born Alive Rule Dies a Timely Death', *Tulsa Law Journal*, **30**, p.539.

King, Patricia A. (1979), 'The Judicial Status of the Fetus: A Proposal for Legal Protection of the Unborn', *Michigan Law Review*, **77** (22), p.1647.

Kitts, Jennifer (1997), 'Commentary on the Drummond Case from Canada', *European Journal of Health Law*, **4** (3), p.289.

Knopoff, Katherine A. (1991), 'Can a Pregnant Woman Morally Refuse Fetal Surgery?', *California Law Review*, **79**, p.499.

Korver, Dawn Marie (1991), 'The Constitutionality of Punishing Pregnant Substance Abusers Under Drug Trafficking Laws: The Criminalization of a Bodily Function', *Boston College Law Review*, **32**, p.629.

LaFave, Wayne R. and Scott, Austin W.J. (1986), *Criminal Law*, Minnesota, USA: West Publishing Co.

Landworth, Julius (1987), 'Fetal Abuse and Neglect: An Emerging Controversy', *Pediatrics*, **79** (4), p.508.

Larson, J. (1990), 'Creating Common Goals for Medical, Legal and Child Protection Communities', in *Drug Exposed Infants and their Families: Co-ordinating Responses of the Legal, Medical and Child Protection System*, Washington D.C., American Bar Association Center on Children and the Law.

Laurance, Jeremy, Health Correspondent (1997), 'Pregnant Women May Drink – In Moderation', *The Times*, 3 March, p.9.

Law Commission Report (Law Comm. No. 60) (1974), *Injuries to Unborn Children* (Cmnd. 5709).

Law, S. (1984), 'Rethinking Sex and the Constitution', *University of Pennsylvania Law Review*, **132**, p.955.

Lazarus, Ellen S. (1994), 'What do Women Want?: Issues of Choice, Control, and Class in Pregnancy and Childbirth', *Medical Anthropology Quarterly*, **8** (1), p.25.

Lehigh, S. (1996), 'Common Sense, or a New Way to Ban Abortion?', *Boston Globe*, 15 September.

Leiser, Burton M. (1981), *Values in Conflict: Life, Liberty and the Rule of Law*, New York and London: Macmillan Press.

Lewis, C.I. (1946), *The Theory of Knowledge and Valuation*, Illinois: La Salle.

Lichtenburg, K. (1990), 'Gestational Substance Abuse: A Call for Thoughtful Legislative Response', *Washington Law Review*, **65**, p.377.

Little, R.E. and Sing, C.F. (1987), 'Father's Drinking and Infant Birth Weight: Report of an Association', *Teratology*, **36**, p.59.

Losco, Joseph (1989), 'Fetal Abuse: An Exploration of Emerging Philosophic, Legal and Policy Issues', *The Western Political Quarterly*, **42** (2), p.265.

Lowe (1980), 'Wardship and Abortion Prevention – Further Observations', *Law Quarterly Review*, **96**, p.29.

Lowry, Steinhorn (1992), 'The Growing Trend to Criminalise Gestational Substance Abuse', *Journal of Juvenile Law*, **13**, p.133.

Lupton, D. (1994), *Medicine as Culture*, London: Sage Publications.

Lynch, Timothy and Grace, Nancy (1996), 'Individual Rights: Is the Prosecution of "Fetal Endangerment" Illegitimate?', *American Bar Association Journal*, December, p.72.

MacCormick, Neil (1982), *Legal Right and Social Democracy: Essays in Legal and Political Philosophy*, Oxford: Clarendon Press.

MacDonald, Victoria, Health Correspondent (1997), 'Prescribed Drugs do More Harm to Babies Than Heroin', *The Sunday Telegraph*, 21 September, p.18(b).

MacKenzie, T.B., Collins, N.M. and Popkin, M.E. (1992), 'A Case of Fetal Abuse?', *American Journal of Orthopsychiatry*, **52** (4), p.699.

Maclean, A.R. (1999), 'Caesarean Sections, Competence and the Illusion of Autonomy', *Web Journal of Current Legal Issues*, **1**.

Madden, Robert G. (1993), 'State Actions to Control Fetal Abuse: Ramifications for Child Welfare Practice', *Child Welfare*, **72**, p.129.

Mahendra, B. (1997), 'Doc. Brief', *New Law Journal*, **147**, p.1387.

Mahendra, B. (1997), 'Medical Treatment Without Consent', *New Law Journal*, **147**, p.887.

Manson, Rebecca and Marlot, Judy (1987), 'A New Crime, Fetal Neglect: State Intervention to Protect the Unborn – Protection at What Cost? (California)', *California Western Law Review*, **24**, p.161.

Marcotte, Paul (1989), 'Crime and Pregnancy: Prosecutors, New Drug Laws, Torts Pit Mom Against Baby', *American Bar Association Journal*, August, p.14.

Marquis, D. (1989), 'Why Abortion is Immoral', *The Journal of Philosophy*, **86**, p.183.

Marquis, D. (2002), 'A Defence of the Potential Future of Value Theory', *Journal of Medical Ethics*, **28**, p.198.

Marshall, Consuelo (1991), 'Plenary Session (Women Prisoners), War on Drugs 200 Years of the Penitentiary: Criminal, Social and Economic Justice', *Howard Law Journal*, **34**, p.512.

Martin, Norma (1987), 'Recent Cases: D (a minor) v. Berkshire C.C.', *Journal of Social Welfare*, May, p.182.

Mason, J.K. and McCall Smith, R.A. (1999), *Law and Medical Ethics*, London: Butterworth's.

Mathieu, Deborah (1985), 'Respecting Liberty and Preventing Harm: Limits of State Intervention in Prenatal Choice', *Harvard Journal of Law and Public Policy*, **8**, p.19.

Mathieu, Deborah (1995), 'Mandating Treatment for Pregnant Substance Users: A Compromise', *Politics and the Life Sciences*, **14** (2), p.199.

McBride, Timothy S. (1993), 'Criminal Law – Should States Criminally Prosecute Mothers For Delivering Drugs to their Newborns During the Birthing Process?', (Florida) (Case Note) *Suffolk University Law Review*, **27**, p.251.

McCormick, Richard (1981), *How Brave a New World? Dilemmas in Bioethics*, London: SCM Press Ltd.

McFarlane, Judith (1989), 'Battering During Pregnancy: Tip of an Iceberg Revealed', *Women and Health*, **15** (3), p.69.

McGinnis, Doretta M. (1990), 'Prosecution of Mothers of Drug-Exposed Babies: Constitutional and Criminal Theory', *University of Pennsylvania Law Review*, **139**, p.505.

McNulty, Molly (1987), 'Pregnancy Police: The Health Policy and Legal Implications of Punishing Pregnant Women for Harm to Their Fetuses', *New York University Review of Law and Social Change*, **16**, p.277.

Meeker, W. (1987), 'Protecting the Liberty of Pregnant Patients', (letter) *New England Journal of Medicine*, **317**, p.1224.

Merrick, Janna C. (1994), 'Paternal Obligations During Pregnancy: Breaking New Ground', *Politics and the Life Sciences*, **13** (2), p.251.

Michalowski, Sabine (1999), 'Court-Ordered Caesarean Sections – The End of a Trend?', *Modern Law Review*, **62** (1), p.115.

Mill, J.S. (1946), *On Liberty*, Oxford: Basil Blackwell.

Mill, J.S. (1948), *On Liberty and Representative Government*, Oxford: Blackwell's Political Texts.

Miller, Lisa (1993), 'Two Patients or One? Problems of Consent in Obstetrics', *Medical Law International*, **1**, p.97.

Miller, Margaret A. (1984), 'Criminal Law – Murder – Intentional Killing of Viable Fetus Not Murder. (*Hollis v. Commonwealth*)', *Northern Kentucky Law Review*, **11**, p.215.

Mills, J.L., Graubard, B.I., Harley, E.E., Rhoads, G.G. and Berendes, H.W. (1984), 'Maternal Alcohol Consumption and Birthweight. How Much Drinking During Pregnancy is Safe', *Journal of the American Medical Association*, **252**, p.1875.

Milne, A.J.M. (1968), *Freedom and Rights,* London and New York: George Allen and Unwin Ltd; Humanities Press Inc.

Mitchell, Basil (1967), *Law, Morality and Religion in a Secular Society*, Oxford, London and New York: Oxford University Press.

Mitchell, E.A. and Milerad, J. (1999), 'Smoking and Sudden Infant Death Syndrome', in World Health Organisation, *Tobacco Free Initiative: International Consultation on Environmental Tobacco Smoke (ETS) and Child Health*, Geneva: World Health Organisation.

Montgomery, Jonathan (1991), 'Legislation: Rights, Restraints and Pragmatism: The Human Fertilisation and Embryology Act 1990', *Modern Law Reports*, **54**, p.524.

Moore, G.E. (1903), *Principia Ethica*, Cambridge: Cambridge University Press.

Morgan, Derek (1992), 'Whatever Happened to Consent?', *New Law Journal*, **142**, p.1448.

Moss, Kary L. (1990), 'Legal Issues; Drug Testing of Postpartum Women and Newborns as the Basis for Civil and Criminal Proceedings', *Clearinghouse Review*, **23**, p.1406.

Moss, Kary L. (1990), 'Substance Abuse During Pregnancy', *Harvard Women's Law Journal*, **13**, p.278.

Murphy, J.C. (1998), 'Legal Images of Motherhood: Conflicting Definitions from Welfare "Reform", Family and Criminal Law', *Cornell Law Review*, **83**, p.688.

Myers, John E.B. (1984), 'Abuse and Neglect of the Unborn: Can the State Intervene?', *Duquesne Law Review*, **20**, p.1.

Myers, John E.B. (1990), 'Intervention: The Best of Bad Options', *Journal of Interpersonal Violence*, **5** (4), p.532.

Nahas, B.M. (2001), 'Drug Tests, Arrests and Fetuses: A Comment on the US Supreme Court's Narrow Opinion in *Ferguson v City of Charleston*', *Cardozo Women's Law Journal*, **8**, p.105.

National Commission to Prevent Infant Mortality (USA) (1988), *Death Before Life: The Tragedy of Infant Mortality*, Appendix 27-32.

Nelken, David (1990), 'Why Punish?', *Modern Law Review*, **53**, p.829.

Nelson, L.J. (1990), 'Intervention Does More Harm Than Good', *Journal of Interpersonal Violence*, **5** (4), p.530.

Nicholson, R.H. (1991), 'No (Pregnant) Woman is an Island: The Case for a Carefully Delimited Use of Criminal Sanctions to Enforce Gestational Responsibility', *Health Matrix*, **1**, p.101.

Nolan, K., Logli, P.A., Mariner, W.K., Glantz, L.H., Annas, G.J., Paltrow, L.M. and Johnson, P.E. (1990), 'Symposium: Criminal Liability for Fetal Endangerment', *Criminal Justice Ethics*, **9** (1), p.11.

Norrie, K. (1985), 'Abortion in Great Britain: One Act, Two Laws', *Criminal Law Review*, **3**, p.475.

'Note' (1988), 'Maternal Rights and Fetal Wrongs: The Case Against the Criminalization of "Fetal Abuse"', *Harvard Law Review*, **101** (5), p.994.

N.V.L. (1987), 'Note on Re D (a minor)', *Family Law*, **17**, p.203.

Oakley, Ann (1980), *Women Confined: Towards a Sociology of Childbirth*, Oxford: Martin Robinson.

Oakley, Ann (1984), *The Captured Womb*, Oxford: Blackwells.

Oakley, Ann (1986), *From Here to Maternity*, Harmondsworth: Penguin.

Oberman, Michelle (1992), 'Commentary: The Control of Pregnancy and the Criminalization of Femaleness', *Berkeley Women's Law Journal*, **7**, p.1.

Packer, H.L. (1968), *The Limits of the Criminal Sanction*, London: Oxford University Press.

Paltrow, L.M. (1989), 'Fetal Abuse: Should We Recognize it as a Crime?', *American Bar Association Journal*, August, p.38.

Paltrow, L.M. (1990), 'When Becoming Pregnant Is a Crime', *Criminal Justice Ethics*, Winter-Spring, p.41 at 42.

Paltrow, L.M. (1994), 'Paternal-Fetal Conflict: An Idea Whose Time Should Never Come', *Politics and the Life Sciences*, **13** (2), p.253.

Parness, Jeffrey A. (1981), 'Social Commentary: Values and Legal Personhood', *West Virginia Law Review*, **83**, p.487.

Parness, Jeffrey A. (1985), 'Crimes Against the Unborn: Protecting and Respecting the Potentiality of Human Life', *Harvard Journal on Legislation*, **22**, p.97.

Parness, Jeffrey A. and Pritchard, Susan K. (1982), 'To Be or Not to Be: Protecting the Unborn's Potentiality of Life', *Cincinnati Law Review*, **51** (2), p.257.

Peak, Ken and Del Papa, Frankie S. (1993), 'Criminal Justice Enters the Womb; Enforcing the "Right" to be Born Drug-Free', *Journal of Criminal Justice*, **32**, p.245.

Permanand, Gavin (1998), 'UK Companies Challenge EU on Tobacco Advertising', *Eurohealth*, **4** (5), p.37.

Perrson, Ingmar (1999), 'Harming the Non-Conscious', *Bioethics*, **13** (3/4), p.294.

Phelan, D.R. (1992), 'Right to Life of the Unborn v Promotion of Trade in Services: The European Court of Justice and the Normative Shaping of the European Union', *Modern Law Review*, **55**, p.670.

Phelan, J.P. (1991), 'The Maternal Abdominal Wall; A Fortress Against Fetal Health Care?', *Southern California Law Review*, **65**, p.461.

Pickworth, Emma (1998), 'Substance Abuse in Pregnancy and the Child Born Alive: Does the *Attorney-General's Reference (No. 3 of 1994)* Increase the Possibility that England and Wales will Follow the American Example?', *Anglo-American Law Review*, **December**, p.472.

Piggott, Mandy (1997), 'Medical Note', *The Sunday Times,* 9 February, p.18.

Poland, M.L., Dombrowski, M.P., Ager, J.W. and Sokol, R.J. (1993), 'Punishing Pregnant Drug Users: Enhancing the Flight From Care', *Drug and Alcohol Dependence*, **31**, p.199.

Pollitt, K. (1990), 'Fetal Rights: A New Assault on Feminism', *The Nation*, 26 March.

Pytkowicz Streissguth, A., Aase, J.M., Clarren, S.K., Randels, S.P., LaDue, R.A. and Smith, D.F. (1991), 'Fetal Alcohol Syndrome in Adolescents and Adults', *Journal of the American Medical Association*, **265** (15), p.1961.

Raw, M. (1997), *Action on Smoking and Pregnancy*, London: Health Education Authority.

Reardon, P. (1989), 'Grand Jury Won't Indict Mother in Baby's Drug Death', *Chicago Tribune*, 27 May, p.1, col.4.

Roberts, D.E. (1990), 'Drug-Addicted Women Who Have Babies', *Trial*, **26**, p.56.

Roberts, D.E. (1991), 'Punishing Drug Addicts who have Babies: Women of Color, Equality, and the Right of Privacy', *Harvard Law Review*, **104**, p.1419.

Roberts, D.E. (1997), *Killing the Black Body: Race, Reproduction and the Theory of Liberty*, New York: Pantheon Books.

Roberts, E. (1994), 'Re C and the Boundaries of Autonomy', *Professional Negligence*, **10**, p.98.

Robertson, John and Paltrow, Lynn (1989), 'Fetal Abuse: Should we Recognise it as a Crime?', *American Bar Association Journal*, August, p.39.

Robin-Vergeer, Bonnie (1990), 'The Problem of the Drug-Exposed Newborn: A Return to Principled Intervention', *Stanford Law Review*, **42**, p.745.

Royal College of Obstetricians and Gynaecologists (1994), *A Consideration of the Law and Ethics in Relation to Court Ordered-Authorised Intervention*, London: Royal College of Obstetricians and Gynaecologists, Ethics No. 1, April.

Royal College of Obstetricians and Gynaecologists (1996), *Supplement to A Consideration of the Law and Ethics in Relation to Court-Authorised Obstetric Intervention*, London: Royal College of Obstetricians and Gynaecologists, Ethics No. 1, December.

Royal College of Physicians of London (1987), *A Great and Growing Evil – The Medical Consequences of Alcohol Abuse*, London: Royal College of Physicians.

Rubenstein, Laurie (1991), 'Prosecuting Maternal Substance Abusers: An Unjustified and Ineffective Policy', *Yale Law and Policy Review*, Spring (9), p.130.

Rush (1987), 'Pre natal Caretaking: Limits of State Intervention With and Without *Roe*', *University of Florida Law Review*, **39**, p.55.

Savulescu, J. (2002), 'Abortion, Embryo Destruction and the Future of Value Argument', *Journal of Medical Ethics*, **28**, p.133.

Schierl, Kathryn (1990), 'A Proposal to Illinois Legislators: Revise the Illinois Criminal Code to Include Criminal Sanctions Against Prenatal Substance Abusers', *John Marshall Law Review*, **23**, p.393.

Schmall, Lorraine (1993), 'Addicted Pregnancy as a Sex Crime', *Northern Illinois University Law Review*, **13**, p.263.

Schott, Lee A. (1988), 'The *Pamela Rae Stewart* Case and Fetal Harm: Prosecution or Prevention?', *Harvard Women's Law Journal*, **11**, p.227.

Schroedel, Jean R. and Peretz, Paul (1994), 'A Gender Analysis of Policy Formation: The Case of Fetal Abuse', *Journal of Health Politics, Policy and Law*, **19** (2), p.335.

Segers, M.C. and Byrnes, T.A. (eds) (1995), *Abortion Politics in the American States*, New York and London: M.E. Sharp.

Seneviratne, Mary (1996), 'Pre-natal Injury and Transferred Malice: The Invented Other', *Modern Law Review*, **59**, p.884.

Shaw, Margery W. (1984), 'Conditional Prospective Rights of the Fetus', *The Journal of Legal Medicine*, **5** (1), p.63.

Sheldon, S. and Thomson, M. (eds) (1998), *Feminist Perspectives on Health Care Law*, London: Cavendish.

Sherman, Rorie (1991), 'Courts Disagree on Mothers' Liability (Drug Abuse During Pregnancy)', *National Law Journal*, **13** (May 13), p.30 col.9.

Sherman, Rorie (1988), 'Keeping Baby Safe from Mom', *National Law Journal*, **11**, p.1.

Siegal, B. (1994), 'In the Name of the Children: Get Treatment or Go to Jail, One South Carolina Hospital Tells Drug-Abusing Pregnant Women. Now It Faces a Lawsuit and a Civil-Rights Investigation', *L.A. Times*, 14 August, p.7; 1994 WL 2332673.

Singer, P. (1993), *Practical Ethics*, New York: Cambridge University Press.

Smith, G.P. II (1988), 'Fetal Abuse; Culpable Behaviour by Pregnant Women or Parental Immunity?', *Journal of Law and Health*, **3**, p.223.

Squier, Susan (1996), 'Fetal Subjects and Maternal Objects: Reproductive Technology and the New Fetal/Maternal Relation', *The Journal of Medicine and Philosophy*, **21**, p.515.

Stauch, Marc (1997), 'Court-Authorised Caesareans and the Principle of Patient Autonomy', *Nottingham Law Journal*, **6** (1), p.74.

Stearns, Maxwell L. (1986), 'Maternal Duties During Pregnancy: Toward a Conceptual Framework', *New England Law Review*, **21** (3), p.595.

Stein and Mistiaen (1988), 'Pregnant in Prison', *Progressive*, **18**, p.18.

Steinbock, B. (1992), *Life Before Birth: The Moral and Legal Status of Embryos and Fetuses*, New York and Oxford: Oxford University Press.

Steverson, Janet W. (1994), 'Stopping Fetal Abuse With No-Pregnancy and Drug Treatment Probation Conditions', *Santa Clara Law Review*, **34** (2), p.295.

Stich, Denise E. (1993), 'Alternative Sentencing or Reproduction Control: Should California Courts Use Norplant to Protect Future Children from Child Abuse and Fetal Abuse?', *Santa Clara Law Review*, **33**, p.1017.

Sumner, L.W. (1981), *Abortion and Moral Theory*, Princeton NJ: Princeton University Press.

Sutherland (1972), *Statutes and Statutory Construction*, USA, C. Sands.

Taylor, D.J. (1993), 'Pregnancy Alcohol Consumption', *Maternal Medicine Review*, **5**, p.121.

Teff, Harvey (1994), *Reasonable Care: Legal Perspectives on the Doctor-Patient Relationship*, Oxford: Clarendon Press.

T.E.G. (1981), 'Constitutional Limitation on State Intervention in Prenatal Care', *Virginia Law Review*, **67**, p.1051.

Temkin, Jennifer (1986), 'Pre-Natal Injury, Homicide and the Draft Criminal Code', *Cambridge Law Journal*, **45** (3), p.414.

Thomson, J.J. (1990), *The Realm of Rights*, Cambridge, MA: Harvard University Press.

Thomson, Michael (1994), 'After Re S', *Medical Law Review*, **2** (2), p.127.

Tooley, M. (1983), *Abortion and Infanticide*, Oxford: Oxford University Press.

Travis, A. (1998), 'Youngsters Targeted in New Heroin Epidemic', *The Guardian*, 15 August, p.1 col.2.

Travis, A. (2002), 'Human Rights "Risk" in Mental Health Bill', *The Guardian,* 12 November.

Treneman, A. (1997), 'Which of the Two Sides will be Left Holding the Baby After the Battle of the Bulge?', *The Independent*, 27 September, p.21, col.1.

United States Department of Health and Human Services (1996), *Clinical Practice Guideline 18: Smoking Cessation*, Washington, DC: US Government Printing Office.

United States Department of Health, Education and Welfare (1979), *Health People: The Surgeon General's Report on Health Promotion and Disease Prevention*.

University of York NHS Centre for Reviews and Dissemination (1998), *Effectiveness Matters*, York.

Vasgar, J. and Hopkins, N. (2001), 'Jurors Confirm Family Murder Verdict on Michael Stone', *The Guardian*, 5 October.

Wadsworth, J.P. (1990), 'Case Note: R v. Tait', *Law and Justice*, **3** (104/105), p.83.

Wagstaffe, Christopher (1998), 'Harming the Unborn Child – The Foetus and the Threshold Criteria', *Family Law*, **28**, p.160.

Walker, Marlen C. and Puzder, Andrew F. (1984), 'State Protection of the Unborn After *Roe v. Wade*: A Legislative Proposal', *Stetson Law Review*, **237**, p.240.

Walton, Reggie B. (1991), 'War on Drugs. (200 Years of the Penitentiary: Criminal, Social and Economic Justice)', *Howard Law Journal*, **34**, p.506.

Warden, John (1999), 'UK Treads Softly on Smoking', *British Medical Journal*, **318**, p.9.

Warden, John (1999), 'NHS to Target Smokers', *British Medical Journal*, **318**, p.1096.

Weiczorkowski, Deborah A. (1993), 'From Mother to Child ... a Criminal Pregnancy: Should Criminalization of the Prenatal Transfer of AIDS/HIV be the Next Step Against this Deadly Epidemic?', *Dickinson Law Review*, **97**, p.383.

Wells, Celia and Morgan, Derek (1991), 'Whose Foetus is it?', *Journal of Law and Society*, **18** (4), p.431.
White, D. (2000), 'The Crack Pot; Vet Joins US Militants Who Want to Pay Scots Junkies to be Sterilised', *Sunday Mail* (Scotland), 6 August.
White, Lesley (1997), 'There is No Right to be Selfish', *The Sunday Times*, 23 February, p.5.
White Paper (2000), *Reforming the Mental Health Act*, Cm 5016, London: The Stationery Office.
Wilkins, Michelle D. (1990), 'Solving the Problem of Prenatal Substance Abuse: an Analysis of Punitive and Rehabilitative Approaches', *Emory Law Review*, **39**, p.1401.
Williams, Glanville (1994), 'The Fetus and the "Right to Life"', *Cambridge Law Journal*, **53** (1), p.71.
Wood, J. (1990), 'Recent Judicial Decisions: Threat to Kill', *Police Journal*, April, p.170.
World Health Organisation (1999), *Tobacco Free Initiative, International Consultation on Environmental Tobacco Smoke (ETS) and Child Health*, Geneva: World Health Organisation.
Wyatt, J. (2001), 'Medical Paternalism and the Fetus', *Journal of Medical Ethics*, **27**, p.115.
York NHS Centre for Reviews and Dissemination (1998), *Effectiveness Matters*, **3** (1).
Young, Ian (1986), 'The Unborn Child and Criminal Proceedings', *The Law Society's Gazette*, December, p.3808.
Young, R. (1986), *Personal Autonomy: Beyond Negative and Positive Liberty*, New York: St. Martin's Press.
Zhang, J. *et al.* (1992), 'A Case-Control Study of Paternal Smoking and Birth Defects', *International Journal of Epidemiology*, **21**, p.273.
Zorpette, Tracey et al. (1993), 'Norplant: Miracle Drug or Threat to Women's Rights?', *Human Rights*, **20**, p.16.

Cases

UK

A, Re (Conjoined Twins: Medical Treatment) [2000] 4 All E.R. 961.
Adomako, R v. [1995] 1 AC 171.
Airedale NHS Trust v. Bland [1993] AC 789.
Attorney-General's Reference (No 3 of 1994) [1996] 2 All E.R. 10, [1997] 3 All E.R. 936.
Ball, R v. (1989) 90 Cr App R 378.
Bolam v. Friern Hospital Management Committee [1957] 1 W.L.R. 582.
Burton v. Islington Health Authority [1992] 3 W.L.R. 637.
C, Re (Refusal of Medical Treatment) [1994] 1 W.L.R. 290.

C v. S [1988] Q.B. 135.

Caldwell, R v. [1982] A.C. 341.

Church, R v. [1965] All E.R. 72.

Collins and Others, R v. ex parte S 2 FLR 728 (May 8 1998) The Times Law
Reports 45 col. 1.

Cunningham, R v. [1982] A.C. 566.

D (a minor) v. Berkshire County Council and others [1987] 1 All E.R. 20
(Div. Court); 27 (C.A.); 33 (H.L.).

DPP v. Newbury [1977] A.C. 500.

F, Re (in utero) [1988] 2 All E.R. 193.

Frenchay Healthcare NHS Trust v. S [1994] 2 All E.R. 403.

Gibbon, R v. [1990] 3 W.L.R 595.

Gillick v. West Norfolk and Wisbeck Area Health Authority [1986] A.C. 112,
[1985] 3 All E.R. 402.

Goodfellow, R v. (1986) 83 Cr App R 23.

Kelly v. Kelly [1997] 2 FLR 828.

Keown [1996] CLJ 207.

L, In Re (An Adult: Non-Consensual Treatment) [1997] 1 FLR 609.

Latimer, R v. (1886) 17 Q.B.D. 369.

M, Re (A Minor) (Care Order: Threshold Conditions) [1994] 2 FLR 77.

MB, In Re (Adult; Medical Treatment) [1997] TLR 427.

McCluskey v. The Lord Advocate [1989] RTR 182.

McWilliam v. Lord Advocate [1992] TLR 06/11/92.

Merton Borough Council and Ors, ex parte Sutherland, R v. [10th July 1997]
I.L.R. Document Number C800046.

Metropolitan Borough Council v. DB [1997] 1 FLR 767.

Mitchell, R v. [1983] 2 All E.R. 427.

NHS Trust A v. M; NHS Trust B v. H [2001] Lloyd's Rep Med. 28.

Norfolk and Norwich Healthcare Trust v. W [1997] 1 FCR 269.

Paton v. The British Pregnancy Advisory Service Trustees [1979] Q.B. 276.

Pembilton, R v. (1974) 12 Cox 607.

R, Re [1992] Fam 11, (1992) 7 BMLR 147.

Rance v. Mid-Downs Health Authority and Another [1991] 1 All E.R. 801.

Rex v. Shephard [1919] 2 K.B. 125.

Rochdale v. Choudhary [1997] 1 FCR 274.

S, Re (adult refusal of medical treatment) [1992] 3 W.L.R. 806.

St. George's Healthcare National Health Service Trust v. S [1998] 3 AER
673.

Seymour, R v. [1983] 2 AC 493.

*Sidaway v. The Board of Governors of Bethlem Royal Hospital and
Maudsley Hospital* [1985] 1 All E.R. 643.

Senior, R v. (1832) 1 Mood CC 346, 168 E.R. 1298.

T, Re (An Adult) (Consent to Medical Treatment) [1992] 4 All E.R. 649.

Tait, R v. [1989] 3 WLR 891.

Tameside and Glossop Acute Services Trust v. CH [1996] 1 FCR 753.

Vickers, R v. [1957] 2 All E.R. 741.
W, Re (a minor) (medical treatment) [1992] 4 All E.R. 627.
West, R v. 2 Car & Kir 784, 175 E.R.329 (1848).

Commonwealth

Kong Cheuk Kwan v. The Queen (1985) 82 Cr. App. R. 18 P.C.
Kwok Chak Ming (No 1), R v. [1963] H.K.L.R. 226.
Lynch v. Lynch and Government Office of New South Wales (1992) 3 Med
   LR 62.
Winnipeg Child and Family Services (Northwest Area) v. G [1997] 3 BHRC
   611.

European Union / European Court of Justice

Ashingdane v. United Kingdom (1985) 7 EHRR 528.
*Dekker v. Stichting Vormingscentrum Voor Jonge Volwassen (VJV –
   Centrum) Plus* Case 177/88 [1991] IRLR 10.
Engel v. Netherlands (1976) 1 EHRR 647 at para. 58.
Guzzardi v. Italy (1980) 3 EHRR 333.
*Handels – Og Kontorfunktionaerernes Forband I Danmark [acting for
   Hertz] v. Dansk Arbejdsqiverforening [acting for Aldi Marked K/S]* Case
   179/88 [1991] IRLR 31.
Osman v. United Kingdom (1997) 29 EHRR 245.
Paton v. The United Kingdom [1980] 3 EHRR 408.
Peters v. The Netherlands (1994) 77A/B D.R.
SW v. United Kingdom (1995) 21 EHRR 363.
Winterwerp v. The Netherlands (1979) 2 EHRR 387.
Witold Litwa v. Poland, Eur. Ct. HR, App. No. 31365/96, 5 October 2000.

USA

AC, Re 573 A 2d 1235 (1990).
Alaska v. Grubbs No. 4FA S89 415 Criminal, slip op. (Sup. Ct. Aug. 25,
   1989).
Alexander, State v. No. Ct-92-2047 Transcript of Decisions (Okla. Aug.
   1992).
Amaro, State v. 448 A.2d 1257 (R.I. 1982).
Ashley, State v. 670 So. 2d 1087 (Fla. 1996).
Baby X, In re, 97 Mich. App. 111, 116, 293 N.W.2d 736, 739 (1980).
Barnett, State v. No. 0220-9308-CF-00611 (Ind. Super. Ct. Allen Cty. Feb.
   11 1994).
Beal v. Doe 432 U.S. 438 (1977).
Blackwell v. DeMaio 503 So.2d 1384 (Fla. Dist. CT. App., 1987).
Bontretz v. Kotz 65 F. Supp. 138 (D.D.C. 1946).

Bouie v. City of Columbia 378 U.S. 347 (1964).

Bremer, People v. No. 90-32227-FH, slip op. (Mich. Cir. Ct. Jan. 31, 1991).

Brown, State v. 378 So.2d 916 (La. 1979).

Buck v. Bell 274 U.S. 200 (1927).

California v. Larve 409 U.S. 109 (1972).

California v. Smith 59 Cal. App. 3d 751, 129 Cal. Rptr. 498 (1976).

California v. Stewart No. M508197, slip op. (Cal. Mun. Ct., San Diego, Feb. 26, 1987).

Carey v. Population Services International 431 U.S. 678, 687 (1977).

Cass, Commonwealth v. 392 Mass. 799, 467 N.E.2d 1324 (1984).

Chavez, People v. 77 Cal. App. 2d 621, 176 P.2d 922 (1992).

City of Akron v. Akron Center for Reproductive Health Inc., 1035. Ct. 2481 (1983).

Cleveland Board of Education v. La Fleur 414 U.S. 632 (1974).

Commonwealth v. Pellegrini No. 87970 (Mass. Super. Ct. Plymouth City, Oct. 15 1990).

Connecticut v. Baez, No. CR089-010-4414, slip op. (Conn. Super. Ct. filed July 31, 1989).

Curlander v. Bio-Science Laboratories 106 Cal. App. 3d 811, 165 Cal. Rptr. 477 (1980).

Davis, People v. Supreme Court of California, 7 Cal.4th 797, 30 Cal.Rptr.2d 50, 872 P.2d 591 (1994).

Dickinson, State v. 28 Ohio St.2d 65, 275 N.E.2d 599 (1971).

Dietrich v. Northampton 138 Mass. 14 (1884).

Drummond, Brenda Case Canada Late 96.

Eisenstadt v. Baird 405 U.S. 438 (1971).

Elaine W. v. North General Hospital (N.Y. Super. Ct. Nov. 23 1989) (No. Index No.).

Ferguson v. City of Charleston S.C. 186 F.3d 469, 485-86 (4th Cir. 1999), rev'd, 532 U.S. 67, 121 S. Ct. 1281 (2001).

Florida v. Black No. 89-5325, slip op. (Fla. Cir., Ct., Jan. 3m 1990).

Florida v. Gethers 585 So. 2d 1140 (Fla. Dist. Ct. App. 1991).

Florida v. Hudson No. K88-3435-CFA, slip op. (Fla. Cir. Ct. July 26, 1989).

Florida v. Jerez No. K89-16257 (Monroe County CT. Jan. 11, 1990).

Florida v. Johnson No. E89-1765 (Fla. Dist. Ct. App., 5th Dist. 1989).

Geduldig v. Aiello 417 U.S. 484 (1974).

Georgia v. Coney No. 14/403-404 (Super. Ct. of Crisp County filed Nov. 6, 1989).

Gray, State v. 62 Ohio St. 3d 514, 584 N.E.2d 710 (Ohio 1992).

Greer, People v. 79 Ill.2d 103, 402 N.E.2d 203 (1980).

Griswold v. Connecticut 381 U.S. 479 (1965).

Grodin v. Grodin 102 Mich. App. 396, 301 N.W.2d 869 (1980).

Guthrie, People v. 97 Mich. App. 226, 293 N.W.2d 775 (1980).

Hardy, People v. 469 N.W. 2d 50 (Mich. Ct. App. 1991).

Harris v. McRae 448 U.S. 297, 324-26 (1980).

Harris v. Vasquez 913 F. 2d 606 (9th Cir. 1990).

Hollis v. Commonwealth 652 S.W.2d 61 (Ky. 1983).

Horne, State v. 282 S.C. 444, 319 S.E.2d 703 (1984).

Hughes v. State 868 P.2d 730 (Okla. Crim. App. 1994).

Illinois v. Green No. 88-CM-8256 (Cir. Ct. filed May 8, 1989).

Ingraham v. Wright 430 U.S. 651 (1977).

Jefferson v. Griffin Spalding County Hospital 247 Ga. 86, 274 S.E.2d 457 (1981).

Jennings, ex parte [1983] 1 AC 624.

Johnson v. State 602 So.2d 1288 (Fla. 1992).

Jones, People v. No. 93-5 Reporters transcript (Cal. Juv. Ct. Siskigou Cty. July 28, 1993).

Juarigue v. Justice Court No. 18988 Rptrs transcript (Cal. Super. Ct. San Benito Cty. Aug. 21 1992).

Keeler v. Superior Court of Amodor County 87 Cal. Rptr. 81, 2 Cal. 3d 619, 70 P.2d 617 (1970).

Kemp, Commonwealth v. 75 Westmoreland Law Journal 5, 11, (Pa. Ct. C.P. 1992) aff'd, 643 A.2d 705 (Pa. Super. Ct. 1994).

Kentucky v. Welsh No. 90-CR-006 (Cir. Ct. Boyd County May 25, 1990).

KH, People v. No. 89.2931.FY (Mich. Dist. Ct., Muskegon County, Nov. 13 1989).

Larsen, State v. 578 P.2d 1280 (Utah 1978).

Linder v. U.S. 268 U.S. 5, 18 (1925).

Liparota v. U.S. 435 U.S. 419, 247 (1985).

Lowe v. State 450 AO. 2d 1191, 1193 (Fla. Dist. Ct. App. 1984).

Maher v. Roe 432 U.S. 464 (1977).

Male R, In re 102 Misc. 2d 1, 10 n. 18, 422 N.Y.S.2d 819 (Fam. CT. 1979).

Massachusetts v. Pellegrini No. 87970 (Super. Ct. filed Aug. 21, 1989).

Merril, State v. Supreme Court of Minnesota, 450 N.W.2d 318 (1990).

Michael M. v. Superior Court 450 U.S. 464 (1981).

Michigan v. Bremer No. 90-1313-FY (Dist. Ct. Muskegon County).

Michigan v. Cox No. 9053535FH (Cir. Ct. for Jackson County filed Jan. 30, 1990).

Michigan v Hardy No. 12845, slip op. (Mich. Ct. App. April 1, 1991).

Mitchell, R v. [1983] 2 All ER 427.

Mone v. Greyhound Lines, Inc. 386 Mass. 354 (1975).

Morabito, People v. 1992 N.Y., 580 N.Y.S.2d 843 (1992).

Moten, People v. 280 Cal. Rptr. 602 (Comm. App. 1991).

Nevada v. Bloxham No. RJC-36887 (Reno Justice Ct. filed Feb. 1990).

Nevada v. Peters No. 90-241 (Sperks Justice Ct. filed Feb. 22, 1990).

North Carolina v. Inzar Nos. 90CRS6960, 90CRS6961 (N.C. Super. Ct. Robeson Cty, Apr. 16, 1990).

Ohio v. Andrews No. JU 68459 (Ohio C.P., Stark County June 19, 1989).

Ohio v. Gray No. CR88-7406, slip op. (Vit. of Common Pleas, Lucas County, Ohio July 13, 1989).

Olmstead v. United States 277 U.S. 438, 478 (1928).

Peabody, In Re 5 N.Y.2d 541, 158 N.E.2d 841, 186 N.Y.S.2d 265 (1959).

Pfannensteil, State v. No. 1-908CR (Wyo. Cty. Ct. Albany Cty. Jan. 5 1990).

Pierce v. Society of Sisters 268 U.S. 510 (1925).

Planned Parenthood v. Casey 112 S.Ct. 2791 (1992).

Powell v. Texas 392 U.S. 514 (1968).

Raleigh Fifkin-Paul Memorial Hospital v. Anderson 42 N.J. 421, 201 A.2d 537 (1964).

Renslow v. Mennonite Hospital 67 Ill. 2d 348, 367 N.E.2d 1250 (1977).

Reyes v. Superior Court 75 Cal. App. 3d 214, 141 Cal. Rptr. 9122 (Cal. Ct. App. 1977).

Reyes, State v. 826 P.2d 919 (Idaho Ct. App. 1992).

Robinson v. California 370 U.S. 660 (1962).

Roe v. Wade 410 U.S. 113 (1973).

Ruiz, In re 27 Ohio Misc, 2d 31, 35, 500 N.E.2d 935 (Ohio Common Pleas, 1976).

Rust v. Sullivan 500 U.S. (1991).

Skinner v. Oklahoma 316 U.S. 535, 541 (1942).

Smith, In re 128 Misc.2d 976, 979, 492 N.Y.S.2d 331, 334 (Fam. Ct. Monroe County 1985).

Stallman v Youngquist 531 N.E.2d 355 (Ill. 1988).

State ex. rel A.W.S. 182 N.J. Super. 278, 440 A.2d 1144 (1981).

Texas v. Rodden No. 37365R (Dist. Ct. Tarrant County files, June 1, 1989).

Torres, In re No. N-3968/88 (N.Y. Fam. Ct., Bronx County Oct. 7, 1988).

Troy D., In re 215 Cal. App. 3d 889 (1989).

Union Pacific Railway v. Botsford 141 U.S. 250 (1891).

United States v. Harris 347 U.S. 612 (1954).

United States v. Vaughn Crim. No. F-2172-88B (D.C. Sup. Ct., Aug. 23, 1988).

Valerie D., In re 595 A.2d 922 (Conn. App. Ct.), *cert.* granted, 600 A.2d 1029 (Conn. 1991), rev'd, 613 A.2d 748 (Conn. 1992).

Wallace v. Texas 7 Tex. Crim. 570 (1880).

Webster v. Reproductive Health Services 109 S.Ct. 3040 (1989).

Welch v. Commonwealth No. 90-CA-1189-MR (Ky. Ct. App. Feb. 7, 1992).

Whalen v. Roe 429 U.S. (1977).

Whitner v. State Supreme Court of South Carolina, Docket No. 2468 (15th July 1996); 1996 WL 393164 (S.C. 1996).

Williams v. State Court of Appeals of Maryland, 316 Md. 677, 561 A.2d 216 (1989).

Willis, State v. 98 N.M. 771, 652 P.2d 1222 (N.M. Ct. App. 1982).

Wisconsin ex. rel. Angela v. Kruzicki 197 Wis, 2d 532, 541 N.W.2d 482, 1995 Wisc. App. LEXIS 1246 (1995).

Wyoming v. Osmus S.C., 73 Wyo. 183, 276 P.2d 469 (1954).

Zaring, People v. Californian Court of Appeal No. F014606, July 22 1992.

Statutes

England and Wales

Abortion Act 1967
Congenital Disabilities (Civil Liability) Act 1976
Children Act 1989
Children and Young Persons Act 1933
Children and Young Persons Act 1969
Criminal Justice Act 1972
Criminal Law Act 1977
Family Law Reform Act 1969
Homicide Act 1957
Human Fertilisation and Embryology Act 1990
Human Rights Act 1998
Infant Life Preservation Act 1929
Infanticide Act 1937
Mental Health Act 1983
Draft Mental Health Bill, (Draft) Cm. 5538-I (London: The Stationary
    Office, 2002).
Offences Against the Person Act 1861
Road Traffic Act 1972
Sex Discrimination Act 1975

European Legislation

Directive 98143/EC *The Parliament and Council Directive on the
    Approximation of Member States' Laws, Regulations, and Administrative
    Provisions on Advertising Tobacco Products.*
European Convention for the Protection of Human Rights and Fundamental
    Freedoms 1950.

USA

ARIZ.REV.STAT.ANN. Section 13-1103(A)(5) (1989).
ARK.STAT.ANN. Section 5-14-123 (Michie 1991 Supp.).
CAL. PENAL CODE 187 (West Supp. 1986).
Child Abuse During Pregnancy Prevention Bill S. 1444 101th Cong. 1st
    Sess. (1989).
DEL.CODE ANN. tit. 16, 190 (1995).
FLA.STAT.ANN. No. 782.09 (West Com. Supp. 1975).
FLA.STAT.ANN. Section 415.503(8) (West 1989).
FLA.SESS.LAWSERV. ch, 89-345, No. 415.5082 (West 1898).
GA. CODE.ANN. Section 16-5-80 (1989).
IDAHO CODE Section 39-608 (1992 Supp.).

ILL.ANN.STAT.Ch. 38 No. 9-1.1 (Smith-Hurd Supp., 1985).
Illinois Juvenile Court Act, ILL.REV.STAT. (1989).
Ill. Legis. Serv. 86-275 (West 1989).
IOWA CODE ANN. No. 707.7 (West 1979).
IND.CODE ANN. Section31-6-4-3.1 (Burns 1987).
MASS.GEN.LAWS.ANN. CH. 119. Section 51A (West Supp. 1990).
MICH.COMP. LAWS Section 333.7401.
MINN.STAT. Section 626.556 (1988).
MISS. CODE ANN. No. 97-3-337 (1972).
MO.REV.STAT. No. 1.205.1C17-(2) (1986).
MP.REV.STAT. 191.725, 191.727 (1994).
N.Y.REV.STAT. pt. IV, Ch. 1, tit. 2 Section 8-9 (1829).
NEV.REV.STAT.ANN Section 432B.330 (Michie 1989).
OKLA.STAT.ANN. tit. 10 Section 1101; tit. 21 Section 846 (West 1989).
R.I.GEN.LAWS 152-3-1 (1994).
TEXAS PENAL CODE ANN. Section 22.012 (West 1992 Supp.).
UTAH CODE ANN. Section 62A-4-504, -509, -511 (1989).
UTAH CODE ANN. 62A-4a-411 (1997).

Index